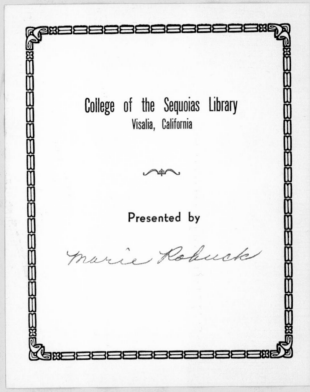

In One Lifetime

In
One
Lifetime

VERNA ARVEY

With an introduction and notes by
B. A. NUGENT

THE UNIVERSITY OF ARKANSAS PRESS
Fayetteville
1984

Manufactured in the United States of America

Designer: Design for Publishing
Typeface: Sabon
Typesetter: G & S Typesetters, Inc.
Printer: Vail Ballou
Binder: Vail Ballou

Library of Congress Cataloging in Publication Data

Arvey, Verna, 1910–
    In one lifetime.

    1. Still, William Grant, 1895–1978.   2. Composers—
United States—Biography.   1. Title.
ML410.S855A78   1984   780'.92'4[B]   83-24226
ISBN 0-938626-31-0
ISBN 0-938626-36-1 (PBK)

*This project is funded in part by a grant from the Arkansas Endowment
for the Humanities.*

Contents

Introduction

I n *Meditations*, Marcus Aurelius wrote, "Remember this—that there is a proper dignity and proportion to be observed in the performance of every act of life." *In One Lifetime* offers the reader a portrayal of William Grant Still as he sought, above all else, to perform his acts with proper dignity and proportion.

This book is not a comprehensive assessment of Still's works. Rather, it is a warm and frank portrait—sometimes with the sharp contrasts of brilliant hues against blackness, sometimes in irenic pastels—of his aestheticism correlated with his personal character and high spirituality. It tells the story of a man whose creative language, eloquent and purposeful, was deeply implanted then rooted in a polyethnic America that he understood better than most. Perhaps this was so because he was truly one of his country's pioneers. Perhaps it was owing no less to his fervent belief that his country's cultural countenance could best be uplifted through the power of beauty and the worth of humankind. He was an exacting diarist whose entries show that he was quick also to give thanks and credit to his God.

If it is true that music is measured by the artistry and stature of those who perform it, along with audiences, who determine whether or not it endures, then William Grant Still's station as a significant American composer is assured. His orchestral works have been performed by nearly every major symphony orchestra in the United States, including the New York Philharmonic, the Boston Symphony Orchestra, the Philadelphia Orchestra, the Chicago Symphony Orchestra, and the orchestras of Los Angeles, San Francisco, Pittsburgh, St. Louis, Dallas, Detroit, Utah, New Orleans, Cincinnati, Minneapolis, and Baltimore. Outside of the United States, the Berlin Philharmonic, the BBC, the London Symphony Orchestra, the NHK, the Tokyo Philharmonic, the Sinfonía de Mexico City, and the Liverpool Philharmonic are among the many which performed his works. The roster of conductors includes Pierre Monteux, Antal Dorati, Sir John Barbirolli, Fritz Reiner, Eugene Ormandy, George Szell, Eric Leinsdorf, Leopold Stokowski, Sir Hamilton Harty, Howard Hanson, and Otto Klemperer. Singers Todd Duncan and Jerome Hines programmed his compositions regularly. During his lifetime, his works enriched audiences and young performing musicians in more than 125 colleges and universities.

Although Still's artifice was forged through years of practical arranging and composing for the likes of Earl Carroll, Sophie Tucker, Bing Crosby, Artie Shaw, and Paul Whiteman, he remains distinct among contemporaries of his race. Unlike Scott Joplin, W. C. Handy, "Count" Basie, "Duke" Ellington, Quincy Jones, and others—all giants—Still remained unswerving in his commitment to writing operas, symphonies, and works of other genres for the concert hall. As the first Negro to write successful symphonies, the first Negro to conduct a major symphony orchestra, and the first Negro to have an opera produced by a major company, he was entitled to wear proudly the mantle of Dean of Negro American composers. In this respect, he was indeed an American pioneer.

William Grant Still's professional career was born in the glittering world of Broadway and circuit theaters with their vaudeville, burlesque, revues, and musicals. If that world glittered with the *Ziegfeld Follies* and *Earl Carroll Vanities*, it also sparkled brilliantly with *Shuffle Along, Dinah, Strutt Your Stuff, Liza*, and *Chocolate Dandies*.

His adolescence as a composer was shaped within a milieu that witnessed the emergence of the radio as a powerful force upon an

America that somehow endured a world war, prohibition, and a depression while learning to travel farther and more rapidly by automobile and airplane. It was also an America that desperately needed to laugh, cry, be entertained and enriched. It was a hopeful nation of families that gathered around radios to share news, presidential addresses, sports, comedy, and music performed by the greatest artists from Europe alongside those of the United States.

Still was at home among such radio shows as the "Deep River Hour," "Old Gold Show," "Maxwell House Coffee Show," "Fleischmann's Yeast" program, "Bell Telephone Hour," and "Standard Symphony Hour." The name William Grant Still was heard regularly on such pioneering radio stations as WGHP, WJZ, WHAM, WABC, KGO, WNYC, KHJ, KECA (the Blue Network), and of course, the youthful networks of CBS, NBC, and Mutual. And he lived to hear his works over NPR and PBS. As cultural ambassador for his country, his works were broadcast over foreign stations and networks such as INR (Belgium), Danish Radio, Swedish Radio, Finnish Radio, CBC (Canada), Norddeutscher Rundfunk (Hamburg), and Deutscher Demokratischer Rundfunk (Berlin).

Finally, it must be said of William Grant Still that through his music he spoke of great pride for his Negro heritage. If there were strains of Choctaw, Spanish, and Scotch-Irish blood also in his veins, they only served to make him all the more American. Moreover, he was a genuine patriot and feared the presence of communism in his country. He believed that racial barriers should be dissolved through exemplary acts and gentle persuasion rather than demolished through the militant explosions of marches and uncivil riots. William Grant Still was a man of extraordinary commitment and resilience who elected to fight racial bias, inequality, and discrimination with intellect, talent, grace, spirituality, and dignity. *In One Lifetime* is the story of two artists—one Negro, the other Caucasian and Jewish—their marriage, their families, their art, and their legacies which bequeath so much to future generations. Above all, it is the story of William Grant Still who never said once, "I cannot achieve because I am a Negro."

* * * * *

The editor wishes to express his deepest gratitude to Miller Williams, Director, Stephanie Brown, and Jeanie Pittman of The University of Arkansas Press; his wife, Clara; Judith Anne Still Headlee; Willard Gatewood, Distinguished Professor of History at the University of Arkansas; Joyce Clinkscales of the University of Arkansas Libraries; University of Kansas Chancellor and Mrs. Gene A. Budig; and the gracious staff of the University of Kansas libraries.

B. A. Nugent

Prologue

As we and Dolores Ardoyno, with her husband, Donald Dorr of Opera/South, sat in the office of William Waller, then (1974) Governor of Mississippi, watching him present a citation to my husband as a distinguished Mississippian, my thoughts travelled back to a time, little more than one lifetime ago, when in the town of Woodville (where my husband was born) there occurred the infamous Woodville massacres in which, quite simply, the colored citizens who thought they had a right to vote were brutally murdered.

In 1976, when I returned alone to Mississippi, the Dorrs drove me down the Natchez Trail to Woodville itself, a charming, quiet little town with friendly people, freshly painted white houses and quaint old churches still in use. It was hard to believe that violence could ever happen in such a beautiful setting. And then I remembered Governor Waller's citation and realized how far some of us have come in so few short years.

Verna Arvey

In my opinion, William Grant Still is one of America's great citizens, because his musical nature has given him the power to fuse into one unified expression our American music of today with the ancestral memories lying deep within him of African music. This blending into one stream of diverse racial cultural origins is most important to the future of our country. For the reason that we Americans come from so many racial origins, we must find a way to harmonize them into one—in our cultural and economic existence, and in our conception of what is the good life that we all can share. Still has succeeded in this to a remarkable degree—and this is what gives deep significance to his life and musical creation.

Leopold Stokowski

I

Prediction

She was a small, very dark woman, and we had known her as a friend, not a psychic, though we were later told that she had spent many Sundays in a church, giving spiritual readings. It was on a day early in January, 1937, when we received word that she had been brought home from work in an ambulance, gravely ill. We decided to pay her a visit.

It happened that Paul Whiteman was scheduled to play a composition by William Grant Still that same afternoon, over the radio. So, of course, we wanted to hear it. While I sat in the bedroom with our friend, her son and the composer went into the living room to turn on the radio. Paul Whiteman came on as planned, but the Still music did not. We were surprised and disbelieving. We had been so happy! Prospects had seemed so bright, and everyone was being so kind. I explained this to our sick friend, whereupon—dramatically—she raised herself up in bed and announced:

"Oh, they'll all be against him now! Everyone will be against him. But you'll see—he'll go on and up anyway!" After that, she never made another coherent statement, and the next day she died. We would come to realize how accurate this deathbed prophecy was and that we were on the threshold of a remarkable adventure.

In the next forty years of that adventure, we would manage to achieve something tangible in our lives and in our work, and come to the great discovery that we had won the respect and even the love of cultured colored and white people alike, North and South. The most important thing we learned was that people are people, and that external differences matter little in the long run.

Our story actually began in Ireland, Scotland, Spain, Africa, among several American Indian tribes and in old Russia's Zhitomir and Minsk—all those colorful places from which our forebears emigrated before mingling their bloods so that we could be born truly American.

The life of William Grant Still began on a Mississippi plantation near Woodville, in the middle of the nineteenth century, when a lonely Scottish overseer named Still (not related to William Still who wrote *The Underground Railroad*) took a slave woman to be his wife. There must have been more than a passing attraction between them, for they became the parents of two sons named, as a true Scotsman might name his sons, Duncan and Milton. They looked like Scotsmen, too, particularly Milton. In his later years, with his fair skin, wavy, sandy hair and long, drooping moustache, he physically exemplified his heritage. He was to become a trustee of the school district in which he lived. Once, it was said, the white superintendent (who was somehow related to the Stills) visited the school, glanced around him at students and officials and caustically remarked that if the color line were to be drawn there, it would be a decided zigzag.

Duncan Still, on the contrary, had a beard and brown skin. He was a large man whom his daugher-in-law called "the old gentleman" and described as the "most handsome man" she had ever seen. It was he who was to become my husband's grandfather.

Duncan and Milton Still were boys in 1863 when the Emancipation Proclamation freed them. Freedom was a new experience for them. They didn't know how to cope with it, so they appealed for help to the white McGehees, owners of Snowden, a fifty-acre plantation six miles east of Woodville. The McGehees were thought of as people who were willing to change with the times, and to become employers rather than slave-owners. They gave jobs to the two brothers at Snowden. There Duncan Still met and married Mary, half Indian, who used to spend most of her time fishing. Their first two children were girls. In November of 1871, William Grant Still, who was to become my husband's father, was born to them.

In order to assess this young man's remarkable achievement in his short life, we must keep his environment in mind. Woodville was a part of the Deep South, with all that the phrase implies. The Woodville of our day was chosen not too long ago by Harvard University Extension workers as a town most typical of the Old South and least changed by industrialization and reconstruction. The Woodville of a bygone day was a fabulously wealthy cotton town: dry, inland and hilly. It was also a town bent on preserving its old habits.

In the lifetimes of the brothers Still, the colored people of Woodville suffered a series of massacres (reported in the official Congressional documents of 1872) aimed at preventing them from exercising the rights guaranteed to citizens by the Constitution of the United States. These bloody events played a great part in shaping the thoughts and behavior of the colored community. Colored people dared only think about white people, never talk. And certainly never take action! If they felt like doing no more than gossip about white folks, they had to do it in whispers. They knew very well that a chance remark might be equivalent to signing their own death warrants.

They well understood that if a colored person committed a crime or was even *suspected* of committing a crime, whether a big one or a little one, any one of his relatives might be shot in retaliation. White residents, on the other hand, did exactly as they pleased. If a white man wanted a colored man's wife, he simply took her. Once, in the Still family, a farm was given to a colored man in exchange for his wife, when one white man tried to be fair.

The colored Stills accustomed themselves to the life they had to lead. They were by no means servile, but they minded their own business and tried to conduct their lives with dignity. They were respected among both races.

My husband's father inherited this dignity. He did not bow or scrape, but neither was he belligerent. He was part and parcel of a prejudiced world and was born at a time when there was both violent and surreptitious opposition to any Negro who wanted an education. Yet he educated himself, became a teacher, ran a little business on the side, and at the time of his death at only twenty-four years of age, managed to leave a small legacy for his baby son. Even in our day, this would be considered real achievement. In his surroundings, it was amazing testimony to his will and to his perseverance.

It's possible that he had a premonition of his early death, because he doubled up on everything: field work as well as study. One of the ways in which he and his friends who lived on adjoining plantations earned their tuition fees was to labor in the fields. They came by every penny the hard way, by sweat and sacrifice, and by casting aside any false pride. Then they hoarded their hard-earned pennies, for they knew as no one else could the toil it had taken to get them.

Once enrolled in Alcorn A&M College in Lorman, Mississippi (oldest of all land-grant colleges for American Negroes), these industrious young men were called "The Alcorn Boys" by their friends and neighbors. Young Still supplemented his college work by taking regular private cornet lessons. Each one cost him a seventy-five mile round trip to Louisiana (near Baton Rouge, where there was a competent teacher) and a night away from home, because he went by train and there was only one train each day. According to Alcorn's old catalogues, he was listed as a student in the preparatory courses when he was fifteen years old. At twenty he was a junior, and a student brass band leader.

He had no use for gew-gaws, no leaning toward extravagance. On the contrary, he practiced many little economies. One was to buy ladies' fifteen-cent hosiery, wear it until holes appeared in the toes, cut off the feet, sew up the hole, wear it until more holes appeared, then repeat the process until there was nothing left of the hose. Then he would buy a new pair.

His sense of humor was delightful, even if potentially dangerous to himself. When he was about sixteen, he and his friend Frank Norwood went hunting together. Nearby were other hunters with a different end in view. Sounds of excitement reached the two boys, then a fox and,

William Grant Still, Sr., Billy's father. Courtesy William Grant Still Estate.

not far behind, a pack of hounds and a group of young Southern aristocrats on horseback. The fox ran across the road near young Still who, on a sudden impulse, lifted his gun and shot it. The white hunters were full of righteous wrath. They threatened a sound whipping.

But young Still, well aware of the proper procedure in a fox hunt but pretending otherwise, blandly stated that he thought they were chasing the fox because they wanted it killed. He had simply obliged them. The hunters, mollified, cautioned him never to do it again and rode on. Frank Norwood said, "Still, you had your gun. Why didn't you bless them out?"

"No, sir, Frank," replied the audacious boy, jokingly. "My mother taught me always to be polite to white folks. And I *was* polite, wasn't I?"

Later in life, Frank Norwood recalled another occasion when he and Still were classmates at Alcorn. "Professor McAdams had his Eng-

Carrie Lena Fambro Still, Billy's mother. Photo by
Harris Studio, Little Rock, Arkansas.

lish class writing poems. Still's poem exceeded mine so much that, schoolboy-like, I became jealous. Professor McAdams was complimenting Still very highly. I rose and tried to clip Still's wings a little by saying, 'Yes, Professor, that *is* a nice poem. I thought so when I read it about a month ago in a magazine.' Still looked at me hard and said, 'Why, Norwood!' I can still see him with that firm, steady look—disgusted, yet dignified. Of course the poem was original."

After his success as student leader of Alcorn's college band, young Still organized one of his own—the only brass band in Woodville at that time. He became the idol of the town when he marched at its head down the street. He was an imposing figure, about six feet, four inches tall with wavy brown hair, even white teeth and skin more like that of an Indian than of a Negro. His band played for all the fairs and festivals, colored and white. His choice of music would be considered corny today—the Quick Steps, quadrilles, and other pieces so popular in the Nineties. He sang too, and in the church choir his "sweet tenor voice" used to ring out in the anthem, "Consider the lilies of the field, how they grow."

In 1892, my father-in-law graduated from Alcorn with a B.S. degree. Because of his musical talent and his genius for mathematics, he was soon recommended for a post in the State Colored Normal School in Normal (near Huntsville), Alabama, later known as the State Agricultural and Mechanical Institute. In 1893, therefore, he said what he thought was a temporary "goodbye" to a Woodville girl whom everyone expected him to marry, and became instructor in bookkeeping and music (vocal and band) at the Alabama school.

Another new teacher came to that school, a beautiful young woman named Carrie Lena Fambro. Carrie Fambro had just parted—temporarily, she thought—from her old schoolmate, Bishop Carey, whom everyone expected her to marry.

They must have fallen terribly, suddenly in love, the young man whose career was just starting and was so soon to end, and the brilliant girl who found in him all that she hoped to find in a mate. They were young and life seemed fresh and exciting and the future stretched out before them. It was a future that they vowed to explore together.

2

Carrie Lena Fambro had roots in Mississippi, too, among people just as forthright and persevering as the Stills. Possibly hers were a little more openly independent and sometimes even pugnacious, but the similarities were clear.

When we think of the dedication and hard work that must have been the lot of those slaves who managed to buy their own freedom, again we stand in awe of a great achievement. Carrie Fambro's maternal great-grandfather apparently married a woman who was still in bondage, for his daughter Anne, my husband's maternal grandmother, was born into slavery on a plantation near Milledgeville, Georgia. It was owned by Irish people, the Fambros, from whom she took her surname.

It was never openly stated, but was nonetheless accepted as fact, that Anne Fambro had actual blood ties with the people who owned her. In those days, only she and her family were allowed to live in the big house with the white people, while the other Negroes lived in huts outside. From here, too, Indian blood came into the family, though how this occurred was never clarified exactly. Yet one of my husband's vivid childhood memories is of his grandmother scolding him when he was naughty by saying, "You're mean! That's your Injun blood coming out."

Another well-kept secret was of the meeting and mating of his maternal grandparents. That grandfather was a Spaniard who owned of a good deal of property in Florida. Perhaps he was a visitor in the Fambro home. Whether or not it was a marriage in the legal sense we now recognize, this man was proud of the child born to him and Anne Fambro and was always glad to see her. Even when Carrie Lena Fambro was grown, she often visited him in Florida, and, because she had beautiful wavy black hair and an olive complexion, never travelled in Jim Crow cars on those occasions. Her father often tried to persuade her to stay with him. As an inducement, he promised her a home and an orange grove in Florida. She never accepted, however; there were probably many complications. She therefore elected to remain with her own culture and its legacies.

The story goes that once, when she was a little girl, her mother bathed her and dressed her in pretty new clothes. As luck would have it, one of the neighboring children took that occasion to yell something offensive. Carrie promptly disappeared, and a half hour later returned home with her hair and clothes mussed, her face flushed and dirty. Questioning revealed that she had beaten up every sarcastic child on the block. When she was taken to task, she faced her family and cried fiercely, "I won't take anything from anybody!"

When the days of slavery were over, Anne Fambro was, of course, thrown out on her own. At first, she had only the necessities of life to consider. Eventually she developed a strong desire to educate her four daughters so that they might meet other people on an equal intellectual footing. If food and clothing cost money, education was even more expensive. She decided to capitalize on her talent for cooking, for she was an expert in the kitchen. It wasn't long before she became the cook for a boarding house on Peachtree Street in Atlanta, and by dint of the same long process of penny-pinching by which William Still survived, the four daughters went to school.

Carrie Fambro's scholarship record was among the highest in her school. Even in recent years her old classmates recalled her as an orator of no mean ability and one of the outstanding students at Atlanta University, from which she graduated in 1886. At one time in her youth she, too, studied music, for she became the organist at the C.M.E. Church in Barnesville, Georgia, and later was soloist with a group of singers of spirituals at Atlanta University. Immediatley after her graduation from the University, she embarked on the teaching career that was to bring her and the elder William Grant Still together and to occupy her for the rest of her life.

Those two young people could scarcely have avoided falling in love. They must have been overcome by the wonder of it all, by the discovery of each other—and surely they must have felt that nothing like this had ever happened before. I say this not only because all lovers feel this way, but also because even today we are struck by the coincidence of two people who were so perfect for each other coming from different parts of the country to that one spot at that time.

The wedding decided upon, Carrie Fambro came to Mississippi for the ceremony. Woodville was surprised, but aglow, on learning the news. Someone asked a lady who was then a complete stranger to the family whether she would have the celebration at her home. She hospitably agreed, and then everyone's plans were upset when the bride's train failed to arrive on time. Nothing daunted, the groom and twenty-five guests made away with the wedding supper, and next day, when the bride finally made her appearance, she joined them in a substitute supper of ice cream and cake.

The young couple made their home in Woodville, where they both taught, he at Chapel Church and she at Bayridge Church, and where the young wife found instant favor among her husband's friends, many of them speaking of her admiringly as being "wide-awake."

Part of the time the young husband taught at Alcorn A&M, the college from which he had graduated. He also taught at Steward and later became principal of a school in a small Mississippi town named Gloster. The way in which this episode was closed is worthy of note.

At that time, he and one of his friends (who taught in a school a few miles away) both carried four-year exemptions from examinations (whereas most teachers had two-year expemptions at best) and first-grade certificates for teaching. As was to be expected, white Southern teachers who had the same qualifications were paid more than the colored teachers. The elder Still's friend got to thinking about this, and the more he thought, the angrier he became.

My father-in-law knew his environment too well. He felt it wiser to remain silent on such a question, but his friend was determined to seek justice. On a Saturday he went into town to visit the Superintendent and to protest against the difference in salary.

A Negro who spoke his mind! The colored people knew that something would happen. Early Monday morning a crowd of stern white people approached the friend's school, bent on showing him how to behave. He saw them coming, quietly dismissed his pupils, got out his gun and fought back. He wounded several of his attackers before he was killed.

Then the mob, knowing of the friendship between the two men and presuming therefore that the elder Still must be an accomplice started out toward his school. My father-in-law was warned, but even had he not been, he needed no special psychic powers to advise him of the coming of these brave people who go in great numbers to capture a lone man. He dismissed his pupils, closed the school and left, never to return. Fortunately for him, the incident also remained closed.

During this time, my father-in-law had another source of income. He was a partner in a small grocery store, a business run by his friend Harry Anderson. As the financier in the enterprise, he would come into town every Saturday to check over the accounts and do whatever else was necessary. Before his marriage he kept the money gained from his various activities for his own education. Afterward he saved it for his son.

On May 11, 1895, less than a year after the parents' wedding, a baby boy was born at the country plantation named Piney Woods, owned in part by the elder William Grant Still. He was named for his father. The young parents were delighted with their baby, as are all parents with their first-born infants. They took him everywhere to show him off—even, the summer after he was born, to a six-day Teachers' Institute in Woodville. Their friends at the Institute that summer could not know that they were seeing the elder William Grant Still for the last time.

A few months later, after a visit to his old sweetheart (who never fully recovered from her disappointment at losing him) my father-in-law was suddenly taken ill. Nobody ever found out exactly what was wrong. Some said it was typhoid fever or malaria. Others said he "ate something that disagreed with him." Still others whispered of jealousy, of mystery and of witchcraft. Almost everybody agreed that the cause of his sudden illness was more complex than it appeared on the surface, but in those days they never asked questions, never investigated. His wife wanted their son to believe that his father had died of a fever, so that was what she told him. In later years, others voiced different opinions.

During the illness, my mother-in-law saw that most evil omen, an owl, around the porch. Time after time she tried to drive it away. It always returned. Finally it came into the house itself. My father-in-law tossed feverishly, prayed that God would hold his little family in "the palm of His hand," then stood up in bed and announced that he saw an angel coming for him.

When he died, soon after that, his young wife seized the baby in her arms and ran screaming into the night. The funeral, they say, will never be forgotten in Woodville.

All his life my husband was conscious of an emptiness that could have been caused only by the absence of a father. His feeling was intensified when he dreamed of him one night, his eyes piercing and unforgettable. Always, his mother held his father up to the boy as an example of fine character and intellect.

After his death, they discovered among his belongings scattered scraps of lined paper covered with bar lines and notes. He actually had tried to compose. There couldn't have been a more valuable bequest than this urge toward musical creation. Very often we have wondered how far he might have gone if life had not been cut short for him, and if he had had greater opportunities for advancement. Surely no one could have made more out of so little in twenty-four years.

—*3*—

Carrie Fambro Still was stunned by the unexpected turn of events. What she had thought was the beginning of a new life was instead the end of a chapter. In little more than a year she had been a bride, a mother and a widow. Bewildered, she didn't know where to turn.

Although she was fond of her husband's family and the good friends she had made in Woodville, she could not forget the sorrow that had come to her in the little Southern town. She turned, as many young women might have done, to the one person who could give her solace and help: her mother. Anne Fambro was then living with another daughter, Laura, in Little Rock, Arkansas, so it was there that the young widow and her baby went soon after the father's passing.

More than a half century later, by a grotesque quirk of fate, Little Rock was to find its name used as a rallying cry for bigots in many parts of the world. Yet the boy William Grant Still grew up in the city

The infant "Babe Will." Courtesy William Grant Still Estate.

liking its people, enjoying its surroundings, and regarding it as an enlightened place in the South.

It was in Little Rock that his mother's new life really was to begin. There she taught English in the schools and there established her permanent home.

Anne Fambro, Billy's maternal grandmother.
Courtesy William Grant Still Estate.

The move was a wise one. Carrie Fambro Still could never have gotten along in Mississippi. She was too outspoken, too much aware of her identity as a person, and her responsibility toward the future. As a matter of fact, she was so intelligent (according to one story) that the Irish people in Little Rock wanted to claim her as their own, and to advance her to a high position in the city schools. She was "too smart to be a Negro," said some. At this, a few of the colored residents were reported to have raised a fuss, calling her a "foreigner" and demanding that she go back where she came from—i.e., to Woodville, where there were fewer opportunities. She sought the advice of the white people in charge of the Little Rock schools. They suggested that she stick it out. She did, ultimately winning honors and acceptance from both whites and Negroes.

She was never a servile woman. She met other people with courtesy and expected to be met with courtesy in return. On one occasion, when a white streetcar conductor in Little Rock called her "Carrie," she gave him such a stern lecture for this familiarity that he never dared to repeat it.

The country around Little Rock was colorful. Masses of vivid flowers contrasted with white dogwood and magnolia blossoms. There were black pine forests and the smell of pine wood burning, women in sunbonnets as in pioneer days, rude cabins, and always new land being cleared. Cotton was grown there, and how hard it was for the boy to pass the gins when he was hungry. They smelled like delicious ham, cooking. Sugar cane grew there too, and often there would be a primitive cane-mill near a home in an outlying village, with horses being driven round and round to extract the juice from the cane.

Even people in the city kept cows. Some boys made a living by coming around in the morning, collecting all the cows, taking them out to pasture, then bringing them back at sundown. City lots were huge in comparison with their more-or-less standard size now. No cows were kept in young Still's backyard, though there were chickens and a sizeable vegetable garden.

Most all positions of service then were held by colored people. In those days, white barbers, waiters or bellboys were unheard of. In Little Rock even the ice men were colored.

Of course, there were also colored professional people: journalists, lawyers, teachers, druggists, and so on. Every sort of business was run by colored people for colored people.

The neighborhood to which Carrie Fambro Still took her infant son was not segregated. White and colored lived amicably side by side in nice houses. All were at home in her house. It was a well-kept, middle-class home with some advantages the average dwelling does not always have: a fine library, musical instruments and, later, a phonograph.

In such surroundings the boy grew up, as a young *American* boy in an *American* community. What he was and how he grew were far from the usual stereotyped concept of a little colored boy in colored surroundings. His was never too far from the simple upbringing that plays an important part in American life. He was taught not to lose sight of the things that really counted, in favor of the fanciness that some people consider necessary. He did, thought and said the things that most American youngsters do, think and say. He was as naughty, as virtuous and as inventive as the next fellow. He followed this pattern, as did Mark Twain's Tom Sawyer, and he was (as boys should be) at once the pride, joy and despair of his mother's life.

To his intense regret, his mother was a firm believer in the old "spare the rod" principle. If his father had lived, she would have expected him to be the disciplinarian, but she knew that she had to be both mother and father. She had a job on her hands, for the boy was so obstinate that sometimes, when he *knew* he'd get a whipping, and that it would hurt, he'd go ahead and be disobedient anyway. Who knows where this stubbornness would have carried young Still if his mother hadn't had the will to tame it and to turn it into constructive channels? She carefully avoided the psychological chasms that swallow so many modern parents, and resorted to the most direct—and sometimes most painful—methods.

Around the age of three the baby developed a love for the pretty red flames that come from matches. Once he locked himself in a room and set it on fire. They had to break the door down to get him out. A spanking followed, but it apparently impressed the mother more than it did the baby, for a few months later he proceeded to wake up hours before the rest of the family and set an embroidered mantelpiece afire. Just in time to save the house from destruction, his mother awoke. The whipping that followed remained a vivid memory through all his life; as did the whipping he got the time they returned from a visit and he nonchalantly called his mother "Carrie," as all the grown-ups had. She took it as a mark of disrespect and dealt with it accordingly.

Nor was he allowed to run around the neighborhood without supervision. On the rare occasion when he was not restricted to his own backyard, she always had to know where he was, and it was she—not he—who decided at what time he should return. It was hard to watch the clock when he wanted so badly to play, but each time he overstayed, his mother's greeting on his return was the ominous, "All right, young man, march yourself upstairs."

This always started a flood of pleading, promises that he would never do it again, and so on. Such pleadings were absolutely useless, however, because when she made up her mind there was no opposing her. That strap of hers cracked furiously. Everywhere he went, it followed him. When he ducked under the bed, it caught him as he disappeared and came back to wallop him as he re-appeared on the other side. It wasn't an ordinary whip, either. A man might have used a razor strap. She had nothing of the sort handy, so she relied on a strap from an old-fashioned trunk.

Young Still's early love for gadgets often brought him into painful contact with his mother's educated strap. Every time she found that her new scissors were ruined because he had used them to cut tin cans, it came his way. She punished him whenever there was even a slight suspicion of his using incorrect English (she was a marvelous grammarian), or of slipping into a slovenly pronunciation. No "Negro" dialect in that household. He knew only too well what it meant to be a schoolteacher's son.

In his manhood, he could still recall vividly the few times that he escaped a whipping. For instance, there was the episode with the sherbet. Servings were never large enough. No matter how much he had had, there was always room for more. Once, taking matters into his own hands, he sneaked into the pantry with the biggest spoon he could find, and went to work. His mother found him there and asked what he was doing. Although his mouth was full, he answered politely, "Nothing," and the frozen stuff slid down into his stomach as he said it. The look on his face must have been remarkable, because his mother and the rather sizable audience that had assembled all burst into laughter.

His mother of course had many things to do besides disciplining a mischievous child. The memory of her holding her head and crying, "Oh, I could scream!" was another of the boy's indelible memories, as was another phrase that became inevitable with her: "Just a little minute!"

The brilliance that had distinguished her in Atlanta University now displayed itself in exquisite needlework that won prizes in county fairs; in colorful paintings (an art which she later abandoned in favor of theatrical activities); in the writing and directing of plays (one in the style of the old morality plays) and pageants; and in speeches. She produced many Shakespearean dramas in Little Rock. She was one of the leaders in the Lotus Club, a literary group dedicated to research and the discussion of matters of the moment. Toward the end of her life she wrote a book which was never published.

She was not a heartless martinet, nor an ambitious woman in whose scheme of life a child had no place. Hers was a warm personality; when she entered a room, she instantly drew attention. She was vivacious, forceful and intolerant of stupidity. Her students adored her. So did her son, though as a teacher and as a mother she clung to her high standards.

She also loved her son so dearly that she had to fight to keep from spoiling him. Every time she went downtown she brought something back for him. When he was hurt, ill, or bitten by dogs (as often happened in his childhood), she was beside herself with grief and worry, and was ready to spend all she had so that he could have the best of treatment. She laughed with him and at him on occasion, and he never thought of her in later years without being grateful for what she did to shape his character and to instill in him the will to accomplish something worthwhile.

A talent that Carrie Lena Fambro did *not* possess was one for cooking. Bluing in the roast was only one of the things the family had to endure when she stepped into the kitchen. When she tried to cook, she used all the pots and pans available, then left them for others to wash. She flavored steaks by spreading over them such a thick layer of pepper that the family was left gasping after every mouthful. No one objected when, for at least a part of each day, Anne Fambro took over the management of the house, the kitchen and the baby.

Grandma, like all true artists, enjoyed an appreciative audience, and her grandson was that. He used to run for her popovers and fritters! They were so hot that they burned his fingers, but he crammed them into his mouth anyway and then "patted his little stomach happily" as his aunt reminded him some forty years later, at which he cast a critical downward glance and remarked that it was not "little" anymore.

He is said to have cried a great deal in those days; certainly he had his share of illnesses, probably as a result of stuffing himself with the good things that came from Grandma's kitchen. Whenever headaches or other ailments hit him, he would see a large, whirling globe, the sight of which would intensify his pain.

Forming a background for his thoughts during childhood were the spirituals and Christian hymns Grandma sang at her work. "Little David, Play on Your Harp" competed with "Nothing But the Blood of

Jesus," but "Little David" was her favorite. Another musical memory of his boyhood came from the community habit of serenading. It was pleasant to be awakened from sleep by such sounds. He felt sorry when the custom was discontinued and knew that the musicians must have regretted the end of it, for it meant that their pockets would go unfilled.

Grandma told the boy stories of slavery days. She spoke of having seen long lines of slaves chained together, going from state to state, herded by a man with a long whip. It wasn't all "Hallelujah" and joyous spirituals then. She dramatized the work of the old-time "patty-rollers" (a corruption of "patrollers") who rode around on horseback at night to keep the slaves under strict control. Colored people feared them and used their name much as we might use the idea of the bogey man, to frighten children who misbehave. "The patty-rollers will get you if you don't watch out!"

Grandma spoke in awesome detail of the weather portents before the Civil War, when the skies were bloody and the days were dull. The slaves expected something momentous to happen.

Every bit of Grandma's affection was returned, although the boy couldn't forget in his younger days that it was she who had saddled him with a horrible nickname. People had called his father "Will," so she called him his likeness in miniature, "Baby Will," altered by his mother to "Babe Will." He despised the name and made no secret of his feelings. When he entered college and learned that all the students were to be known by nicknames, he made haste to tell his classmates a different one, lest someone from Little Rock appear and inflict "Baby Will" on him for the rest of his college days. Even in later years, when some friends from the old days impulsively called him "Baby Will," he found that his feelings hadn't changed a bit in more than eighty years. He still despised it as much as he did "Booger," a name given him by playmates at Union School.

Although they never moved from the South, the family took many train rides to other cities. It was fun, going to Milner, Georgia, (where his mother was born) with Grandma, probably because the boy had learned to make the trip pay. At home at the age of three he used to chirp to visitors, "Want to hear me sing? Want to hear me sing a song?" They all said that they did, and were properly appreciative when it was over. The very first time he tried this on adult fellow train passengers, they handed him money and candy in return. Thereafter he happily (and expectantly) sang for everybody.

Train rides to Atlanta with Grandma always ended interestingly, for his cousins there welcomed them with shouts of joy, principally because of Grandma's cooking, and they hoped that she would spend most of her time in the kitchen. The cousins were less than joyous over Baby Will's visits, for they considered him spoiled and knew they would have to give way to him every time he cried, or else incur Grandma's wrath. They enjoyed so much hearing his reedy, high-pitched voice threatening, "I'll tell my Grandma on you!" that they devoted themselves to tormenting him.

Cousin Norman was the one who conceived the most masterly plot to put him in his place. He pretended to eat a pretty red pepper. He smiled, licked his lips and patted his stomach with evident pleasure. The baby watched covetously until Norman said, "Want some candy, Baby?" Of course he did. Norman wasted no time in handing it over, and even less time in running away so that Grandma couldn't find him when Baby started howling.

Visiting with his mother in other cities was a different matter, for she was still young, beautiful and popular. Many of the young men called on her. In one town, a minister persisted in courting her even though she discouraged him because, she said, he preached all the time. To Grandma she would say with emphasis, "I wouldn't have him. I wouldn't have him." Accordingly, when he came calling, Baby Will was sent to the door to tell him that Mama was not at home.

Once, Baby Will announced affably instead, "Oh, come right in, Reverend. Mama's here. She's hiding under the bed!" The Reverend believed the first part of the statement but not the last. It was fortunate for the baby that Mama's sense of humor overcame her embarrassment.

It was in Barnesville, Georgia, where he would learn to make corn-silk cigarettes, and sit on the curbstone opposite the C.M.E. Church to hear the congregation sing Spirituals. It was there that he saw a man howling because he had been shot in the hand, and never understood why Grandma didn't want him to talk about it. It was also there that he saw his first mob, out for the blood of a Negro accused of rape. He sat calmly on the front porch and watched grizzled white farmers emerging from the woods with their guns.

These were memories of events only half-understood when they were happening, but they helped to shape the youngster growing out of his early childhood.

—4—

With school babyhood ended and boyhood began. All the while his mother was teaching him elementary facts, encouraging his creative efforts in drawing, constructing and so on (but forbidding him to copy anything, lest that destroy his originality), she was holding out to him—like the promise of a new toy—the schooldays ahead. How he looked forward to them, and what careful planning he did.

He watched the children already attending school, walking by with whole armloads of books. So he raided his mother's library with a collection of books that would have astonished a scholar.

Miss Alice, his first teacher, along with his mother (who taught in the high school department at the same school) explained to him that things had to be taken as they came, slowly, and all in good order.

At first, his contact with his mother at school came only at lunch time, when he would have to eat with her, whether she was on ground duty or in her room. Usually, he gobbled his food as quickly as possible and rushed out to play in the tree-filled, rocky schoolyard. Later, in his high school years, he was assigned to some of her classes. In some ways this was fortunate; his mother was determined not to let anyone accuse her of partiality, and in her fierce maternal pride, she insisted that he do better than all the others.

It was fortunate in another way also, because the other students sympathized with him wholeheartedly. Many times, for the slightest error on his part, he was punished by being made to stand in the corner, or was given demerits. One day, for example, while reading Chaucer's *Canterbury Tales* aloud to the class, he came to the word "dung" and laughed involuntarily. She cracked her ruler over his fingers and he started to pout. "Stick that lip in, young man!" she commanded. So, even if he lost the argument, he won—as they sometimes say in politics—for as he proved himself to be the opposite of a teacher's pet, his popularity with his classmates increased accordingly.

It was easier for Babe Will to get good grades than to stay out of mischief. He was willing to work for the first, but not so eager about the latter. One day he sneaked into the room where his uncle's embalmed body lay in state and tried to open the eyes. He was glad that no one found him there, for it was a gruesome experience.

Not so gruesome, however, as to deter him from going to see a big bold bandit with a large bullet hole visible in his chest when the body was put on display in the window of a funeral parlor. He had tried to hold up a railway clerk, and had been rewarded with death instead of the diamond stickpin he wanted. He was white. There was also a colored bandit who had been killed, embalmed, and put on public display in Little Rock, sitting upright in a chair. He made more of an impression on young minds in death than he ever could have in life.

During the summers when most people were on vacation, Carrie Fambro Still took her little son along when she taught school in the back country, many miles from the railroad. That was the only time of the year that the half-dressed children there could go to school, and then only for a few weeks each time. Their schoolhouse was about as big as a modern living room in a middle-class home, built of log walls chinked with mud and covered with branches and leaves. When it rained, school had to be dismissed for the day. The teacher was frightened—but not the pupils—when a large green scorpion once decided to attend her classes. A barefoot boy unconcernedly killed it and she had no more trouble.

Of course there were no hotels in the back country, so while they were there the boy and his mother lived as those simple people lived, in mud-daubed houses. One night, after he had seen a woman writhing and groaning from a tarantula bite, the boy found a tarantula of his very own when he pulled back his bedcovers. It disappeared quickly, not to return. It took courage to climb into bed after that, but he made it!

Since the contact with primitive life on those occasions was first-hand, the boy's mother was constantly vigilant to make sure that he did not copy the personal habits and uncouth speech of the back country people. They would say, "fah" for "fire," for instance. When one day he pronounced "far" with the usual Southern soft "r," she thought that he was saying "fire" as they said it and gave him a sound whipping. She was only, she insisted, trying to keep him from "following the path of least resistance."

It was in the back country that they attended a basket meeting where everyone brought a basket filled with pies, cakes and other good things. Everywhere he was allowed to eat whatever pleased him. He divided his time between eating and laughing as the folks sang spirituals and shouted in ecstasy. The emotional import completely escaped him; he regarded it as a show put on for his benefit. He had yet to learn about the beauties of Negro folk music, even though he had heard it from his beloved spiritual-singing Grandmother.

No one was happier than Grandma when the boy learned to read. Anne Fambro was only a spectator among the educated members of her family, for she had been so busy giving them an education that she had forgotten herself and didn't even know her letters. Yet she dearly loved the imaginative world of books and welcomed her grandson's reading aloud to her by the hour, hesitatingly at first when he could only spell out the words, but more fluently as he gradually became proficient.

Even on dark, cold mornings before anyone else was awake, he'd be up, making fires in the stoves and preparing to read his favorite book of the moment. This was, of course, a situation in which Carrie

Fambro Still exercised guidance. So careful was she in helping him to choose worthwhile books that she had her friends laughing, because such a small boy was being made to wade through *The Scarlet Letter*. He found it far from engrossing.

Dumas, on the other hand, was exciting. He and Grandma were kept in suspense from day to day and from chapter to chapter. They liked ghost stories, too, though afterwards he imagined that the ghosts were lurking in all the darkest corners. There was only a slight interest in another of his mother's literary musts: *Gulliver's Travels*. The boy and his grandmother had fun picturing the Lilliputians as animated dolls, but were content to leave the giants alone.

After Dumas, the boy's real love was literature about the Wild West, which his mother saw as a weakness. When she found out about it, she promptly forbade all Wild West books, along with detective stories. In their place, she substituted Horatio Alger and other such works. For days, the boy roamed the house aimlessly, unable to develop any interest in the new books. Grandma, herself melancholy over the unexpected turn of events, came to the rescue. Together they searched for the hidden Diamond Dick novels, found them and put them in a closet where they could get them when they wanted them. Grandma promised not to expose him, so that his mother remained— or pretended to remain—unaware of this crime against the laws of good taste.

Babe Will had gone to his mother's own library for the bulk of his reading, for there was no public library in Little Rock open to colored people. It was not long before his mother resolved to do something about this. She recruited the graduates of the school for a benefit performance of a Shakespearan play. During long days and evenings she drilled her young actors. The resulting performance brought in several hundred dollars at the box office, and with that money the library in Capital Hill School was started. Later performances brought in more money to expand the library.

It was during one of his mother's theatrical performances that Babe Will discovered something about himself: He felt a difference between himself and other people. In one of the presentations his mother directed, he was cast as the boy Hiawatha. Immediately preceding him on the program was a student who brought down the house with a

Charles B. Shepperson, Billy's stepfather.
Courtesy William Grant Still Estate.

snappy Buck-and-Wing to a song called "I'm goin' back, back to Baltimore." When Babe Will followed with his little Indian dance, so seriously, the audience laughed. He wondered a long time about that, not only because he wanted some nickels and dimes and approbation, but also because it somehow told him that nothing he did would ever be completely understood; he wondered whether there was something wrong with him. Often when he was grown, he would feel bewildered that his most sincere offer of friendship would be cast aside as if it didn't matter. Gradually, he came to understand that some people are not meant to be members of a herd, and he was one of them.

For some time, Babe Will had noticed that most of his mother's admirers no longer called as frequently as before. The reason was that she had shown unusual interest in one of them, Mr. Charles B. Shepperson by name, a railway postal clerk who roomed nearby. Mr. Shepperson also ranked high with the boy. On one occasion when grown-ups were visiting his mother and their children were visiting

him, the youngsters decided to play a game of choices, each child naming the adult he liked best. Babe Will's instant choice was Mr. Shepperson. So when his mother told him that she had decided to marry again
and that Charles Shepperson was the man she had chosen, he was
overjoyed.

They were married at home, but since Grandma insisted that children should be seen and not heard, the boy didn't get any nearer than
the outskirts of the festivities. It was probably soon after they returned
from their honeymoon at the St. Louis World's Fair that Will became
bold enough to ask Mr. Shepperson what the mysterious middle initial
"B" stood for in his name. He laughed. "*B* for buttermilk," he replied,
and that's all he would say on the subject during the many years thereafter. He knew how to keep a secret!

Mr. Shepperson was another colored person who carried himself
with dignity. Everyone who knew him—colored and white—called
him "Mister." He earned that respect and was to become one of the
strongest and most constructive influences in the boy's life.

Mr. Shepperson was a comparatively young man when he married
Carrie Fambro Still, so he remembered well all the things that little
boys like. He fired his stepson's imagination by telling him marvelous
tales of the time he was a mail clerk on the train that Cherokee Bill
tried to hold up, of the marshalls fighting with the bandits, and of
mailbags made of buffalo hide so thick and so full of mail that they
turned the bullets. He took the boy to Coffeyville so that he could see
the last bank the Dalton Boys had tried to rob, and could witness a
trial where a man who had merely stolen a horse was sentenced to the
amazing term of twenty years in prison. Horses were still valuable assets in those days. To a boy already fascinated by books dealing with
these same subjects, this was Paradise, for here were scenes and characters transplanted directly from imagination to reality. And a sympathetic companion like Mr. Shepperson made it all more exciting.

In a creek south of Little Rock, Mr. Shepperson and his stepson
went fishing, after which the boy spent many hours lamenting the little
fish that got away.

Having a turkey dinner for Thanksgiving wasn't then the routine
matter it is now, for Mr. Shepperson used to go into the Indian country
to get theirs and bring it back alive. One year it was so frisky that the

boy had to chase it up a pole before it would agree to be their holiday dinner.

When the circus came to town, Mr. Shepperson and his stepson would watch the parade together. How excited the white crowd would get when the band played "Dixie!" How the rebel yell would ring out! (Even today, visiting entertainers in the South can provoke an enthusiastic response with "Dixie.") When Theodore Roosevelt came to Little Rock on the Rock Island Railroad, Mr. Shepperson was careful to see that this opportunity was not missed by his stepson. He took him to the depot and placed him as close as possible to the train. When the great man came out to make his speech, the boy was positive that he was speaking and smiling just for him.

The Sheppersons attended the Cole and Johnson shows, which were in reality operettas, whenever they came to town. Afterwards, at home, they would describe the music, relate the plots and laugh again at the jokes. In those days of successful Negro shows that had been created by Negroes, colored people could laugh at comic portrayals of themselves, because they were true to life and lacked malice. It is only the white man's concept of the Negro that is unfunny to the Negro.

Sometimes Mr. and Mrs. Shepperson went together, but at other times the boy was the one who was allowed to accompany his stepfather. His mother would say that she had to correct examination papers, or would give some other excuse. So together Will and his stepfather saw stage shows like *Ben Hur*, *The Wizard of Oz*, and *Robin Hood*. The music was glorious and the whole atmosphere of the theatre fascinating to the boy. He even loved its smell, that musty, incomparable odor that is found nowhere else. When he was sent downtown on errands he'd go out of his way to pass by the theatre so that he could sneak backstage and be a part of the glamor.

It's easy to see how such a child could be influenced by a man like Charles Shepperson. His employment was prosaic, and he was not artistic in a creative sense, but he was a lover of beauty who responded to the same things that his stepson loved. After the daily work was done, the two of them would sing duets at home and discuss the plays they had seen and the music they had heard. When that startling new invention, the phonograph, came on the market, he bought one and began what was to become a sizable library of Red Seal records. These gave the boy his first chance to hear real operatic music, music such as he had never heard before save in his dreams. He neglected his chores to play the records over and over. As they revolved on the turntable, he knew that he had to become a musucian.

At their house even their pranks took a musical turn. They owned a stack of the fancifully titled sheet music so popular after the turn of the century. One of the most evocative titles was "The Burning of Rome." Mrs. Shepperson pulled this piece out and proceeded to play it with gusto. Rome was burning gaily away when Mr. Shepperson walked in with a pail of water. "What's that?" she asked. "Oh, that!" he replied, on his way out of the room. "That's in case the fire gets out of control."

In those days the boy made his own violins. They were toys, but they were varnished, had strings, and were capable of producing sounds. He liked his own handiwork better than the things that could be bought, so he made other toys too, out of stray materials he got by barter, plus such items as he found by crawling under old houses and in other out-of-the-way spots, material no store could offer. There were mud forts with homemade cannon to shoot down boats, soldiers, and balloons that rose into the air, and roller coasters made from planks. There were also piquant chemical experiments like nitrate of grasshopper, as well as electrical experiments.

Of all his creations, though, the ones that most impressed the family were the toy violins. When the time came for him to begin study on a musical instrument, the piano (which was already in the house) wasn't even considered. As a matter of course, his mother bought a violin and paid for his violin lessons with Mr. Price, a short, cross-eyed man who was never—within anyone's memory—without his long black coat.

The days of Will's first musical instruction were magical days. He was absorbed in the new world that had opened up to him. In school he had been taught to read music, but he never really learned his notes until he began to play the fiddle. And as soon as he learned to read them, he wanted to write them. Since there was no manuscript paper at hand, he made his own, laboring to get each group of five lines symmetrical and evenly spaced. When he began to jot down little melodies, his mother gave him immediate encouragement. At school, while other students doodled in their spare moments, he scribbled musical notes.

Music students are often asked to display their abilities in public; they thrive on the applause they receive at club meetings, school assemblies, and the like. Young Still didn't. His public performances were seldom successful, to hear him describe them in later years. Self-consciousness may have been at the root of this, for once (when he was scheduled to play *The Angel's Serenade* at a literary meeting) he began to tremble and sweat profusely long before the time for his solo arrived. This moistened the violin, so he was then in agony as he played. The angels could scarcely have been pleased, and surely his mother must have sat there wondering why she was bothering to pay for his lessons. He suspected later that there was more truth than was intended in the observation of an admiring girl that "Billy used to play the violin so that it almost made you cry."

During grammar school days he became interested in the Episcopal choir. Here was glorious music in which he could participate, so he joined. He sang for several Sundays, discovering that an Episcopal choir did not devote itself solely to music. It was kneel down, rise, kneel down, rise, and so on. That involved too much effort. He reluctantly left that music behind and concentrated on the violin, without calisthenics.

There was no fifth grade for him in school. He skipped it entirely. Then, for the eighth and ninth grades, he was sent to the Union School (because they lived in that district), away from his mother's watchful eyes. At that time the gratitude he would later feel for her rigorous training had not begun to make itself felt, so he regarded his sudden transfer as a deliverance and immediately ran wild, joined by his friend Leo. They played hookey to watch the trains pass and to dream of the day when they would travel. They went to watch the horses being shod in the blacksmith's shop. They had a wonderful time. To their shocked amazement they found, on returning to school, that the principal, Mr. Watkins, was waiting for them. He applied the regulation strap and proved to be an energetic substitute for Mrs. Shepperson.

Another lesson learned outside of classes was equally painful and no less instructive. One day he teased a little boy and tried to take his apple away from him. The boy grabbed something hard, threw it and hit young Will in the head. It made a bad cut which had to be treated by a doctor.

In addition to learning not to be a bully, he learned how to treat bullies. Down their street one day came a little boy, being chased by a crowd of much bigger boys. Young Still faced the pursuers squarely with all the determination he could muster. They dispersed. He wondered later what would have happened if they hadn't.

His own neighborhood bully was Walter. He tormented young Still on every possible occasion. One night Will dreamed that he had fought Walter and been victorious, so that Walter had never tried to bother him again. Next morning, it seemed that this wasn't a bad idea. He wrote Walter a formal note. Later, in the presence of witnesses, he announced that he would fight him after he'd had lunch with his mother. The other children were eager to see the promise was carried out. They escorted both boys to the battlefield, where they squared off. Will had no idea what should happen after that, for fighting was something quite outside his experience. Walter fixed that. He made a dive for Will. Will responded by blacking his eye. That ended the fight.

Mrs. Shepperson never mentioned the subject, but she knew about it and was pleased that Will had shown courage. Josie, the pretty little girl of whom he was enamored at the moment, admired him, too. He was happy because she was happy. Next Christmas, when someone gave him a dollar, he used it to buy a doll for Josie.

When he fell in love with Fredricka he learned not to be overconfident. He wanted to impress her, but couldn't find the words. He decided to go back to established precedent. If he had won one fight, why not another? In Fredricka's presence, he picked a fight with his ordinarily peaceable friend Leo. She wailed excitedly, "Oh, please don't fight! Don't fight!" At which he saw himself again a hero and was more determined than ever. He collected some stones and threw them at Leo. When Will ran out of ammunition Leo was still well-supplied, and began a barrage that ran Will home. Fredricka was not impressed.

Another little girl inspired him to show off by riding a bicycle before he was old enough. He ran into a building and cut his forehead so deeply that he was ill for several weeks afterward.

Many of the Sheppersons' friends were not colored. As a matter of fact, Will's two best friends, Stanley and Clifford, were sons of one of Mr. Shepperson's white coworkers. The three of them played together regularly and attached an elaborate flag signal system to their houses, visible to all three.

Many years later, when the three were grown men and Will returned to Little Rock for his mother's funeral, Stanley came over from North Little Rock, where he was living then, to visit him. It was good to see him again, and it made Still realize that it's impossible for *all* the little white and colored boys and girls who play together in childhood to grow up hating each other.

But what of the little boys and girls who *don't* play together? There was another white playmate, a boy named Boone, the son of a railroad conductor. He and young Will played together until the day Will passed his home as he was entertaining other white boys. Said Will, "Hello, Boone!" Said Boone, "Hello, coon!" After that they never even greeted each other any more.

A German family in the neighborhood was the only family that held itself rigidly aloof—with the exception of their son, who played with young Will until the day someone called him a "nigger-lover." Their friendship ended then.

Once, walking home from school, Will was ambushed by a large group of white boys who threw rocks at him. He ran back to school so that he could walk home with his mother. This same matter of rock-throwing had been the cause of some trouble in general between the white and colored boys in Little Rock. One white boy was said to have been killed as a result, so thenceforth many of the white boys were allowed to carry rifles to school to "protect themselves." Although Will had been the one attacked in his own instance, no one suggested that he have any such means of protection.

On another occasion, Will happened to board a streetcar just after a colored chauffeur, driving his employer, had injured a white pedestrian. A white bystander boarded the streetcar and became furiously angry at the boy, swearing at him and calling him ugly names. Another white man passed the boy walking, pushed him off the sidewalk and said matter-of-factly, "Get out of the way, nigger!" Little Rock's Center Street was the scene of another incident, long a bitter memory. There he saw two white officers strike a colored man with their sticks until his blood dyed the pavement a deep red.

There was a knock at the Shepperson's door one morning. When they answered it, they found a colored man in tattered, dirty overalls. He was a sharecropper who had come all the way from Louisiana; he asked for enough food to help him along until he could get to St. Louis and freedom. Although Emancipation had come long years before, to him it was still a dream. He had been working for nothing all his life. One day, hope and ambition made him decide to leave, but they sent bloodhounds after him and brought him back. This time he hopped a freight train and made good his escape.

One of Mrs. Shepperson's friends, a well-to-do lady who had a large house, well-staffed with servants, was very handsome and very fair of skin. Had she not lived in a city where she was known to be colored, she could easily have passed for white. One day she just got tired of being colored. She moved herself, her family and her belongings into the fashionable white suburb of another city, hundreds of miles away.

Some years ago, we received a letter from my father-in-law's old business partner, telling how he had had to flee for his life from Mississippi. He had bothered no one. He had simply worked hard and acquired property, which angered those white people who didn't want to see a colored man get ahead. There actually were places in the South where a colored man dared not appear in ordinary street clothes, lest he be called a "dressed-up nigger" and meet trouble, no matter how circumspect his actions.

Incidents such as these became a part of his consciousness despite the efforts of his family to shield him from prejudice and to keep his mental outlook broad and clear by giving him all sorts of contacts and by never discussing racial differences in front of him. Nevertheless, on his first visit to St. Louis, where there were no Jim Crow laws, he felt bewildered. Imagine going into a washroom with no sign to tell you whether it was for colored or white! Will had not realized before that this distinction had been made a fundamental part of his being.

—5—

Eventually, elementary school became routine, merely something to be sandwiched in between periods of play. Then, as Will entered high school, he discovered that school was not only learning—it was competition, and that competition was fun.

Like his father, he made good marks in mathematics, much to his own astonishment, for he was never very fond of the subject. When one considers the affinity between mathematics and music, however, it may not be so surprising after all. Many people who today call themselves composers are really mathematicians in disguise, a fact that becomes all too apparent on listening to their music.

Not surprisingly, history turned out to be a favorite subject. It was as fascinating and as dramatic as a story book. Literature, however, was the subject in which, by command, he was forced to excel, for his mother was the teacher.

His love of competition was so strong that young Will even went out for the football team. In less than a minute, someone ran up against him and gave him a hard blow to the head. For a boy who had withdrawn from the Episcopal Choir because he disliked kneeling and rising, this was too much. He made a lightning decision to leave football alone. He had demonstrated that he had courage when it was needed, but going out of his way to get hurt didn't strike him as being at all necessary. Perhaps that was the reason that in later years he looked with awe and admiration on one of his own young relatives who became a football star in school and later played the game professionally.

During the high school year, his mother offered another ultimatum: that he should go to work during his vacations and learn to assume responsibilities. He resolved to combine business with pleasure; he got a job in an ice cream factory. It lasted exactly one day. Next time, he managed to work at a soda fountain. After that came a Coca Cola job.

Once he tried waiting table, but lost count of the dishes he broke. Working in an electrotherapy establishment later, he nearly drove the doctors crazy, experimenting with their machinery. His mother wasn't very happy, either, about his accepting their leftover sulphuric acid for his own use at home, when the bottle fell off the dresser and the contents ate up a large part of their white bearskin rug.

His first pair of long trousers was bought with the money he earned one summer, making barrel heads in an Arkansas heading factory. The work was exacting, because the slightest dent in the wood spoiled the piece. To add to his worries, the heat was almost unbearable, and the thick dust of the factory hurt his lungs, but he stuck it out. The resulting pair of trousers amounted to a special triumph for him, the product of his own painful labor.

His mother was in her element when he was named valedictorian of his graduating class. She wrote his speech and coached him on delivery, gestures and stage deportment. But she encountered unexpected difficulties when she insisted that the paper be memorized. She threatened to take away his violin, and this brought quick results. The speech was committed to memory in record time, and commencement proceeded as planned.

Though the violin was still important to him, somewhere along the line Will had forgotten his desire to be a professional musician; his aim now was to go to Tuskegee Institute and learn how to raise chickens. His mother had other ideas. Her choice was Wilberforce University in Wilberforce, Ohio, where he could take military training and cultivate a good posture and prepare to enter medical school. The young man himself finally had to admit that he wasn't cut out to be a poultry farmer.

Once at Wilberforce, he began to discover what he rediscovered often in the following years, that the community he had left was one of the most enlightened he would ever know, among colored people and among many white people. There, cultural and intellectual pursuits were held in esteem; Negro achievement was praised; Negro artists were engaged to give public programs. Clarence Cameron White, the composer, gave a violin recital. (In later years, he remarked that his composer friends usually considered him a fine violinist, while his violinist friends regarded him as an excellent composer.) Mme. Azalia Hackley, who helped so many colored students get scholarships, gave a vocal recital. Richard B. Harrison, later to win fame as The Lord in *The Green Pastures* was then earning a living by travelling around to give readings. He read a Shakespearean play in Little Rock.

But it took a little growing up and a great deal of visiting other places for young Will to be able to make just comparisons.

He enrolled in Wilberforce University in September of 1911 in a course designed to lead to a Bachelor of Science degree. The official records of Wilberforce reveal that "Mr. Still maintained a slightly above-average scholastic record." The fact that it was only "slightly" above average was owing—not to the absence of his mother, as one might suppose—but to his sudden realization that music, not science, was to be his life. All the energy that otherwise might have gone to make him a brilliant doctor was poured into music which, for a student with a science major, was an extracurricular subject.

There was much more musical activity at Wilberforce than Still had ever known before, and he was eager to make himself a part of it. He was surprised and flattered to find that his violin playing was enjoyed. He hadn't been especially proud of it before, but now the admiration of the people at Wilberforce made him outdo himself. There were students who played better than he, technically, but he tried to play with the soul and style he had caught from the Red Seal records at home. Then he began to diversify and learn to play other instruments.

A band was then being organized in the college. Instruments and instruction books were bought and students were invited to join. There was more than one reason for Still's interest. Not only did he enjoy music, but he disliked the military drill in the open air on cold mornings—drills from which the band members were excused. So, courageously, he signed up for the clarinet. He took the instrument and instruction book and set out to learn by himself; it wasn't long before he knew enough about it to be able to take an active part in the band rehearsals.

Having introduced himself to this new instrument, he put it to further use by playing in the choir, near the girls who sang so sweetly. This resulted in his learning to improvise and to transpose at sight. Adapting the choral lines to a clarinet pitched in B flat required that he transpose each note, a skill that he rapidly developed, and one that would later prove valuable.

When something happened to take the bandleader at Wilberforce away, the post was offered to young Still. He accepted, and his study of different instruments began in earnest. A good many more were needed to supply the sounds the boy wanted to hear in the new band arrangements he made. A piccolo, for instance, was a necessity. Wilberforce had the instrument but no one to play it. It was up to young Still to teach a student-recruit to play, but first he had to learn to play it himself. He learned about the saxophone the same way. He also taught himself to play the bass viol, viola and cello, not well enough to become a soloist, but well enough to be familiar with the possibilities and limitations of the instruments.

It was the oboe, which he also taught himself at Wilberforce, that made the deepest impression on the faculty. The professor in charge of the dormitory had reason to be annoyed at its woeful sounds when the budding performer used to march up and down the dormitory halls, practicing all the way. "Are you at it again?" the professor would cry in depression, as he burst through the door. Sometimes, to escape a scolding, the young bandleader would run and jump into bed with his

Billy with school friends. (*Left to right*) Louis Perkinson, Billy, Orson Bean, Billy's "Man Friday." Courtesy William Grant Still Estate.

clothes on. The angry professor would find him there, apparently sound asleep.

Many years after his Wilberforce days were over, the man who had been registrar wrote a letter in which he referred to Still as being "a great man," and Miss Hallie Q. Brown, who had taught him English and who had also been one of his mother's teachers, went on record as saying that, in his college years, young Still was "studious, alert, and gave promise of a bright future." Still enjoyed these comments immensely. "My, my!" he remarked. "They certainly didn't think I was great when I was learning to play the oboe up and down their halls!"

Every month before his allowance came, the music books he wanted were checked off in his precious Carl Fischer catalogue. The Fischer firm received practically all his spending money. Little did he dream that one day this big New York publishing house would be handling his own compositions and that the royalties would go far to balance the money he had spent with them in his youth. Once bought, scores like Weber's *Oberon* and Wagner's *Flying Dutchman* and books containing stories of famous symphonies would be placed inside his regular textbooks during classes, so that he could read about music instead of studying his assignments. He also attended concerts and operas in nearby Dayton.

Soon a string quartet was formed at Wilberforce and for this group, too, he made arrangements hoping to improve on those he had heard. He hadn't yet heard a real symphony orchestra. When at last he did, he knew at once that this was the way a combination of instruments should sound. His ear was satisfied at last.

It was only a small step from there to his first compositions, which were of a religious nature. Mrs. Marvin (wife of one of the professors) was interested enough to play over on the piano the things he had written. Hearing the music and observing it, as it were, through the eyes of someone else helped him to develop his critical faculties. Mme. Florence Cole-Talbert, a colored soprano who had been introduced to Little Rock in a pageant written and produced by Mrs. Shepperson, came to Wilberforce and supported his creative efforts. So when the composer Clarence Cameron White also came to Wilberforce and later said that he had "discovered" young Still, Still remarked, "I'd like to know how he could have avoided it. I dogged his footsteps until he *had* to pay attention to me!" Dr. White listened patiently, advised, and remained a friend during the years to come.

The boy had decided to become a composer in the serious tradition. He had thought a good deal about the music he had heard and had concluded that what separated the works of the masters from pieces like "The Burning of Rome" was their *spiritual* content. He wrote music feverishly, trying to rise to great heights, but was never wholly satisfied with the results. He was searching.

At that time, he was not particularly fond of Negro music. Years passed before he felt that it was actually a part of him and he could devote himself to a thorough study of it. In the meantime, he heard it in all its phases and absorbed it subconsciously. He travelled all over the South, from the backward areas to the intellectual centers, and the things he heard were never forgotten. It was just as well, though, that there was a period when European music was highest in his affections, for the tools of his trade had to be mastered before he could apply them to the music of colored Americans.

After a recital of his first compositions (some songs and band pieces) was given at Wilberforce, the enthusiastic reaction of those very kind people made him decide to throw his scientific studies out the window. He wrote his family a letter, announcing his decision to leave Wilberforce in order to go to Oberlin and begin musical study in earnest. The family ignored the letter and the decision. When he went home on vacation he discovered why.

His mother, despite her leanings toward the artistic, realized—as he in his youthful enthusiasm did not—that he was inescapably a Negro. What future, she wondered, could a Negro find in serious music? With fine scorn, she pictured her son as a poverty stricken musician, hungry, with the elbows of his jacket and the seat of his trousers patched. In her day, so many of the Negro popular musicians were a disreputable lot. They drank (or at least, she thought they did) and they were illiterate and immoral. They frequented cheap dives and honkytonks. The better colored people thought of them only as entertainers and didn't invite them into the finer homes. Carrie Shepperson felt that for her son's own good, she had to take a strong stand.

Her son understood eventually, but at the moment he couldn't see why he was unable to convey to her that he was determined to succeed in a different sort of music; he couldn't see why she wouldn't believe that this was possible for a colored man in America. She was deeply disappointed that he didn't want to be a doctor; he was equally disappointed that she wouldn't stand behind him in his chosen profession. By now his mind was made up: nothing but music would do. He returned to Wilberforce to continue his other studies, but both he and his mother knew that this was only a formality.

He read every book he could find about musicians. First, he chose Samuel Coleridge-Taylor as his model and even tried to make his hair grow straight up as his did. This was a problem that was never completely solved, because young Still's hair was straight naturally, while Coleridge-Taylor's was bushy. After months of trying, he began to ask himself why he should copy someone else. Why not be himself? He wrote to his aunt in Canada to promise that someday he meant to be greater even than Coleridge-Taylor, and to wear his hear in his own way.

One of his books told how Beethoven used to go into the woods to compose. Since there were many spots around Wilberforce where nature invited communion, the young man decided to see if it would work for him as it had for Beethoven. He went into the woods, lay down with a grassy mound for a pillow, heard birds singing and leaves whispering, and saw some wild strawberries. The more he looked at them the hungrier he grew. Finally he picked them, bought some sugar, concocted a dessert and forgot all about Beethoven for a while.

Beethoven and the other masters of music were never very far from his thoughts, however. At school and at home on vacation, he composed furiously, trying to get several pieces ready for submission to national contests for composers. His mother thought this absurd for one so limited in his musical education, but he saw nothing peculiar in it. He was anxious only to avoid her scathing comments, so he would compose at night—almost all night long—sitting in his pajamas at the dining room table. He would beg anyone who found him not to tell his mother.

One contest was for a three-act opera. He mailed in a piano score totalling exactly twenty pages. The judges wrote back to ask what on earth he had sent! Another set of critics, for another contest, replied to an overambitious effort by saying that the music had merit, though they regretted they couldn't completely understand it.

None of this got in the way of his interest in girls.

He enjoyed dancing, especially the tango and schottische, which his mother had learned in order to teach him, but he had to know the girls with whom he danced. He usually felt ill-at-ease in public places with all the bars let down, where it was customary to ask total strangers to be one's dancing partners. He also felt strange among people who drank or gambled. This made all the more mysterious young Still's disappearance from Wilberforce two months before graduation, with his cap and gown already bought and his scholastic work almost completed.

Some of the girls had suggested to several of the boys that they all take a walk into the woods. They thought it would be fun, but they all knew that it was against the university's strict rules. They decided to go, nevertheless, and someone warned the faculty that this walk was about to take place.

Young Still was paired off with a girl whom he had known casually. When the little group of walkers had almost arrived at its destination

(Still didn't even get as far as the woods), members of the faculty suddenly appeared from behind bushes and trees where they had been hiding and threatened all with expulsion. Since nothing immoral had happened—indeed, there hadn't been time for anything of the sort—the students were bewildered at the turn of events and couldn't imagine why so much fuss was being made.

Still decided that they were going to expel him, so he simply packed his things and left for Columbus, taking only a suitcase, his fiddle and his oboe. Back in Little Rock, Carrie Shepperson was hurt and disappointed, but she accepted her son's written explanation with a measure of sympathy and from time to time sent him small sums to help him out.

He instinctively turned to music to support himself. And here, in retrospect, one might see the hand of Providence at work. He might have been writing an entirely different sort of music in the years to come, if he had not pushed himself into the commercial world in the spring of 1915, for a sheltered musician has a completely different viewpoint from the one who makes himself a part of the contemporary world. Jazz, folk idioms, the music of the dives as well as of the conservatory and concert hall, all these were to mingle with his formal training as the years passed, and all were to become parts of his musical experience.

6

The closing of the Wilberforce days found the boy stunned, discouraged and lonely. His troubles were so close that he could not see them as anything but monumental. He felt cut off from his family; he felt that he had done very little to justify his mother's hopes for him. For the first time in his life, a job had become a necessity instead of a lark. Always before, he had been secure in the knowledge that a comfortable home and plenty of good food awaited him if he chose to quit. The world now had a mighty different appearance.

He was still more discouraged when Tom Howard heard him play the violin and reluctantly told him that he wasn't good enough for professional work. He had to tide himself over the rough spot with a job which paid six dollars a week for cleaning up a club and racking pool balls. Then Tom Howard heard him practicing the *William Tell* Overture on the oboe and gave him a job with an orchestra that played in Cleveland's Luna Park—at fifteen welcome dollars a week. Howard liked his cello playing too, and let him play that as well as oboe. Work soon became more plentiful and he saved all he could out of his salary. He went into the National Guard Band, played oboe and fiddle in various orchestras and joined a group of musicians then playing at the Athletic Club. All of this was done in Mr. Shepperson's cast-off dress suit, which had to be held in place with safety pins because it was so very much bigger than Still was.

The professional musicians with whom he played in Columbus spent their free time Sundays playing over standard music just for the love of it. Not symphonies, however, for the group wasn't large enough. Just overtures, operatic excerpts and other concert music. They also made it a point to hear good music whenever possible, even though they had no assurance that they'd ever be able to put what they were learning to any public use.

Not only did he learn by joining these practice sessions, but he also enjoyed the companionship of men with kindred ideals. Besides these musicians, he had only a few friends in Columbus. Most memorable was Nimrod Allen, a Wilberforcean who had graduated long before and who became a most constructive force in the field of social service in America. He was then in charge of the Columbus YMCA and was later Executive Secretary of the Columbus Urban League. The warmth of his friendship and that of his wife Clara meant a lot to the lonely Still.

Often he just sat for hours alone in his room, so when letters began to come from the girl with whom he had walked into the woods at Wilberforce, they found him vulnerable. They intimated that it was he who had been responsible for everything that had happened, (he didn't know then how often he was to hear that refrain in the years to come!) and that he owed it to her to redeem her reputation. Gradually the full purpose of the letters became clear, and like a knight or Don Quixote, he rushed to the rescue. They were married in the fall of 1915.

His mother was upset—much more than she had been over the escapade that drove him away from college. In the interim, with her characteristic thoroughness, she had been asking questions and doing some investigating on her own. She had come to the conclusion that things were not what they seemed. She and the new wife met each other and immediately felt jealousy, envy and mutual distrust. Still

Grace Bundy, Still's first wife. Photo by Cloud's Studio.

Billy and Grace had four children during the years they were married. Courtesy William Grant Still Estate.

soon discovered that he and his wife's mother disliked each other just as intensely, yet he was forced to have her living in his house for many years. Few members of his family ever met his wife, a woman with her own friends and her own ways, to which she expected him to conform.

Next spring, she went to live with her parents in Danville, Kentucky, where he had to go whenever he wanted to see her. Again, he was bewildered and lonely. She would not come to live with him, and there was no outlet for his talents in Danville, where only lowly positions were open to colored people. So, until 1922, he lived mostly alone and lonely even though children began to arrive as early as November of 1916. There were four in all.

His mother seldom wrote; she would not forget that he had not confided in her. If she had drawn a little closer, she might have saved him years of misery, for he was lukewarm about the situation into which he had allowed himself to be drawn. One word from her might have given him the strength to assert himself, but that word never came. Both were too proud to make the first move.

Lacking close friends, the boy turned instinctively to God. One day alone in Columbus, he began to feel that he was meant to use whatever talent God had given him in His service. He dedicated himself to that end. It was a promise never to be forgotten. It has been felt in everything he has written, in some form, since that day.

The young man was delighted when W. C. Handy, after some correspondence, invited him to come to Memphis and work with him one summer, to arrange and play cello and oboe with Handy's Memphis band. This group travelled the length and breadth of the South, performing for both white and colored audiences. Beale Street showed Still another world, the tough element from which he had been sheltered. Among those people and in those sordid surroundings where Handy found beauty and was inspired to recreate a vital folk art, Still began to perceive the beauty in a different sort of Negro folk music— the blues. He did not see the blues as an immoral or sexy outpouring, as many people then seemed to think of it, but as something that expressed the yearning of a lowly people, a poignant appeal for solace and hope, but with little promise of fulfillment. In the blues he discerned a distinct and unmistakable musical form. In later years, he was to elevate the blues form and to present it in symphonic dress as no one, before or since, has done. In those later years, Handy reminded Still that he had played in his band at the time he wrote Beale Street Blues. "You were making history and didn't know it," he said. "Neither did I."

Mr. Handy was that rarity among people, a man of importance who was truly generous in spirit. There wasn't a spark of jealousy or meanness in him. If there were some who resented the accomplishments of their former associates or pupils, Handy was not one of them. Like Paul Whiteman, he was always ready to extend the hand of friendship and to take pride in the fact that he had once worked with someone who later succeeded on his own. Because of this, the homage paid to Handy while he lived and after he passed on was the sort that came from the heart.

And not to be forgotten was the encouragement young Still received from his fellow musicians, those the university might scorn. These men would gather around to play over, offer suggestions about, and praise the little pieces that he wrote. Every so often during our married years, one of those early friends would turn up, to say how proud he was of Still's success. Probably none of them will ever fully realize how much their early encouragement contributed to that success! They didn't know what it was to be jealous, either. Only proud. And it was through many of them that the young man learned that his mother had been wrong when she placed all popular musicians on a low level. It wasn't always fair.

When Still came of age, he received the legacy that his father had left. During those years at Wilberforce, he had wanted to study at the Oberlin Conservatory of Music, so now, perhaps realizing that he would never rest until he did, his wife suggested that this would be a good way to use his legacy. In 1917 he began private lessons there, but his small fund was soon exhausted. He had to find a way to make enough money to return to the Conservatory for the regular session.

He got a job playing in a local theatre for fifty cents or a dollar each week and another helping the Conservatory janitor clean the rooms. He was quite businesslike about it, but before long he would disappear into some offices for hours at a time. He had discovered piles of orchestra scores, many by Richard Wagner; they acted like a magnet. He spent all the time he could spare reading through them.

Though he was at long last attending his beloved Oberlin, the schoolboy in him had not disappeared. He never understood how he managed to pass his examinations in Figured Bass, for at that time he couldn't play the piano at all. All he recalled was that he used to wait until class was about to be dismissed, then agreeably walk to the piano. He timed it so that when he was on the point of beginning, the bell rang.

Then there was his violin teacher, Maurice P. Kessler. Kessler would ask to have a certain lesson prepared, but his student would be so busy concentrating on theory and composition that he would fail to practice. When lesson time arrived, he would diplomatically ask his teacher to demonstrate, which Kessler, kindly and sympathetic as he was, would do. The result was that young Still spent the lesson hours listening to his teacher play perfectly the exercises and pieces that had been assigned to him. Some thirty years later, when Kessler and his wife, a gifted artist, again crossed our path, he remarked with a puzzled expression, "Bill, it's the funniest thing—but I can't remember your violin lessons with me at all!"

Another beloved Oberlin instructor was F. J. Lehmann, author of a treatise on harmony and another on counterpoint. He never had to complain about Still's attentiveness, for in his classes the young man worked determinedly (sometimes so hard that it made him dizzy) and succeeded in cramming a lot of work into a short space of time. Lehmann demanded strict conformity to the rules he had expounded in his books; when he would find too many mistakes in his students' notebooks, he'd become impatient, scratch the books up and tell the offenders to go home.

One day Lehmann gave the class Dunbar's poem "Good Night" to set to music. After he had seen Still's setting, he called him aside and asked why he didn't go on to study composition. The young man said it was because he didn't have the money. Those were months when it was a physical sacrifice to pay for musical instruction. The fact was that he was planning to withdraw from Oberlin, with only one semester's work in Theory and Violin completed.

Lehmann promptly called a conference of the Theory Committee. A few days later, he told the young composer that he had been given free tuition in composition, under Dr. Andrews.

They were part of a long line of generous white people in his life, to whom he has been able to close his letters truthfully with the phrase: "Gratefully yours. . . ." They have been the people uppermost in his mind during the years when so many considered it fashionable to protest and protest and protest. Often protests are justified and necessary for progress to be made. But who can forget the people who offer so much, asking only that their beneficiaries work hard?

Although he was still at Oberlin in 1918, away from the great centers, the first World War was brought very close. It brought to the young man's attention a newspaper interview with a colored artist who had just returned from Brazil. She was so enthused over the friendliness of the people and cultural advantages of that country that she inspired many young colored Americans to want to emigrate to a

One of Grace's and Billy's children was born during World War I, when Billy was in the Navy. Courtesy William Grant Still Estate.

great nation in the making, a nation where it was said that a man could be judged on his ability and not on the color of his skin. Still, at loose ends because he continued to be at odds with his family in Little Rock and could not consider his wife's family home in Danville his own, began to share these thoughts. He went so far as to buy a little Portuguese dictionary in a secondhand bookstore in Oberlin, then went to New York with the intention of working his way from there to Brazil.

En route to New York, reservations began to form in his mind. How did he know if he would like Brazil? If he didn't, and wanted to come back to the United States, wouldn't his own government then consider him a slacker? It was a sobering thought. He decided to serve his country first, then go to Brazil.

Serving his country meant—to him, if to no one else—music. He tried to join an Army band, but none had room for him, so he enlisted in the United States Navy as a mess attendant, third class. Mess attendant was the only position available to Negroes in the Navy at that time.

While waiting for his orders, he lost no time in visiting the Metropolitan Opera, one of his musical shrines. There, having bought standing room for the price of $1.10, he heard *Rigoletto* in its entirety for the first time. The famous Quartet was well known to him from the Red Seal records and amateur performances back home, but this—this was different! This was magic! The costumed singers, the glamorous stage settings and the thrilling voices. Then and there he decided that one day he wanted to hear one of his own operas as he heard *Rigoletto* that night, not as a successful composer taking a bow, but leaning over the rail in the family circle, among kindred music-loving souls.

A few days later he was put on a transport and sent to a training station near Norfolk, Virginia. The colored men were supervised by Dick Cherry, who was then a relic of a happier time in the Navy, when Negroes weren't merely mess attendants. Dick Cherry was a colored retired gunner's mate. He taught them how to fix a hammock and sleep in it, and inflicted on them as a matter of course all the old jokes, such as whether or not they wanted ladders for their hammocks.

As soon as the USS *Kroonland* was outfitted as a transport, young Still was assigned to it, where he was to remain until a month before his discharge. Memories included breaking a tooth on biting into an unmoistened sea biscuit, being struck with terror during submarine attacks, picking up extra pennies by selling lemons to seasick sailors and by laundering some of the officers' clothing. After finally proving that he was the world's messiest mess boy, he was relieved of his ordinary duties so that he could play the fiddle for the officers at dinner time, to the piano accompaniment of a white yeoman. He never waited table again.

A troop transport never carried the same group of men twice, so there were always among the troops new faces and different ideas. The young musician was puzzled that all these men, white and colored, were fighting to "make the world safe for democracy," while there were countless incidents of discrimination, subtle and blatant, showing how far off democracy was.

For instance, all of the colored enlisted men were resentful when a colored enlisted officer once made a trip over on the *Kroonland*. He was given an entire side of the dining room to himself, and as the colored mess attendants passed and re-passed the solitary figure, they went out of their way to give him extra service and to find good things for him to eat. All of them felt the snub keenly.

One day, as Still was lying in his bunk reading and some colored soldiers were shooting dice on the floor, a white officer came in, removed his belt and flogged the gamblers severely. They all knew this violence was against regulations, but no one said a word.

Ashore in Europe, people were generally friendly, except for occasional fights between British and American sailors. Some English people had not, at that time, become aware of differences in color. Young Still was amused when several very pleasant English sailors at last asked him innocently, "But I say, old chap, why are you so brown?"

A few weeks before his discharge, Still was transferred as an entertainer to a station in Newport News. During his stay, he went to visit the Negro composer, Robert Nathanial Dett, who was teaching at Hampton Institute. He took with him a little piece he had written at Oberlin and dedicated to Dett. The older composer invited him to dinner, then took him to the Institute to hear the singing in the evening. He was disappointed by two things that evening: the colored girls sat apart from the Indian girls, carefully segregated, and Dett's music was not performed. Not until many years later was he told that Hampton Institute didn't want Dett to program his own works during his tenure there.

After the Armistice and his honorable discharge from the Navy, the young musician wasn't able to get musical work, so he took a job in a shipyard at Port Newark, New Jersey, helping to clean out the rust in the dark, cold spaces between two of the ships decks. Shortly afterward he received a telegram saying that his wife was dead. He quit his job in the shipyard and went to Danville, only to find that his wife was very much alive and that her father was completely unaware of the telegram which had been sent in his name. Again the round of arguments started: He knew he would have to give up any hope of a musical career if he stayed in Danville; she refused to come away with him. By now they had one child.

So, again he returned alone to Columbus. There, despite the general lack of employment, he did find work because colored orchestras were then in vogue. He had only a dollar in his pocket, no savings, no prospects. Nothing lay ahead, as far as he could see. Yet, as he was to discover on so many occasions, God always took a hand when he was nearly at the end of his rope.

This time, there was a musical group called the "Whispering Orchestra," whose violinist was usually drunk. One winter night when he was too drunk to play, they offered Still the job. He started the next night, playing at the Kaiserhoff Hotel. However, when the group left to tour the Ohio and Mississippi Rivers, he stayed behind to continue his studies.

Part of the money he saved from working in the "Whispering Orchestra" went to pay for more lessons in composition with Dr. Andrews at Oberlin, for that was the way he spent his Wednesdays and Saturdays in the latter part of the 1918-1919 spring semester.

This study didn't last long. He had begun to look at the academic world with new eyes. He had learned the rules; now they wanted him to follow a pattern. Do it this way, he was told, because that's the way Brahms or Beethoven did it. But now he had to ask himself if he wanted to say over again what they had already said. The harmony he had learned in the Conservatory began to seem narrow and confining. He was eager to make experiments of his own. Already he was filling notebooks with theories on orchestration that he wanted to try out. The traditional variety of counterpoint, written intellectually, for its own sake as counterpoint, began to strike him as being artificial and forced. He wanted to discover a more effective way of writing counterpoint for the day in which he was living, a form that would rise naturally from the nature of the human ear.

Moreover, the musical life in Ohio no longer satisfied him. Certainly there was more there than in Danville, but in neither place was there a future. In Danville, he would vegetate. In Ohio, he would go on and on till the end of his days, playing in orchestras—an engagement here or there—jumping from one place to another, dreaming of another life but never having strength enough to reach out for it and, as he grew older, being replaced by smart youngsters who would refer to him as "Pop."

Once more he had come to a place where the road forked. What his life would be if he took the known path was only too clear. He didn't know what would happen if he turned toward the unknown, but it was important that he have the courage to do it.

—7—

Next stop: New York. His wife decided, finally, to join him. There was too little money to support two households any longer. His only problem now was how to crack the unscalable wall that surrounded the music business. Once again he turned to W. C. Handy, who had moved to a little office in New York's Gaiety Theatre Building, and once again, Mr. Handy came through. He offered Still twenty-five dollars a week for playing in his newly-organized band, and for arranging as well. The young composer was quick to take advantage of Mr. Handy's generosity; the relationship lasted for several years, until the Pace and Handy Music Company was dissolved.

Not only were there important and stimulating concerts to be heard in New York, but also there were personal contacts to be made. The Handy office was a rendezvous for most of the colored musicians of the day. Colored songwriters would frequently drop in and tell how

Pace and Handy Music Company in the Gaity Theatre Building, New York City, 1920. Still (*seated left*). Photo by Underwood and Underwood, New York.

they'd just sold a song to such-and-such a white composer for the bare price of a meal. The song would later appear with the white composer's name on it.

In those days many serious colored musicians worked hard and excelled but got nowhere because there were then no symphonic opportunities for them. Allie Ross, for example, was a good violinist, arranger and conductor. Every morning after his regular coffee and toast Ross read conductor's scores. He knew the business thoroughly, but died without having had a chance to prove it. There were many colored men who became topnotch instrumentalists, but had to find other ways to make a living. Some of them lived to see their art cheapened by aggressive amateurs; others lived to see the beginnings of opportunities, but by then they had become so steeped in commercial music or in outside activities that they were no longer capable of realizing their dreams.

Sometimes in later years the colored musicians Still knew then got together and talked about that life. One remarked, during such a discussion, "In those days colored musicians had ambitions and no place to realize them. Now if they can sit up and hold a saxophone in a nightclub they think they've reach the pinnacle of success." He continued by telling the story of a man who, after spending more than a year as a successful arranger for modern bands, became so intrigued with what was unfolding before his eyes that he exclaimed, "Say, this is great! I think I'll go study harmony!"

This isn't to say, of course, that it's impossible to learn while working, because that is what Still did. He couldn't imagine a time when it would be possible to stop learning. One of the reasons his years in New York were important was that there he taught himself to orchestrate—studying, experimenting, trying out new ideas which he would retain or discard.

Like form in music, orchestration was something he had to learn by himself, unhampered by teachers and rules. Unlike some young students of orchestration who rely on textbooks, Still used the orchestra as his laboratory. He had firsthand experience with the ranges, intonations, moods and characteristics of many of the instruments. When he didn't play one, he would experiment on it anyway. He was always asking the players questions.

Even after he became known, he used to buttonhole players wherever he met them, to ask more and more questions. In later years, whenever he began a new orchestration, he did it with an open mind, as if he knew nothing whatever about orchestration, for he felt that there is never an end to what a person can learn.

In many respects, the fact that he didn't learn to play the piano increased the scope of his work. Too often, the composers who were also brilliant pianists were limited when scoring, because their orchestrations had a tendency to sound like piano music expanded.

At first, of course, he imitated other orchestrators, but he always tried to choose the best to imitate. As soon as he dared, he broke away and began to try out different orchestral effects on his own. He was not surprised to learn that many combinations forbidden by teachers were quite interesting and were, when used with regard to the limitations of the instruments, very musical.

One of the first things he tried out was his fantastic layer-cake theory. How would it sound, he wondered, if he orchestrated in layers, one bank of sound above another? Would it sound like a layer cake looks? It certainly did not, as he soon discovered, because sound can't be treated that way. It's like a very liquid liquid, he decided, about the most fourth dimensional thing we have. Until this became clear in his mind, some mighty strange sounds came out of the orchestras that played his arrangements.

Another of his problems was to find the best way to get force out of an orchestra. He tried various methods, of which the worst was scoring differently for every instrument in a *tutti* passage. He had never dreamed that anything could be so ineffective. But it was something he had to find out for himself. Another ineffective device was to have the entire orchestra playing in unison. He did that once, confident that it would achieve a grand effect. To his astonishment, the whole thing fell flat in performance. The problem of force was finally solved by putting the instruments two or three octaves apart, but the fact that he had found that solution didn't change his opinion that orchestrating in unison is one of the most difficult of feats.

While all such details were being filed away in little notebooks and in his mind for future reference, he spent a good deal of his time composing. Most of those early efforts are now lost, which is probably just as well; he would not have been as proud of them in later years as he was at first. Many were written as jokes, to amuse his fellow musicians, though some were played over the air. The titles of some of them attest to the genre: "The Tumblebug's Lament," "Sister Heavy Hips," "Brother Lowdown," and "The Cross-eyed Monkey."

His love for opera had not been forgotten. He wrote whole operas and parts of operas and destroyed most of them. When, finally, one did seem to him to be worthy, he telephoned Harry T. Burleigh to ask him if he would help in getting it to the attention of the people at the Metropolitan Opera House. Burleigh was very kind, but he told the young man that the manuscript should be submitted directly to the Met.

Still was disappointed. Burleigh had been one of his heroes, with so much influence (he imagined) that he would have only to say a word and all the doors would open. It was an unexpected rebuff. Not until many years later, when he knew Burleigh better, and when he too was receiving similar requests from other young composers, did he understand how right Burleigh had been. The Metropolitan would not listen to Burleigh—not even to people with far more influence and more money. It goes its own way. Burleigh knew too, as Still later learned, that a composer has to succeed on the merits of his music first, not through friends or influence. In the following years, Burleigh was friendly and encouraging, often going to concerts where Still's works were played and then sending programs, clippings or firsthand accounts of their reception. Our program of the New York Philharmonic concert where Pierre Monteux conducted *Old California* bears the words, "'Twas a triumph!" in Burleigh's handwriting. It is worth saying that the opera—the one Still wanted produced so badly—was eventually thrown out by its composer. Years later, he couldn't even recall its name.

When the Pace and Handy partnership dissolved, Still played with Deacon Johnson to keep his pocketbook from getting too flabby. One of Deacon's jobs was to play in a west side movie studio in New York where silent films were being made. One day during the filming of a scene, the comedian took his violin and broke it for one of the comedy sequences! It may have seemed funny to him and to the audiences who were eventually to see the picture, but it was far from funny to the young man who was barely paying his bills. When he recovered from the shock, he tried to persuade the company to pay for the instrument, since it was indispensable for his work. No one made a move to reimburse him, and he had no choice but to buy another fiddle.

On another occasion, a tall viola player named Hall Johnson (who hadn't even begun to think of directing a choir in those days) met him on the steps of the YWCA cafeteria. He said that he was going to play in Eubie Blake's orchestra for *Shuffle Along*, and asked whether Still wanted a job, too. Certainly he wanted a job. Any good musical job would do. None of them guessed that that pleasant little show was going to make theatrical history as the most successful all-Negro show ever.

Shuffle Along was like a preparatory school for colored artists. If

Eubie Blake (*seated at piano*) and his "Original Shuffle Along Orchestra,"
1921. William Grant Still (*seated, 5th from left*).

the people who appeared in that show could be gathered together
today, the salary list would be tremendous. None of them was well
known at the time. Harold Browning, Paul Robeson and Caterina
Jarboro (who had a comedy part) were in it. A little chorus girl named
Josephine Baker was tucked away in a back row. Her biggest assets
were her ability to make the most of any opportunity that presented
itself, and her willingness to work hard. When she was given an unexpected chance to dance in the front row of the chorus, she did things
that attracted so much attention that her career took off from that
night. The authors of *Shuffle Along* took a chance on a young singer
and dancer named Florence Mills, to replace Gertrude Saunders, who
had left the show. Rehearsals weren't overly promising, so the ushers
were instructed to applaud at the end of Miss Mills' number, to make
sure it wouldn't be a total loss. They applauded all right, and so did
the audience. Florence Mills had stopped the show!

Still played oboe in the orchestra. Bored playing the same score
over and over, night after night, the musicians began to improvise.

They improvised so much from night to night that if, at the end of the run, they had played the score exactly as written, the cast wouldn't have recognized it. Sometimes Eubie himself would add something unusual for the piano, or Still would write out something for the rest of them to try.

On one of Eubie's visits to Los Angeles many years later he phoned us and hummed a tune by way of greeting. "Why are you humming 'I Got Rhythm'?" Still asked. And Eubie answered, "That's not 'I Got Rhythm.' That came before 'I Got Rhythm.' It's one of the tunes you used to improvise in *Shuffle Along*. Remember?"

Many revues that followed *Shuffle Along* were modelled after it. It was the first colored show to have a real love story, the first that didn't rely solely on comedy and fast music. It was the first to present choruses that sang and danced with zest and sparkle. When Flournoy Miller, one of the authors, talked about *Shuffle Along* later in his life he was most proud of the fact that it was a good, clean show and that the players responded enthusiastically to his plea that everyone in the cast be morally straight. Miller—one of the pioneers who gave starts to many who later became famous—knew that good offstage conduct would help the show's prestige. *Shuffle Along* went to theaters where no colored show had ever played before, and where the theatre managers were deeply prejudiced. Everywhere it did big business and everywhere the managers admitted later that "they certainly were a fine group of ladies and gentlemen."

Still learned something valuable about race relations from being involved in *Shuffle Along*. He discovered that contributions to race and to nation were ineffectual unless they were couched in an over-all effort to create friendship and understanding between the races. This became a chief and lifetime goal.

When *Shuffle Along* went to Boston, Still realized that he could now afford to pay for music lessons, so he filed an application at the New England Conservatory of Music for study in composition. On returning to the Conservatory for his answer, he was sent to talk to George W. Chadwick, a trailblazer among American composers. He had been thoroughly grounded in European methods, which he used, not to imitate Old World musicians, but to create something typically American. As they talked, Chadwick looked over some of the compositions Still had brought. Then he said, impulsively, that he would like to give the lessons free of charge. Still protested that he could afford to pay and that he wanted to pay, but Chadwick had made up his mind.

Chadwick's method of teaching was wise and unusual. The student merely worked out his own ideas, which the teacher afterward criticized and discussed in detail. Chadwick never forced his own judgments, never asked his students to change their styles of writing to conform to his own or others' styles. He merely suggested improvements or changes, then left their acceptance to his pupils' discretion.

George Chadwick was a man who looked ahead to fresh and effective means of musical expression, but who refused to be carried away by a desire to innovate. In other words he kept his balance, always aware of the difference between the creation of music and the mere collection and distribution of sounds. In addition, without any display of patriotism, he did recognize and liked to use in his writing idioms which are particularly associated with the United States. Still was so interested in what he was learning from Chadwick that the only personal trait he remembered later was his teacher's smoking. Chadwick's pipe was always in his mouth, except when he took it out to refill it.

When it came time for *Shuffle Along* to leave Boston, Still went to this considerate old gentleman to say goodbye and to thank him. He never saw him again, but he never forgot his generosity, his good musical common sense, or his warm encouragement.

Back in New York, Still took the recently vacated job of recording director for the Black Swan Phonograph Company, at thirty dollars a week. The Black Swan office, like the Handy office, was a gathering place for Negro artists and other Negro visitors to New York, because it was a Negro-owned and Negro-operated company.

Ethel Waters came to record some of the delta blues she had heard down South. A frequent visitor was Richard B. Harrison, looking seedy and doing menial work to keep alive, but never losing sight of his dreams, and never allowing himself to believe that his big opportunity would not arrive. As a result, when the big chance to play the role of the Lord in *The Green Pastures* came, he was ready, and he played it with reverence and simplicity, so that it would not appear to be a farce. Harrison's understudy, Charles B. Winters, recorded some

William Grant Still directing the "Black Swan Orchestra." Courtesy William Grant Still Estate.

recitations at the Black Swan. Robert Nathaniel Dett, one of Still's early idols, came in while some of his Spiritual arrangements were being recorded, and he heard Tourgee de Bose playing some of Still's first compositions on the piano. His audible and scornful comment was "Junk!" In later life he was friendly, as he had been many years before, but at that time and in that place he seemed to regard the aspirations of younger Negro composers solely as a challenge.

Indirectly, the Black Swan proved to be the gateway to another important phase of Still's life. And this incident, in turn, served to show that in our confused times, a Negro is a representative of a race, and the impression he makes on people of other races may have a direct bearing on the lives of other Negroes.

Colonel Charles Young, whom the budding composer had never met, though he had passed his home often while at Wilberforce, had a great effect on the life of Still. Colonel Young was a distinguished Negro who had seen thirty-four years of active service in the United States Army. Before his death in 1923, Colonel Young met Edgar Varèse on a transatlantic voyage, and made such a favorable impression on the French composer that the latter decided to offer a scholarship to an American Negro composer. He asked a friend to write to several people in Harlem in an effort to find such a person.

One of the letters came to the Black Swan. The man who received it sat down to write a reply, saying that he knew of no one suitable. Still walked into the office at that moment, happened to glance over the man's shoulder and said quickly, "You can just tear your letter up. I want the scholarship!"

That was the way he met Edgar Varèse and "modern music." Varèse's teaching was important in two aspects. First, he pointed the way toward individual musical expression. He felt that Still's style was sugary, too conventional. He used to repeat over and over, "Don't get soft! Don't get soft!" As a result, his pupil went overboard in the other direction for a time. Then Varèse was what might be termed today a "promoter." It was he who introduced his pupil into the Composer's Guild, to Leopold Stokowski at his home, to Eugene Goossens, Georges Barrerre and Quinto Maganini—all of whom performed his music when he desperately needed to be heard. It was through Varèse and Frank Patterson (of the *Musical Courier*) that he met that giant of American composers, Howard Hanson, whose friendship and support continued until the end of his days. Still learned a great deal from Edgar Varèse and recognized that debt; he would come to reject the modern orchestral music Varèse championed, though the older man's influence would remain strong for some time and Still would have to battle against it.

It was also during this period that Still met many of the people whose names were then—as now—mentioned frequently among the elite of the music world, again with Varèse acting as intermediary. There was Arnold Schoenberg, on his arrival in America; Carlos Chavez and Miguel Covarrubias, who came to the Still house for dinner; Carlos Salzedo; Olin Downes; Ottorino Respighi and Alfredo Casella, among many. One invitation was to a gathering where guests sat in a darkened room whispering about the "Revolution." Another was to witness a sculptor making a bust of Paul Robeson.

Still never forgot the looks on the faces of Mmes. Respighi and Casella, wives of the Italian composers, to whom he was introduced at a Guild concert during his period of study with Varèse. In great surprise, one turned to the other and exclaimed, "Tres gentil!" Who knows what they had been told about the black barbarians over here?

Like George Chadwick, Varèse never commanded when he taught. He looked over what his pupil brought to him, advised, suggested harmonic alterations, and so on. He may be said to have opened the way, instead of pushing his pupil along. In the sense that it is possible to teach simply by commenting from one's own point of view, everyone who listens and comments is a teacher, but Chadwick and Varèse were so much better equipped to do this than many others that their opinions assumed greater importance.

It was not long before Still began to think as much about what he was going to say in music as how he was going to say it. He was not as self-satisfied as he had been, nor did his compositions seem to him as good as they had seemed before. There were many months during which he began things and left them unfinished, or completed compositions and then tore them up. He was both prolific and destructive. Many works became no more than self-imposed exercises.

Some of the few titles of that era which did remain in his memory were *Three Fantastic Dances* (for chamber orchestra—never finished); *Death*, a choral work for mixed voices *a capella* on a Dunbar poem (finished and then discarded); *Puritan Epic* (finished and then discarded); *Three Negro Songs for Orchestra*: *Negro Love Song*, *Death Song* and *Song of the Backwoods* (discarded); and *Black Bottom*, a discordant tone poem for orchestra (also discarded). The *Log Cabin Ballads* were written for and played by Georges Barrere, but the score is now lost. There was also a song called "Mandy Lou," which belonged to but did not appear with the set later published by G. Schirmer (*Breath of a Rose* and *Winter's Approach*), principally because the publisher feared it might conflict with another song of a similar title. There was also the setting of Dunbar's "Good Night," a holdover from the Oberlin days.

Black Bottom was his anonymous entry in a NFMC composition contest. It didn't win. One judge made it as his second choice, however, and offered a comment which proved to be most discerning. "'Black Bottom,'" he said, "is conceived in the so-called ultra-modern manner, a somewhat international one, and therefore not very original. It is written with a sure hand and is interesting program music and, in this respect, most expressive. If this composer will ever succeed in putting his heart into his work as much as his imagination and intellect, he will be a master."

It was not long before Still horrified the music lovers of New York and caused ultra-modernists to hail him as someone worth thinking about. His first big serious work, *From the Land of Dreams*, was played in concert in New York City. In it, he tried to suggest the flimsiness of dreams which fade before they have taken definite form. It was scored for chamber orchestra and three female voices treated as instruments and was played at one of the Composers' Guild concerts where, in fair weather or foul, Carl Ruggles would come striding down the aisle in galoshes!

This big performance, Still's first, produced a strange reaction in the composer. He seemed unable to hear what was going on, imagined all eyes were on him and felt more like hiding than standing up to bow. People asked him then, as they continued to ask through the years, whether the music sounded as he thought it would. It seldom did. The composer and the playwright are the only creators who must depend on an interpreter for the final result.

This was Still's first exposure to formal criticism. Olin Downes thought that *From the Land of Dreams* was terrible; Rosenfeld liked it. Most of the critics and members of the press took sides, one way or the other. As for the composer himself, as soon as he could get a proper perspective, he began to agree with Downes. His opinion was strengthened during succeeding years. He was happy when the score was lost and hoped it would never be found, or performed again. It was then that he realized that if he followed Varèse too closely he would be limiting himself to an idiom foreign to his individuality.

Like most young artists, he studied every word in those newspaper criticisms carefully. It was a long time before the meaning of what John Barbirolli later told him actually penetrated—that if an artist has a real, a deep and an honest conviction about his work, nothing any critic can say should be allowed to change it. For years he looked at criticisms, some of them discerning, some of them totally inaccurate but smug, some of them witty at everyone else's expense and some of them obviously written colorfully but carelessly in order to make a deadline. Alternately he would glow with pride or grow cold with anger at the wise or silly things he read. Gradually he came to understand that not even the finest critic in the world can grasp everything on a first hearing, and it's a rare observer who is capable of admitting that it's only his own reaction he is reporting.

During all this study and soul-searching, life was anything but smooth for the ambitious young man. There was so much discord, deception and difference at home that it was a pleasure for him to be away. He often stood on streetcorners and dreamed of having a wife and family, all of them established in a real home. It never seemed incongruous to him that he was wishing for what he already had. There were money troubles too. His thirty dollars a week didn't last very long when ninety dollars a month went for rent. Then he lost his current job and once again was penniless, this time with a wife, children, mother-in-law and an expensive apartment to support. He hadn't the slightest idea which way to turn, except that he still knew that nothing but music would do.

The only possible step was to strike out on his own. He rented an office downtown and went into business as an arranger. Initially, he made a few hundred dollars on arrangements for a little flop show. Then when Florence Mills' show, *Dixie to Broadway* came along, Will Vodery offered him a place in his orchestra, so he gratefully gave up his office to go with the show. He stayed with *Dixie to Broadway* for many months, all the time cementing his friendship with the star and her husband, "Kid" Thompson, and increasing his admiration for Florence Mills' artistry and personality.

She was another artist who never feared competition and was never jealous. She believed in surrounding herself with the best of talent and in giving her associates their just share of applause. Everyone loved her. She didn't say much and wasn't particularly good-looking. She was little and skinny and had none of what we nowadays call "sex appeal." But who could be critical where she was concerned? She didn't have to wiggle her hips in order to sell a song. Her charm, her magnetism and her complete lack of conceit did it for her.

Sometime in 1925, Still had asked Florence Mills whether, if he wrote some music for her, she would sing it in concert. She agreed, and so did her manager, Lew Leslie, even though she was not to be paid for the concert. The resulting performance not only occasioned newspaper reviews, but was mentioned in several books on music. Many famous people attended, among them Arturo Toscanini and George Gershwin, the latter always on the lookout for new sources of material to use in his own work.

So it happened that Still wrote *Levee Land*, consisting of four songs with orchestral accompaniment. With his one-finger piano technique, he taught the songs to Florence by rote, doing them over and over until she had mastered them. She never even heard the basic harmonies until the first rehearsal with the orchestra. She was so patient, so willing to learn and to accept suggestions that many times since, when certain other artists felt that they were doing him a favor to perform his works, he thought back to one of the biggest of them all, who counted *Levee Land* a milestone in her life.

Florence Mills hadn't sung with anything but a jazz band before. On January 4, 1926, when she stepped in front of the International Composers' Guild Orchestra in Aeolian Hall and faced Eugene Goossens' upraised baton, she was frankly nervous. She had been before the public constantly since her childhood, but this one time she was afraid. Nonetheless, her performance was such that the audience called upon Mills to repeat it. The critics praised Miss Mills, and the composer agreed heartily. He felt as if he had found a co-creator, and as if the piece had been composed for chamber orchestra and Florence Mills, rather than for soprano and orchestra, as it might otherwise have been described. The composition has never been performed since that time. Sometimes it has been suggested, but the composer's inevitable reaction was, "Where can we find another Florence Mills"?

While Still was traveling with the Mills show, he found it hard to keep up his composing. There was so little time, and all too often a piano wasn't available. He regularly arrived early, and alone at the darkened theatres went into the orchestra pit and played softly the musical themes that had occurred to him. These went into that little notebook that served him well throughout his life. He also followed a custom that he had established some years before, of going to small Negro churches and revival meetings wherever he found himself, in order to make a mental record of the little-known Spirituals and to learn as much as he could about Negro music firsthand as possible. In those little gatherings the musical material is usually new because it is constantly revitalized. Still preferred not to use the themes that he heard in such places in his serious creative work, but they often came in handy for commercial purposes.

Still's love for and understanding of Negro music was growing. He was further on his way to identifying himself with it, and to absorbing its color and flavor as a basis for some of the creative work that was to come. Even then, as in later years, he considered it merely a single facet of his musical personality, and not by any means the only one.

There was virtually none of what might today be considered color-ful and exciting in that period, for this was a dedicated young man who didn't enjoy playing cards, drinking and carousing to pass the time away between engagements. He was learning. For him, that was excitement enough.

8

In retrospect, the years 1926–27 marked a very real turning point in the composer's life, though at the time he didn't realize what was happening. It was during this period that the ferment which had been growing in his heart finally culminated in that most certain of decisions, one not shaken by the pressures he felt then, or in the years to follow.

His decision was that, as a composer, he was ready to be himself, and that the discordant idiom of Edgar Varèse was not and never could be a part of his individuality. He was still grateful for the contact; he was well aware of the fact that he had learned a great deal from it and that his music would always be richer for having had it, but he was positive that the idiom itself did not belong to him.

It did appear to the composer that he was supported in his decision and in his work by spiritual forces, for this is an entry in a notebook that he kept in 1926, detailing a dream: "I beheld a host of angels.

They approached me like a mighty cloud and sang a song of over-whelming beauty; one that I have been unable to remember though I am a musician, and usually retain with ease any melody that appeals to me. As the angels sang, I broke into tears and awoke to find myself sobbing with joy." He was sure that the dream had a deep meaning, but at the moment, he couldn't imagine what that meaning could be. He said later that the angels in the dream had been black angels.

Similar experiences followed, such as the time he saw an owl who talked to him and the time later when he was lying on a bed, half-asleep and half-awake, and saw a faceless Being clothed in white entering the room. The Being told him to get up and when he did so, he looked back and saw himself still lying on the bed. The Being showed him wonderful symbols, such as lush green foliage, crystal clear water, and then explained the meaning of each symbol. The feeling of exaltation was almost overpowering.

Having consciously allied himself with God and with His constructive forces on earth, these experiences indicated to Still that he had chosen the right course, so he went ahead with confidence. On his subsequent scores, he inscribed: "With humble thanks to God, the Source of inspiration."

His first excursion into symphonic racial music was *Darker America*, in which a listener could easily detect the struggle between the young composer's ideals and the teachings of Varèse. He had not quite liberated himself. Yet *Darker America* won a publication prize at the Eastman School of Music in Rochester (which was to play an important part in Still's life) and was described as the "high spot" of its New York concert by the *Musical Courier*, which told its readers that "there is no doubting the man's power."

The Eastman School of Music and its distinguished director, Dr. Howard Hanson, became increasingly important in Still's life. One of Hanson's compositions in the Twenties, *From the Journal of a Wanderer*, had won recognition, but no prize, in the Chicago Symphony Orchestra's competition. One critic thought it had elements of "stunt" writing. On hearing it played in Rochester, Hanson agreed. He had written many clever orchestral effects into the score—effects which looked fine on paper, but didn't sound fine. It did much to teach him restraint in orchestration. "It was a good lesson," as he later put it, "in what not to do."

This lesson and many others were by-products of Hanson's now-famous American Composers' Concerts at the Eastman School. They had been started in 1925, and proved to be Godsends for Still and many another American composer, eventually having a lasting effect on the entire panorama of serious American music. At first, their purpose was to give an opportunity for the initial performance of any worthwhile work by any American composer. Then they were expanded to include performances (not necessarily premieres) of any outstanding American work, and further expanded to include publication of manuscripts. In the Twenties, Hanson went out of his way to recommend Still's music to others and to perform his works, and when the composer didn't have money enough to come to Rochester to attend the performances and hear the results of his long hours of toil, Hanson engaged him to lecture to some of the classes on orchestration and paid him enough for this service to cover the cost of the trip to Rochester. His friendship never faltered.

Reviews of the first major metropolitan performances had reached Little Rock, where Carrie Shepperson lay dying of cancer. She was, as always, proud of her son, and at last in 1927 (the same year which brought the untimely passing of Florence Mills) she understood what her determined son had set out to do, and she approved. Finally she knew that such an achievement was indeed possible for an American Negro, and that her ideals, her loving and stern discipline, had helped to bring it about.

Mr. Shepperson had already met his death by drowning, so, as his mother's body was consigned to its grave, the young man felt that his ties with the past were almost completely severed. He returned to New York, to his composing and the commercial work which kept a roof over his family's head.

After 1926, enough arranging work came his way that he no longer found it necessary to play in orchestras to make a living. He had gone through a period of playing in nightclubs, such as the Plantation (when he needed a job so badly that he promised to play the banjo even though he had never touched one before; he bought one in a

pawnshop, and made good!), and at Ciro's with LeRoy Smith's orchestra, in which he again played the oboe—an oboe that was usually
out of commission and was held together with rubber bands. When he
finally had it repaired, its correctness seemed so strange that he had to
get acquainted with it all over again.

At the Plantation, the orchestra conductor was again Will Vodery,
a colored musician who was then a successful orchestrator for Broadway shows. He had a name in that field and Still did not, so he gave
some of his work to the ambitious young man, who was of course
grateful. What Still didn't know until years later was that Will Vodery
had not only put his own name on the Still arrangements, but had
copied them out in his own handwriting so that no one could guess the
deception.

After scoring some of the music for the Earl Carroll Vanities, Still
asked Vodery if he could go along to a rehearsal to hear how the music
sounded. Vodery made no objection. He took him along and introduced him to the conductor, Don Voorhees. The latter realized instantly that the arrangements were, in fact, Still's (because, as he later
remarked, Still's orchestrations had a new color, while Vodery's were
in the old style) and promptly asked him to make all the arrangements.
Vodery accepted the change with good grace, remained a friend, and
continued to give Still some of his work to do on occasion, while shar-
ing the credit. He was also generous enough to help make ends meet in
the days when such help was badly needed.

When LeRoy Smith's musicians went to play in Atlantic City, Still
went along as part of the group. Soon he received a wire from Don
Voorhees asking him to give notice immediately and return to New
York to score the new Vanities; Jack Robbins was publishing the music. A substitute was ready to take his place, so off he went. Never
again did he have to play professionally; it was a relief for him not to
have to play every night, all night long, not getting to sleep until after
6 A.M. His first thought was that he would have more time for composing, but so much work came in that his composing time seemed
again cut short. He made up his mind to take just enough work to
keep him in basic funds, no more.

Don Voorhees and Still were linked through a couple of historic
occasions. When the Columbia Broadcasting System network started,

Voorhees broadcast an entire program of Still arrangements on the opening day. And it was Voorhees who recorded (on a Columbia disc) Still's Fantasy on the "St. Louis Blues," the first such arrangement of what is now an American classic ever to be recorded. Years later, W. C. Handy heard the recording again after many years and wrote to Still, "It's a novelty these days, because you can hear the melody in it!" Other notable Still arrangements include the first one of "Dinah," for Ethel Waters, and several for Sophie Tucker. He scored a number of shows, including *Rain or Shine*, one edition of J. P. McEvoy's *Americana*, and *Runnin' Wild*, the show that contained the first Charleston. Jimmy Johnson and Cecil Mack wrote the tune; Still was first to orchestrate it.

Even royalty touched the composer's life in 1926, for it was then that Crown Prince Gustavus Adolphus of Sweden and his Princess were guests at the Long Island home of Mrs. James A. Burden. The Prince, known for his love of music, was entertained by William Grant Still and an orchestra of Negro musicians playing serious compositions by Negroes and some arrangements of folk songs. It was a first in racial terms, certainly, and it was also a departure from custom because no dance music was included. The royal couple asked for several encores.

The concert accented young Still's friendship with another important figure in American music. John Alden Carpenter, one of the country's foremost composers, a generous soul with no room in his heart for jealousy, had suggested the younger composer's appearance at Mrs. Burden's soiree. Through him and his artistic friends in Chicago, Still also became acquainted with that famous dancer and ballet master, Adolph Bolm, and with the latter's pupil, Ruth Page. It was from this association that Still's ballet, "La Guiablesse" was born. Ten years later, Carpenter wrote to one of his correspondents: "Still is easily the best composer ever produced by the Negro race, and without regard to color, one of the most interesting of the younger men working today. From a technical standpoint he is thoroughly adept and sophisticated."

In the immediate post-Varèse years in New York there began to come from Still's pen music which so clearly indicated the trend of his thinking that one critic reviewed his suite, *From the Black Belt*, by saying that he had "probably written the little pieces while his mentor,

Mr. Varèse, had his back turned." The ingratiating music was so well received when George Barrere played it in concert that he played another Still suite, *Log Cabin Ballads*, and was gratified when the critics noted that Varèse's influence was fading away. He was even more pleased when the appreciative young composer dedicated his new orchestral suite, *Africa*, to him. This, too, he played with success.

On Jack Robinson's recommendation, Paul Whiteman came into Still's life first as an employer, then as a mentor of sorts and a guide. Not only did Still become acquainted with such jazz greats as Bix Beiderbecke and Bing Crosby (then one of the Rhythm Boys), but he was profoundly impressed by Mr. Whiteman's businesslike approach to music. The "King of Jazz" believed in paying well and promptly, a virtue not manifest in everyone. Somehow it didn't always work out that way.

When Paul Whiteman went to Universal Studios in 1929 to make the film, *The King of Jazz*, Still had been making several arrangements each week for the "Old Gold" radio show and went along as one of his arrangers. As the film was in progress, Bix Beiderbecke came out to join the orchestra. Being on the West Coast impressed young Still more than he realized at the time; from entries in his notebooks made a year later, it was apparent that he had begun to think of going west to live.

In the late Twenties, about the time that his first European notice came (a radio concert in Frankfurt-Am-Main), the idea of expressing himself racially in music was still uppermost in Still's mind. He asked the Negro poet, Countee Cullen, for a libretto which he could set to music, and didn't get one. Alain Locke sent him the scenario for an African ballet, *Sahdji*, however, and asked if it interested him. It did indeed, and Still plunged enthusiastically into the work. His 1930 notebook shows that he completed the sketch on July 7 and began scoring on July 8. The score was completed on July 22, after which he started work on the piano score. This was finished on July 30. A month is surprisingly little time for the creation of a major work for chorus, orchestra, ballet and bass soloist, lasting for almost an hour. *Sahdji*, which Still dedicated to Howard Hanson, became the first ballet produced as a part of the American Music Festivals in Rochester, and starred Thelma Biracree as choreographer and soloist. Its success paved the way for productions of other ballets by other American composers at the Eastman School.

Buoyed by an October 24 (1930) performance of *Africa* in Rochester, Still launched another ambitious venture, his now-famous *Afro-American Symphony*, which he constructed on an original theme in the blues idiom. Ever since his work with Handy in Memphis, he had felt that the blues were more than an earthy, sensual outpouring. He saw much more in them, and set out to elevate them to the highest musical form, exemplified in a symphony. His success was evident in the worldwide acclaim won by the *Afro-American*, particularly in the approval of European critics who considered it a bridge between the old world and the new.

He started work on this symphony on October 30th, 1930. Ideas came to him so rapidly that he could hardly record them. Being able to create so steadily and so constructively occupied him to such an extent that he didn't realize there was an economic depression. He discovered it at the same time he learned that his wife had paid a bill with what was left of the money Paul Whiteman had paid him. There were other bills and nothing with which to pay them. He didn't have nine dollars to cover a check he had written, and couldn't collect the money people owed him.

There were by now scenes at home so unpleasant that sometimes he felt like walking away from it all. He asked himself what God would have him do, and decided to stick it out.

He had another dream. In it he saw a large building, in one office of which he found Don Voorhees, Johnny Rehauser and another man. The following day, Don Voorhees telephoned and asked him to make some arrangements for the Maxwell House Coffee radio show which he was then conducting. Still went to Voorhees' office and there were the three men, just as he had dreamed of them. The arrangements not only brought in the much-needed money, but inaugurated a totally new and unexpected experience.

This experience seemed to have evolved routinely. The orchestrations so pleased Willard Robison, the guest soloist on the show, that he asked Still to orchestrate his new radio program, the "Deep River Hour." Still agreed. The "Deep River Hour" gained an immediate and enthusiastic following among musicians, partly because of the unique orchestral effects. What few of them realized was that its orchestrator was using it as a musical training ground: trying out new tone combinations, experimenting with harmonies and rhythms, and in general bringing to it the freshness of his youth and his creative ideas.

He had an orchestra of real professionals to practice on, and within the space of a few days—often only a few hours—he would conceive a new orchestral device and hear it tried out. It was the most effective way to learn orchestration, and it succeeded in establishing Still as an innovator in the field—one whose inventions became almost legendary and were so widely copied that after a while their originator soon was rarely credited with them.

He was credited, though anonymously, in the book *Music in Radio Broadcasting*, edited by Gilbert Chase in 1946, part of the NBC-Columbia University Broadcasting Series. Page 78 contains this comment: "Another who must be mentioned in speaking of the development of arranging for radio is Willard Robison, who conducted a show called 'Willard Robison and his Deep River Orchestra' on most of the networks some years ago. Mr. Robison's orchestra was a small one, but the effects he attained with it were so unusual and distinctive as to gather great attention, not only from the public, but from other radio conductors and arrangers. I am told that the distinctive quality of his orchestra was set by a then unknown symphonic composer, who is currently on the West Coast."

Even now people who do remember who orchestrated the old "Deep River Hour" write to ask whether they can beg, borrow or steal the orchestrations used on the show. Still's work on the songs involved actual composing, and was far more than what is usually meant by "arrangements."

In the choice of music as well as in the making of arrangements, Still was given a free hand, so that the show took on a slightly different character after he joined it. Before, Robison had specialized in spirituals and music of a popular nature. Still added all sorts of music, ranging from Handy's "Memphis Blues" to MacDowell's "To a Water Lily" and other music of a more serious nature. There were also Negro spirituals, of course, and folk tunes, along with the better popular songs. Still made an effort to present everything in such a way that listeners would feel uplifted when the program came to an end.

That, simply, was the quality which set the "Deep River Hour" apart, and which made it virtually impossible to imitate, though quite a few tried. It was the underlying spiritual theme which was sensed rather than clearly identified.

There was some difficulty over conductors during the course of the "Deep River" broadcasts. For one reason or another, none of them worked out well. Finally, the men in the orchestra went to Mr. Robison and asked why he didn't let their orchestrator conduct. It seemed to Still to be a workable solution. After all, the faculty and students at Wilberforce had approved his conducting of the band; John Alden Carpenter and the Crown Prince and Princess of Sweden had also accepted it. So Still became the first Negro ever to conduct a white radio orchestra in New York.

One of the players in the orchestra explained to the management that he was from the South and simply could not play under a colored man. Very quietly, he was allowed to leave the group. But before the programs ended, the musician returned and asked to be reinstated in the orchestra, after which he became a loyal friend of the new conductor.

Still had had no formal training in conducting, therefore very little knowledge of baton technique. All he knew was what he wanted to hear from the orchestra, so the orchestra members became his teacher. Move by move, they showed him what they had to see him do in order to get the effects he wanted.

Learning to conduct also helped him in composing; he had never before known how things look to a conductor. It was an entirely different point of view.

When a foreign-born musician decided he wanted to play a certain passage in his own way, instead of the way Still wanted it, the rest of the players took sides with their conductor and the assertive musician had to give in. The result of this rapport came out in the New York *World Telegram* when it described the "Deep River" program as a "half-hour of truly native American music, adroitly conducted."

Eventually the "Deep River" moved from CBS to NBC, where the officials adamantly refused to have a Negro conduct the orchestra, so someone else was called to do it.

A sordid side of the world of music was manifest at about the same time, something that over the years would cause Still great sadness. In the Twenties, Deems Taylor (another staunch and generous friend) was on his way to becoming America's top serious composer, having proven himself outstanding in many fields. Then murmurs started; the aggressive composers began to paraphrase his name and to call him "Damn Stealer," suggesting that he was a plagiarist. At first, the whispers were shrugged off, but they persisted. It was not until much later that the sad results became apparent. Deems Taylor became known to the general public as a radio commentator and musicologist, but not as the fine composer he actually was.

Still would hear the same type of whispering campaign directed against other American compoers, with varying degrees of success. Still himself became an intended victim. But disturbing as they were, such campaigns did not assume their most sinister proportions until much later. In the late Twenties and early Thirties they were only hints of what was to come. Meanwhile, young Still was excitedly and emotionally involved in his own creative development, which zoomed ahead.

Around this time (1932) Still's wife, obviously as discontented as he, took her four children and her mother and went to live in Canada. She was going there, she said, to write for a magazine, though the job never materialized. Still never saw her again, but he did continue to see the children. On one occasion they came to him and reported a terrifying experience. Their mother had been resting in bed, fully awake, when a hand suddenly materialized out of thin air and started to strangle her.

Thanks to Howard Hanson, Still didn't lack performances of his work, and the results were gratifying. After the first rehearsal of *Sahdji* in May of 1931, Hanson wrote to say that the orchestra members put down their instruments and applauded, as the audience applauded after the performance. In the 1931-1932 season, Hanson also played the *Afro-American Symphony* and then repeated it at a subsequent concert, after which its composer was given a standing ovation by the audience. One of the critics wrote that it seemed "a much more important work on second hearing." In January of 1933, Hanson played the Third (Scherzo) movement of the *Afro-American Symphony* with the

Concert in Paris, 1933. Photo by George Manuel.

Berlin Philharmonic Orchestra, where the audience ignored tradition and refused to let the concert continue until the Scherzo was repeated.

That same year, *Africa* was played to a thunderous ovation by Richard Lert and the Pasdeloup Orchestra in Paris. Some critics hailed the composer as a true musical spokesman for the Negro, though one of them didn't care for the dissonance in the composition. Today, with our ears so accustomed to cacophonous sound, *Africa* seems relatively mild and entirely consonant.

Randall Thompson, himself an American composer of great distinction, writing on "The Contemporary Scene in American Music" at this time, said, "William Grant Still, himself a Negro, has treated of his race in many authentic pages without literal quotation." It was this way in the West Indian ballet, *La Guiablesse*, which Still had completed in the intervening months and for which, lacking material from Martinique, he developed his own idiom. He later found it to be completely true to the drama, characters and locale. Both Howard Hanson and Thelma Biracree in Rochester—as well as Ruth Page in Chicago—produced this ballet successfully in 1933, Ruth Page repeating it at the Chicago Grand Opera the following year, with Katherine Dunham as soloist—her first major opportunity.

Still's scrapbooks of this period are given over in great part to programs on which his music was played, among them Paul Whiteman's, Martha Graham's and Quinto Maganini's, and to letters from people asking to perform his compositions after they had heard the music elsewhere. As a young pianist, I was one of those; I played his work in concerts in southern California and in Mexico City.

On February 7, 1934, George Fischer of the publishing firm of J. Fischer and Brothers made an appointment to discuss publication of the *Afro-American Symphony*, initiating a friendship which lasted even after Fischer's death, when his sons took over the business.

George Fischer was a rarity in music publishing circles, a man who was able to recognize something new and valuable when he saw it, and who was willing to underwrite it personally. When he died, there was one catalogue of compositions owned by J. Fischer and Bros., and another catalogue published under the firm name, but owned by the George Fischer Estate; this was the catalogue on which he had risked his own funds, and which included the *Afro-American Symphony*.

In these days of aggressive lawyers and agents, and mutual distrust of nearly everyone by nearly everyone else, the business arrangements made for this publication might be considered quaint. It was an oral contract, including an agreement that the composer would receive no royalty payments until the expenses of printing and promotion had been met. The score sold well and was played frequently. The United

States Government used it as part of its international public relations campaign.

Still never requested any sort of accounting from the publisher. After several years had passed, a simple note came from Fischer saying that the symphony had paid for itself and that, from then on, royalties would be paid. This promise was meticulously kept.

It was George Fischer who brought his new protégé into ASCAP (the American Society of Composers, Authors and Publishers) in 1936, and who recommended him warmly to his colleagues in the elite musical fraternity, particularly Gene Buck, a man of great integrity whom everyone admired.

During these years, the young composer's strange dreams continued, inspiring him on occasion and sometimes proving to be prophetic.

In one, he was walking away from Willard Robison toward a forest where a group of hostile white people were standing. There was some obstacle to his entering this forest, but a white man unexpectedly came and removed it. Then he entered and seemed to be working quietly among the white people, whereupon a colored child nearby, lying bound in a blanket, stopped crying. Throughout the dream he was impressed by the humility that he felt for God's benevolence, and for the work he was convinced that God had assigned to him.

Still continued to dream, in his waking hours, of being an operatic composer, for he still loved the stage and the sound of operatic singing. His work in the symphonic field was in part a substitute because he had been unable to make any headway in opera. He had written many operas and torn most of them up; he had tried to make contact with major producers such as the Metropolitan Opera Company, and failed. He had applied for a Guggenheim Fellowship so that he could have a year free in which to work on an opera, but he had been refused. Dr. Hanson was visibly surprised to learn of the refusal, and suggested that he try again the following year. He did, and this time he was awarded one.

On May 22, 1934, he did walk away from Robison and the "Deep River Hour," drove to Los Angeles, and settled down to composing his new opera.

Here we met and began to work together.

9

My family background was of a different sort, but in a way we shared an important experience with my husband's family. Out roots were in old Russia, where the Jewish people have long been persecuted, and from where so many have emigrated to distant lands in order to enjoy the good things God had granted to the people of the earth. Many believed what they had been told: that in America gold was lying in the streets; some were so disillusioned when they got here they didn't even want to learn the new language. What they found instead of gold was a democratic way of life they had not known before.

Often the old world families would educate only that child who showed the greatest promise of achievement. But in old Russia among the Jews, it was evidently different. My maternal grandmother Annie (or Hassie) Mann was deliberately not taught to read and write because she was so smart. Her parents were afraid she might go over to the Nihilists, to whose terrorist groups so many of Russia's nineteenth-century restless youths gravitated. My great-grandparents wanted none of it for their offspring. Yet, despite the fact that she couldn't read or write, my grandmother became one of the "bankers" of her day, ably and quickly changing money in one of those sidewalk operations which do not exist in this country, keeping all of the accounts in her head. She married Jacob Meyer Tarkowsky, a man who was as impractical as she was practical: a dreamer, an avid reader, and a student of religions. His recipe for getting ahead in the world was to "go where the silk hats go."

The Tarkowskys began to raise a large family, of which my mother, Bessie, was the second baby who lived. My mother was born in Zhitomir on February 26, 1883 (though her passport listed it as March 18; there were many difficulties in reconciling the old world calendar and the new). The family owned a vineyard from which they produced more than a hundred gallons of wine every year.

Well before the turn of the century, Jacob Meyer Tarkowsky brought his family to America; they settled eventually in Chicago.

In Turetz, Minsk, my father's family, the Aryevichs, had been busy making its way in the world and dreaming of a better future. Israel Aryevich was an industrious man who went from job to job, trying to better his lot. Knowing he could not make enough money in Russia to pay the fares of a wife and three sons to America, Israel Aryevich emigrated first, alone, and worked for three years before sending for the rest of them. Bela, or Beulah, my grandmother, sold everything she had to help meet the expenses of the trip. My father, David, who was born September 15th or 17th, 1882, was about twelve when the Aryevichs made their way toward Chicago.

After having lived in the United States for some time, both families noted that most of the Americans they met had difficulty in spelling the family names, so the Tarkowskys became the Tarks and the Aryevichs became the Arveys. Grandfather Tark was naturalized in Chicago on September 24, 1896 (a proud day for him!). Impulsive Grandfather Arvey promised to become a citizen, but procrastinated, promised and procrastinated while my father and mother met, fell in love and—on December 2, 1902—were married. They moved to Los Angeles to start their home, and there my father received his own naturalization papers.

In her childhood my mother learned to embroider and to crochet beautifully, and to paint. When she was in the eighth grade in school, she was removed from her classes so she could make drawings for the 1900 Paris Exposition Universelle. I still have the set of Victor Hugo's books which my mother bought with her first paycheck after she had gone to work as a young woman. As an exploring teenager, I recall getting into those books and being fascinated by *Les Miserables*. Daily as I read, and with the exuberance of youth, I would recount the story to my father, always trying to impress him with the magnitude of my discovery. My surprise and chagrin were clear when one day he remarked pointedly, "You know, Verna, I have already read all of those books."

I also came across the program of Shakespeare's *King Henry V*, which had starred Richard Mansfield in Chicago. It was my father's program, and he got it the way most poor and enterprising young men would get it—by ushering in the Grand Opera House. He saw all the attractions there: Weber and Fields, M. Beaucaire and the other great names of the time.

I was born on February 16, 1910 in the old Crocker Street Hospital in Los Angeles to parents who, with no pretense, enjoyed the good things of the spirit. I don't recall ever having heard the word "culture" used in our home. Therefore, piano lessons seemed the most natural thing in the world for me.

My younger sister, though, successfully resisted all attempts to make a musician out of her. When she was in school, her teacher asked her to write a composition on "My Musical Experience," and this was the result: "About four years ago I started to take violin lessons, but my teacher was very inconsiderate. He actually wanted me to practice occasionally, so therefore I took only one year of it. My teacher, Mr. Benkert, was first violinist in the Philharmonic Orchestra. When my brother took cornet lessons he had a teacher with an unspellable name who plays in the Philharmonic. My sister's former piano teacher who is my brother's present one played in the 24 piano ensemble at the Hollywood Bowl. Before I started violin, I took two or three piano lessons but decided to take violin because I only used four fingers there while in piano I used ten. My sister is a radio artist, etc., so therefore I have had the pleasure of listening to 57 varieties of scales for the past six years. Although I've never heard a real opera in my life, my sister has been so kind as to try to be one for me, but I'm afraid that I'm terribly unappreciative. Several times I have shivered in great distress at the Bowl till midnight, when I finally fell asleep." Eventually my sister became part of the business world.

On the other hand, our brother, the youngest child, learned to play the piano with very few lessons. He did well, in fact, at everything he attempted. He developed into a scientist, an educator, a linguist of prominence and became internationally known as a paleontologist.

After my homework was done, I usually had so much leftover energy that I would raid the neighborhood library, taking several books at a time, reading them in a single afternoon, returning them the following day and taking out more. These were not always the sort of books which would introduce me to the classics of literature; I gained nothing from them except a pair of worn out eyes. The optometrist fitted me with glasses, then had me removed from school for a year, to give my eyes a rest, but he didn't think it would hurt me to read music.

A year away from school was all right. It was part compensation for having skipped two years which had put me into grades with others who were several years older than I.

Somewhere along the line I had gotten tired of practicing exercises, so my parents decreed that the piano lessons should stop, though they were willing to continue my subscription to *Etude* music magazine. After that, I used to close the doors to the den, where the piano stood, and read for hours all the new music that came monthly in *Etude*, or that I could get from the library, or borrow from friends. This went on for about a year, when again I became hungry for the routine of piano study. To everyone's astonishment, including my own, my musical explorations had turned me into a capable sight-reader, a skill that was to be of great value in the days to come.

When I was about nine years old, my parents became interested in Spiritualism. Whereas they had previously scoffed at it, something dramatic happened one day to change this attitude.

Some time after the death of a Norwegian neighbor, a kindly soul with a strong accent, my parents were persuaded to go to a trumpet seance. They were convinced in advance that it would be nothing but fakery, but when the trumpet flew all by itself to my mother's ear, and the voice of our Norwegian neighbor, accent and all, came through it, my parents (never ones to do things by halves) plunged into their own investigations of psychic matters mornings, noons and nights at church, where I usually had to play hymns for the services. Even our vacations were spent at a Spiritualist camp in the southern California mountains.

That I had existed before I came to earth and would exist after I had passed on seemed to me to fit in with the natural order of things. I saw no reason why people who had loved each other in life would not be able to communicate after death, given the right conditions. Nonetheless, even as a child, I began to have my doubts about some of the people who presented themselves as purveyors of such messages. Sometimes one who seemed to be authentic would come along, but for the most part they were just one phony after another.

After about six years of this sort of thing, I was fed up and so were my parents. We stopped our active participation in Spiritualism, though they continued their interest and study of the occult. I considered myself through forever and became rather hostile.

During my years at John Muir Junior High School I found myself studying Spanish with Evarose Griffin Lloyd, who was an aunt of the film actress Bebe Daniels, and whose mother was Colombian. Her method of teaching was to start immediately with conversational Spanish, and fit the grammar into the framework later. We acquired some fluency before we even knew what we were doing. I later won a prize in Spanish in a city-wide competition. Other activities in junior high school indicated that even at that early age, my interests were beginning to take a permament form. The Scholarship and Self-government clubs in which I participated were routine. But playing in the school orchestra and accompanying one of the vocal clubs helped me carry on my practical musical training, while a major interest in journalism gradually took form. I wrote for the school newspaper and was on the staff of the school's annual.

One of the reasons that I attended Manual Arts High School was so that I could study journalism under an instructor who was then legendary in educational circles. My father, a paper salesman who sold exclusively to printers, had heard R. A. "Daddy" Maynard's name time and time again around the city, and agreed that I should take advantage of the opportunity to work with him. Maynard was himself an ex-reporter and staunch exponent of the old way of doing things in the newspaper world. As each new class entered his room, he would solemnly issue textbooks. When he saw that each student was supplied, he would open his own book, glance scornfully at the first page, then close it and launch into a firsthand account of the way things should be done in newspapers. The textbooks were never again consulted.

I learned one hard lesson from "Daddy" Maynard that stayed with me through all the years to follow. We had in school one young musician, and only one, who was trying his hand at serious musical composition. I wrote an article about him for the school paper. A few months later, when another serious musical work of his was performed, I wrote another story. This time "Daddy" Maynard called me in, showed me the story and said, "This boy is a Negro, isn't he? And didn't you write about him before?" I admitted it. "Well," said he shortly, "he's had enough. We don't have to give him any more publicity." And he handed me back my story.

Mrs. Lloyd had followed our class to Manual Arts High School from junior high, to teach Spanish. As our friendship resumed, she decided it would be nice for one of Los Angeles' big newspapers to carry a story about me. She suggested it to her sister Georgia, then a reporter for the Los Angeles *Examiner*, who said she would like to do one. The only trouble was that there was really nothing remarkable about me on which to base a news story; but Georgia was undaunted. When the story came out, I discovered that I had won a gold medal for musical composition in a nationwide contest! For weeks I had to make all kinds of excuses to people who couldn't understand why I wouldn't show them my medal, or play my composition for them.

During this time I had been studying piano privately, first with Marguerite d'Aleria and Rose Cooper Vinetz, then with Alexander Kosloff and Ann Eachus. In school I had taken most of the music courses offered; harmony, music history, sight singing and others, and I did indeed try my hand at composition.

When our class graduated (the same year my mother graduated from Chiropractic College in Los Angeles) we gave the school a new grand piano. I played Mendelssohn's "Capriccio in F Sharp Minor" on it as a commencement piece and it came off well.

__IO__

In January of 1931 the first of my contributions to *Etude* found its way into print. I wrote about the music used as an accompaniment for films and as far as I can ascertain, it was the first article to treat this type of music seriously. I did a number of topical articles and interviews for *Etude*, and also for *Opera*, *Concert*, and *Symphony*, some on my own initiative, some on assignment. It was in this way that I met and wrote about Sir Hamilton Harty, Alfred Hertz, Bernardino Molinari, Ernst Toch, John Charles Thomas, Russell Bennett, Deems Taylor, Erick Wolfgang Korngold and Sir John Barbirolli.

Writing for *American Dancer* magazine I interviewed people in whose lives the dance had played a part, including such Hollywood film notables as Mary Astor, Olive Borden, Antonio Moreno, Maurice Costello, Tom Patricola, Betty Blythe, Jeanette MacDonald, Doris Kenyon, Louise Fazenda, Betty Bronson and Ramon Novarro.

My interest in the dance had begun in a much earlier interview with

Bertha Wardell, a Manual Arts alumna, for the school weekly. A concert dancer and a dance instructor, she introduced me to the role of the pianist as accompanist to dancers. Eventually I accompanied Norma Gould, Waldeen, Eleanora Flaig, Benjamin Zemach and Charles Teske, among others. Accompanying dancers (sometimes writing music for them) was far more interesting to me than accompanying singers, which I also did from time to time.

It was from my experience as a dance accompanist and composer that I later developed a series of lectures, tracing the history of music for the dance, and it was from those lectures that my book, *Choreographic Music* evolved, though it wasn't published (by Dutton) until 1941.

Co-incidentally with my writing activity, I was still playing the piano (teaching sometimes) but principally in concerts (some in women's clubs) and over the radio. After one of the broadcasts, I was told that Charles Wakefield Cadman had telephoned to say he was listening and enjoying the performance. He was not then a personal friend, so I was touched and grateful for his thoughtfulness. In later years he did become a personal friend and I interviewed him for *Etude*. He was showing his home movies at our house to guests just a few days before our daughter Judith was born, and he brought Christmas gifts for both of our children shortly before his fatal illness. We had reason to remember him as a person of great compassion.

One of my favorite motifs for concerts was "Music of the Americas"—this before the general public had become as much aware of the other Americas as they are now. There was a strong below-the-border attraction for me, which was intensified after I had visited Mexico and had learned the background of this entrancing music. When I was en route to Mexico, traveling alone, one of our Latin American consular officials warned me, "Señorita, beware of bandits!" He need not have worried; I was quite safe all the way. Indeed, instead of bandits, I met some of the people prominent in Mexico's creative life, and wrote about them: Carlos Chavez, Manuel M. Ponce, José Rolon, José Pomar, Antonio Gomezanda, Julian Carrillo, Candelario Huizar, Luis Sandi, Silvestre Revueltas, Salvador Ordoñez, Vilma Erenyi and Diego Rivera. I had already met that very great Mexican artist, Alfredo Ramos Martinez, before leaving Los Angeles.

During those happy post high school years, I tried my hand at many things, including the translation of some plays from the Italian. I was not at all familiar with the language; I simply adapted what I had learned of Spanish and plowed in. Then I used to take groups of my performing friends out to the Veterans' Hospital in Sawtelle, to give concerts for the ex-servicemen. They were such an appreciative audience that it was a pleasure for us and we, in turn, were a novelty for them, because we gave them serious music which they could understand but which was a step above the tap dancers and popular ensembles to which they were accustomed.

When an opera company was established in Los Angeles, some of us discovered a new occupation. We would go backstage, put on costumes and get paid one dollar per performance for being supers in the productions. I was an angel with a ghastly canary yellow blonde wig in *Hansel and Gretel*, and a mobile part of the Spanish scenery in *Carmen*. I recruited thirty boys for supering in *Il Trovatore* and six for *Manon*, so that we were all able to see and hear the operas from a new vantage point.

Crazy things often happen to crazy people. Once, at some sort of social function, a charming little lady introduced herself to me as a syndicated columnist for newspapers throughout the Western Hemisphere. She admired my friends, she said, and would like to interview all of them for her papers. Would I mind getting them together at my home for that purpose? I spoke to my friends, who were pleased over the prospect of being quoted all over Latin America, so we set a date.

The first indication that something was amiss came on the morning of the gathering, when one of my mother's friends phoned to say, "Well, I see you are entertaining some distinguished people tonight." Mama asked how she knew, and it turned out that she had read it in that morning's *Times*. We bought a copy of the *Times* and, sure enough, there was an excellent photograph of our lady's daughter, dressed in an Aztec costume, with the announcement that we were going to give a party in her honor. No one could have been more surprised than we.

Early that evening, our lady arrived at the house, bringing a huge box of delicious Italian cookies to serve as refreshments. Later, we were to have other surprises. The doorbell rang, and there stood two handsome gentlemen in tuxedos, representing the Mexican Consulate.

Verna Arvey, 1933. Photo by A. Brisgaloff, Hollywood.

They entered, stayed for a few minutes, then left. The next ring of the bell announced the Dominican Consul himself and his secretary, both dressed formally. They came in and stayed, and it was from them that we learned that all the consulates had received engraved invitations to our party.

As the evening wore on, it was evident that our pseudocolumnist was not thinking about interviewing at all. She was circling among the male guests, asking them to dance with her daughter.

The party broke up after midnight. We were wearily cleaning up about 2:30 A.M., when the doorbell rang again. Three ebullient young men said they were members of Carlos Molina's orchestra, then playing at our Ambassador Hotel, and that they had come to entertain our guests. No other guests remained to be entertained, but we invited the young men in anyway, gave them our leftover refreshments and then, for want of other entertainment, played some of their own Carlos Molina recordings for them.

We never did find out whether our lady columnist was trying to promote a husband or a film career for her daughter, for we never saw or heard of either of them after that night.

It was a varied life: I found myself touring for the Santa Fe Railroad with a small group of artists (giving concerts at stops from Los Angeles to Chicago); appearing in a Pasadena Playhouse production, speaking one line, and doubling offstage for the star, Harrison Ford, who was supposed to be playing the piano onstage; and accompanying my Nisei friend Teru when she danced for a Japanese celebration of Buddha's birthday. I also accompanied a choir in a Japanese Protestant church which engaged me as its accompanist. To my astonishment, one choir would always come to rehearsals, while an entirely different choir showed for the Sunday services. I also did research into serious music by Negro composers, devoting several concerts to it.

I still thought of myself as a student and regarded my activities as part of my training—for what, I didn't yet know. Today, I consider most of my early efforts inadequate in many ways. But each had a part to play in the preparation for what lay ahead in my life.

I I

The young Negro composer about whom I had written in high school had been asked to supply part of the libretto for the opera William Grant Still had planned to write as the first work on his Guggenheim Fellowship. He talked about it so enthusiastically that by the time Still arrived in Los Angeles on May 22, 1934, a veritable fever of excitement had been worked up among his friends. Many of us were on hand to greet the composer soon after he came to town—not only the legitimate friends, but also the hangers-on, the baskers-in-reflected-glory, the wakers-up-at-all-hours-of-the-night with requests for entertainment, and the consumers of other people's liquor. The latter four categories were soon made unwelcome, for the composer had come to the West Coast with a great hunger to work and with a job to do. He intended to do it.

Now, for the first time, I saw a real composer at work. He would accept or initiate an assignment with enthusiasm, then agonize until the form, themes and treatments were clearly outlined in his head. After he started putting things down on paper, he would go slowly (just a few measures a day), but steadily every day. He would be alternately uplifted (thanking God for his inspiration), or downcast (sure that he was being unworthy of the help he had been receiving). At some point in the creation, he usually decided it was no use—he just couldn't go on with it—but then he would pick up where he had left off and bring the composition to a logical conclusion, at which point he would decide it was terrible, not fit to be performed, and he wouldn't change his mind until it had been played, until the audience had approved it and until he could hear it objectively. It took him over twenty years to approve his own *Festive Overture*, even after it had won an important prize and had been applauded by audiences and critics alike. He just didn't care for it, he said, until he heard Izler Solomon conduct it. Then an astonished look came over his face and he decided that it did sound good, after all.

As the months came and went, it became apparent that composing wasn't all there was to being a composer. Letters arrived, a lot of them. All had to be answered. People requested biographical information, photographs, program notes, speeches, material for theses, and so on. If a composer were to take time out for all of this, he would have neither time nor energy left for composing; it was a problem that had to be solved. It seemed to me that my own talents might be of use here, so I volunteered to handle the public relations and promotional side of the work. Still (who by then was called Billy by his West Coast friends) agreed, so I started to work. In addition to the secretarial and literary aspects of my labors, I often played over what he had written when his day's composing was over, because, although he could find his notes and chords on the piano, he was still far from being a performing artist on that instrument. I also included some of his music in my own piano recitals, often lecturing about him and his compositions in the process.

He paid me for all this, but not very much, since he was keeping only fifteen dollars a week for himself and sending the major part of his Guggenheim Fellowship money for the support of his family in the East. He did this despite the absence of a court order requiring him to do so. He continued to send money until the last of the children came of age.

The Guggenheim Fellowship was renewed for another year. After a brief period, Billy requested and received a Rosenwald Fellowship which also was renewed. This gave him four worry-free years, and he made the most of them.

The opera he had come to write was *Blue Steel*, based on a story by Stills' friend, Carlton Moss. This was full of beautiful melodies, lush harmonies and stirring choruses. After finishing it, he decided it was not strong enough as a drama and put it aside. He was therefore delighted when Langston Hughes offered him a libretto on the life of Jean Jacques Dessalines of Haiti. Still had previously asked some of the Negro poets for opera libretti, but they had not responded. Langston himself had written this first as a play, and had then offered it to Clarence Cameron White for a possible musical setting, but White had turned it down in favor of another poet's libretto on the same subject. So now Langston proposed what was to become *Troubled Island*, and he made a trip to the West Coast to outline the work.

After he had completed the script, Langston left Los Angeles for Spain, and then Billy was really upset. From time to time, changes in the script became necessary, but he could not reach his librettist to discuss them and had to rely on his own judgment. At last, a major change had to be made at the end of the second act. New lines had to be written to fit the music and the new turn in the drama. After an exchange of many letters, during which he received the new melodic line and made an effort to fit appropriate words to it, Langston wrote that I would have to do it because he couldn't. I was apprehensive of course, because this was all strange to me. However, I worked and worried for days until the missing text was finally supplied.

Now we both knew that I could write words to fit music. Thereafter I wrote libretti for all of his operas and other vocal works. It was a more comfortable arrangement than collaborating with someone at a distance. It also allowed Billy free rein in composing, for I followed his music far more often than he followed my texts.

Some months after he came to Los Angeles on the first Fellowship, Still made a trip to Chicago to see the second performance of his ballet, *La Guiablesse* at the Chicago Opera. This time Ruth Page (who had danced the leading role before) gave the part to a newcomer, Katherine Dunham. The program included works by two American composers, both of whom were on hand for the performance. Still was happy when the rehearsal went well. His good humor left him at performance time, when the conductor stood up and beat time in silence for a number of measures. No music came out, though the ballet was supposed to open with a trumpet solo. After the performance, it was discovered that when the music was passed out to the orchestra, the trumpet's part was missing, so the trumpeter had no music to play. When the parts were returned to Still later on, the trumpet part was among them.

The other composer's work went flawlessly, in rehearsal and in performance. In later years, we were to hear of many such incidents of sabotage of other composer's works, but this was Still's first. He was pleased, though, that in spite of the disheartening opening, the rest of the ballet went off well and was received warmly by the audience.

During this period, Mrs. Claire Reis, always a friend and champion of American composers, commissioned from Still a new work for the League of Composers to be introduced by Eugene Goossens and the Cincinnati Symphony Orchestra. With his typical enthusiasm, Still turned out two works instead of one, and let Goossens take his choice. These were *Dismal Swamp* and *Kaintuck'*, the latter dedicated to me, and both for piano and orchestra. Goossens decided on *Kaintuck'* for geographical reasons. Cincinnati is almost a Kentucky town. He called it a "grand piece of tone painting." He said he placed no importance on the "fetish of first performances," so another pianist and I presented it first, for two pianos, in a Los Angeles Pro Musica concert. Howard Hanson also played it in Rochester, along with *Dismal Swamp*.

After *Afro-American Symphony* appeared in print, thanks to Fischer's diligent promotion, it was played with increasing regularity. Sir Hamilton Harty, to whom I had mentioned Still's music when I interviewed him at the Hollywood Bowl, broadcast it in London and wrote that it had created a great deal of interest. Karl Krueger, a cherished friend whom Still had met in Hollywood through the intervention of Isabel Morse Jones of the Los Angeles *Times*, gave inspired performances of it with several symphony orchestras in this country and abroad, and later twice recorded it in its entirety, the last time for his Society for the Preservation of the American Musical Heritage. It had its first performance with the New York Philharmonic Orchestra; and in Chicago it was played under the baton of Hans Lange. It was a success everywhere.

Many of the Still performances were so far away that it was financially out of the question to travel to hear all of them. So it was not until Lt. Benter and the United States Navy Symphony Orchestra broadcast the *Afro-American Symphony* over the NBC Network that I actually heard one of these major compositions in its orchestral form, having been limited until then to more or less inadequate piano reductions.

Now it burst on me in all its glory: rich, emotional, and at the same time spiritually satisfying. I had just noted a controversy in some American magazines over who could be considered a genuine American composer. All sorts of names had been offered, but none had been convincing. Suddenly, I wondered what all the shouting was about. Here was their American composer, truly a product of our own soil, both himself and the music he created. Why were none of the frantic journalists aware of him?

But they were not, so I felt especially honored when one early morning, around two or three o'clock, I was awakened out of a sound sleep at my home by the ringing of the telephone. It was Billy. He said that he had just gotten the theme for the second movement of his *G Minor Symphony*, and wanted me to hear it. He put the telephone as near the piano as possible and played the theme. It struck me then, as it has ever since, as being one of the most lofty and inspired symphonic themes I had ever heard.

Possibly Still's symphonic music received its greatest North American publicity when Leopold Stokowski played the fourth movement of the *Afro-American Symphony* on his cross-country tour with the Philadelphia Orchestra, for this tour was advertised extensively. Contrary to the general impression of Stokowski as a temperamental, flamboyant individual, we found him to be thoughtful and quite meticulous. When he studied a score he studied every bit of it. He even took note of Billy's concluding phrase on every score: "With humble thanks to God, the Source of inspiration." In one of his letters there was this paragraph: "I am so interested to see that you dedicate these works to the source of inspiration. How mysterious and yet how definite is this source! It is strange how many people seem to be so far away from it, and not to have any contact with it."

Publicity in the Los Angeles papers brought Still a contract with Columbia Pictures for six months, and an option which was never picked up, for understandable reasons. Billy was out of his element in the studios. The man who brought him in (Howard Jackson, an old friend) soon lost his job as head of the studio music department.

Time and time again during the six months, the new studio music director would ignore Still and call in outside composers to do the work. He was not given a real chance, until at the very end he was asked to orchestrate some of Dmitri Tiomkin's music for *Lost Horizon*. As a joke, he asked the copyist to pencil in a hot trumpet playing "The Music Goes 'Round and 'Round" over the solemn choral music in the funeral procession of the dead Lama. He knew it could quickly be erased after the first rehearsal. Well, at that first rehearsal, the joke was highly effective, with one reservation. Everyone laughed heartily except Tiomkin and the music director, who asked plaintively, "Was that supposed to be in there?"

They took revenge by not picking up his option, and the music director told the heads of music departments in other studios that Still couldn't do the work—a statement belied by the fact that several times in later years Tiomkin himself asked for Still to orchestrate his scores. In the studio Still had also had the experience of passing an open doorway and hearing one of his colleagues remark loudly, "A nigger in this line of work?"

Quite a few of the composers who did get all the film work would call Billy on the phone from time to time, asking for help in finding native African themes or rare Negro Spirituals. (This was true even of a very important foreign-born composer, who in public deprecated all American composers, loudly and with finality.) Some others asked Billy to teach them orchestration. He always refused these requests, though he often gave time, advice and recommendations to students and other young composers.

The open-mindedness of Mrs. Leiland Atherton Irish, then manager of the Hollywood Bowl, brought us to another milestone. She invited

Still to conduct some of his own compositions at the Bowl on July 23, 1936. The men in the film studio, unaware that he was accustomed to conducting an orchestra, proceeded to instruct him in the art. He accepted their advice without comment. They must have thought, when they saw him in action, that they had an exceptionally bright student.

Before the concert, I had pointed out to Isabel Morse Jones that this would be the first time a Negro had conducted a major symphony orchestra in the United States. Mrs. Jones kept this to herself until her review appeared in the Los Angeles *Times*, so the event's historic importance was not revealed until the concert was over. Approximately a year after that, Dean Dixon conducted a symphony orchestra in New York, and for months afterward I was kept busy reminding journalists that he was not the first Negro to do so. Even as late as 1966, *Time* magazine repeated the error and refused to correct it.

The Hollywood Bowl concert was shared by Fabien Sevitzky, who was later to play an important part in our lives, and who for many years routinely included an American work in almost all of his concerts. Another bright spot that night was the presence of Stepin Fetchit. He had often been criticized as an Uncle Tom, exemplifying the worst kind of Negro stereotype, but that night he bought five extra boxes and two hundred extra tickets so that he and his guests could watch a colored man conduct the Los Angeles Philharmonic Orchestra. For that gesture, even though we never met this man in person, he always had a place in our hearts.

A new kind of music was requested for Still's next composition when CBS, under Deems Taylor's guidance, decided to commission six leading American composers to write compositions especially for radio. It was a relatively new medium for serious music, so the project was considered experimental. Still composed a series of pieces—actually a suite—for orchestra, piano soloist, chorus and narrator, inspired by street scenes in Harlem. He called it *Lenox Avenue* and tied the musical episodes together by a continuity which I supplied. It was the first piece performed in the CBS series because it was the first of the CBS works to be completed. It elicited about one hundred and thirty letters, telegrams and postcards from listeners (of which fewer than half a dozen were disapproving). One man likened his response to the surge of emotion he felt on first hearing Charpentier's *Louise* in Paris.

Still (*left*) and Handy stand in front of the Perisphere to discuss
Still's theme music for the 1939 World's Fair in New York.
Courtesy 1939 New York World's Fair, Inc.

Indirectly, this led to another commission, for when Kay Swift and the other members of the New York World's Fair in 1939–40 Theme Committee wanted to select a composer to write their theme music, they went to the CBS offices and there heard aircheks of all the serious American composers' work which CBS had in its files. None of the composers was aware of this at the time. The Theme Committee itself did not know the names of the composers of any of the works. They found two (*A Deserted Plantation* and *Lenox Avenue*) and agreed that whoever wrote either one of them could be their composer. William Grant Still had written both.

On February 1, 1938, Still dreamed of his grandmother. She seemed to be trying to impress on his consciousness the words, "Watch February 5th." This was so vivid that he could hardly wait for February 5th to come, to see what would happen. But it came and went, and nothing out of the ordinary occurred. A few days later, he received a letter written and mailed in New York on February 5th, inviting him to compose the theme music for the Fair.

The next composition for the concert hall to win acclaim was the Second (G minor) Symphony, subtitled "Song of a New Race"—the Symphony with the particularly inspiring second movement theme. Leopold Stokowski introduced this in Philadelphia and New York with his usual flair, so it was well-publicized and well-received, though there were some people who were so steeped in the Negro stereotype that they assumed anything by a Negro composer had to be in a popular vein.

Among congratulatory notes and wires were those from Charles Wakefield Cadman, Clarence Cameron White, Alain Locke and Harl McDonald. "Your symphony," McDonald wrote, "is strong and spontaneous music. Such beauty and honesty must live a long time and enrich the lives of many people, for it comes in a period when composers have devoted too much time to superficial tricks." This was in contrast to printed remarks by reviewers in the opposing camp, who wrote that Still's music was "dull," "pretentious," and reeking of "swamps and alligators."

In the Thirties, Still was visited by the older Negro composer, R. Nathaniel Dett, and a younger composer, Ulysses Kay, then fresh from the University of Arizona. Still was impressed with Kay's potential and was happy to recommend him for various fellowships throughout the years. Dr. Dett shared an entirely different experience with us, for we drove him and another friend to Negro Day at the San Diego Fair. As we walked around the Fair grounds, we were awed by the large number of people who followed us to get Dett's autograph. His was a large and loyal following. When lunch time approached, we were told to go to a particular restaurant on the Fair grounds. We did, and there we sat, the four of us (two white and two colored), while waitresses passed us several times, with no sign of recognition. At last Dett asked to see the manager, who informed him that they would not serve Negroes. We left and, like the multitude of other Negroes who had paid their admission fees, ate hot dogs and hamburgers at lunch stands. This was Negro Day at the Fair, in sunny California.

Always in demand as a conductor and educator, Howard Hanson was another whose path crossed ours when he visited California. One incident involving him stayed especially vivid in our memories. An organization of southern California composers decided to honor Hanson with a banquet at Homer Grunn's home. One of the members phoned me to say that they would like to invite Mr. Still too, because it might help him to know Dr. Hanson. It seemed best not to embarrass them by telling the truth—that the Hanson-Still friendship was then well along in years—so we simply showed up at the banquet. As luck would have it, Hanson arrived at the same time. We walked in together.

He was given the place of honor as a matter of course, while we were asked to sit at an auxiliary table out on the service porch, along with some WPA workers and others. We thought nothing of it since we could see that there was an overflow of guests, many unexpected. Hanson evidently made a mental note of it, however, and must have thought we were being slighted. He said nothing until they asked him to make some remarks after dinner. Then he rose and said, "You ask me why the American Composers' Concerts in Rochester have been successful. Well, they have been successful because all along we have played the music of composers like William Grant Still." Then he paused and looked all around the room. When he was sure that his remark had penetrated, he made another remark about William Grant Still and again looked around the room—then a third remark and another long look. Then he went ahead with his speech.

Hanson was a monument in American music not only because of his creative work, his conducting and his educational prestige, but also because of his integrity and forthrightness. Years later his wife (seeing him from backstage while he was conducting a children's concert) said, "Isn't he beautiful?" I looked at him and agreed.

During the Thirties there was a series of odd events which had not occurred before and never occurred afterward, yet we did not appreciate their significance until much later. The doorbell would ring several times and there would stand someone with a crystal ball—someone different each time—asking if we would like to have a reading. As a matter of curiosity, we usually said "yes," and sometimes these impromptu readings turned out to have real meaning. The fact that they were positive encouraged us to go to one of our friends, then a well-known psychic in the Los Angeles area, for readings. They also helped me to overcome the feeling of hostility I had developed after the spiritualist experiences of my childhood. Much later, we realized how this spiritual help from our psychic friends and from wandering crystal-gazers had bouyed us up during a period of crisis.

All of our readings pointed to coming trouble which would last for years, but all of them assured us that if we continued to fight, and did not abandon the struggle, we would be victorious in the end. Since those were golden years, as far as we could see, it was difficult to accustom ourselves to dark thoughts, but things happened exactly as predicted, and it became clear that precisely because of the golden years and our successes, some people were planning to try and thwart us.

First came a series of anonymous, nasty letters: some to Billy, some to me, some to newspapers and even (we have reason to believe) to film studios who might have wanted to employ Still. Ours began with the ominous statement that there was no one so big that he couldn't be torn down, and they lasted for about two years, each one uglier than its predecessor. The police thought they were part of an extortion plot and assured us that we would soon receive a demand for money, but this never came. Apparently the worst accusation in the eyes of the writers, was that Billy and I were planning to get married.

Several themes ran through the letters. They all made strong attacks against me and defended the wife who had deserted him some years before; all contained a great deal of misinformation, most of which was quickly spotted by friends who had known one or both of us over the years. The plot had the appearance of having been conceived and carried out by several colored women in particular, but we know that they were not the only ones involved.

One day our psychic friend phoned and said in great agitation, "Mr. Still must get out of that house!" Billy immediately rented a post office box to which his mail could be sent, then arranged to move into a bungalow a short distance away, not telling anyone but a few close friends where he was going.

Sure enough, before leaving the old house, he became ill. We discovered that someone had been going into his refrigerator on the service porch and putting something in his food. He kept the door locked but the intruder had poked a hole in the screen, and gone into the refrigerator again, leaving in such haste that the refrigerator door was left open and the neighbor's cat got into it. This or another trespasser ransacked the glove compartment of his car. Clearly our psychic friend had foreseen such things.

The night before moving, when the house was in a dishevelled state, there was a knock on the front door and in came an unexpected but most welcome guest: Arizona composer Robert McBride. He shared our delicatessen supper and swapped stories about mutual friends such as Ulysses Kay and Leopold Stokowski, who had played both his and Billy's music in recent concerts.

It actually hadn't occurred to us that we might marry, though I suppose we had been falling in love all those years we had been working together. The odds against marriage seemed too strong. Billy had not thought about divorcing his first wife, though in his mind he was already divorced from the woman who had walked out on him. But the letters changed his mind. When the children in New York began to write letters implying that he had forsaken them, his feeling of consideration for his former family was sharply modified. Only then did he initiate divorce proceedings. In California at that time, this was a long and involved process; it was quite a while before we were able to carry out our plans.

As for myself, I had long forgotten any ideas about racial differences—if indeed, I had ever had any in the first place. The more colored people I knew, the more I realized that they were like other people: some wonderful, some terrible, some in between. I realized, too, that pigmentation had nothing to do with the inner qualities of an individual. As our son Duncan carefully explained to me, when he was about eight years old, "Mom, I'll tell you about colored people. When you know them and like them, they're not colored anymore."

I've often felt that some people's prejudices are owing to their lack of acquaintance with the better class of colored people, and when I say "better class," I am not referring to the amount of money they make, nor the the darkness or lightness of their skins. I'm referring to the sort of colored people I know who, by virtue of their intelligence and good breeding, could go into any elite gathering and be perfectly at home.

So the usual doubts about marrying a Negro didn't occur to me. As a matter of fact, it seemed exactly right. One of the people we took into our confidence was Norma Gould, who had welcomed us into her dance studio on more than one occasion, and who had presented there a choreographic version of our *Lenox Avenue*. When she heard the story, she looked me straight in the eye and said, "Your *friends* will stick by you!" And so it was.

The year between the granting of the interlocutory and the final divorce decrees went rapidly, because there was much to do: preparations for the World's Fair and trips to New York, with Billy posing for photographs with Grover Whalen and other dignitaries; dinner at the home of Henry Dreyfuss (designer of the Theme exhibit); and conferences with Kay Swift and others involved in the music. Billy went alone to New York, but in California there were trips we made together, when we gave concerts in various places (he conducting the orchestra, I playing the piano). From each event, we brought back stories.

In San Diego a prominent white lady honored our concert with a reception afterward. We enjoyed it, until we returned to Los Angeles and encountered an indignant colored woman who wanted to know why we had not visited any colored people in San Diego. When we told her that no colored people had invited us, it didn't seem to make any difference to her. Apparently we should have barged in on someone colored, invited or not.

In northern California, where both of us lectured, I was introduced

to a white woman, said to be a Communist, who "just loved Negroes."
As soon as she could get me alone she informed me that she disap-
proved of Still because he was too sophisticated. I replied that he
couldn't be anything but what he was, and she asked, "Do you know
(naming a particular colored character actor)? Well," with a smirk,
"he's just a *nigger!*"

Also in northern California we renewed our friendship with Sis
and Walt Gordon. Walt's early friendship with Earl Warren may have
been a factor in the later Supreme Court desegregation decision.

Ralph Bunche, William L. Dawson, Paul Williams (the distinguished architect), Camille Nickerson, Josephine Harreld, Jester Hairston, Sargent Johnson and Richmond Barthe (the artists), Dorothy
Maynor, Mattiwilda Dobbs, Georgia Laster, Philippa Schuyler, Harold
Browning, Ethel Waters, Ulysses Kay, Hale Smith, Frederick Douglas
Hall, Theodore Phillips, Todd Duncan, Georgia Ryder, Alison Davis
and Arna Bontemps were among many other noted colored people
whose paths crossed ours as the years went by. Arna showed us his
films of Haiti, while Ralphe Bunche showed the pictures he had taken
in Bali and Africa. He convulsed us with the story of his teaching the
Africans to "truck" (one of the dances popular in the United States at
that time) in return for their teaching him their tribal dances. His films
also dramatized the frustration experienced by the Africans at the
hands of their colonial masters.

On another occasion, Florence Cole-Talbert, the soprano, was entertaining some friends. These were mostly colored, but among them
was a white woman—a poet—who had brought a mousy little man as
her escort. When the hostess asked them if they would like to say a few
words, the poet responded as a poet would, then her escort rose and,
in some embarrassment, blurted out. "I don't know why I'm here—
unless maybe it's because she (pointing to the poet) thinks I like to go
to funny places." I looked at the faces around me. They were impas-
sive. Not an eyelid flickered; not a word was said. The man sat down;
the other guests applauded softly; the evening went on.

So that year did pass quickly. The final decree came through, and
we made our plans to buy a house, build a fence around it and get
married in Mexico because interracial marriages were illegal in Cali-

fornia at the time. We got a ticket for speeding, driving home from the Border, but it didn't dampen our spirits in the least. We had managed our marriage, and now we had to manage the new cycle that was beginning.

12

Back in Los Angeles, we hired a moving van and took all the things from my apartment and all the things from Billy's rented house to a bungalow on Cimarron Street, where we would live for twenty years. For the first seven years there we had the companionship of our beloved dog, Shep, who became the official announcer of visitors. He traveled with us, had his picture in the papers, and even had a piano piece, "Quit Dat Fool'nish," dedicated to him. When he died, we acquired gentle little Ozma and finally, Princess, whose resemblance to Lassie made her a celebrity to the children we met.

Our marriage took place on February 8, 1939. As if in celebration, and again through the good offices of Mrs. Irish, on February 17 and 18 of the same year, I was soloist with the Los Angeles Philharmonic Orchestra, performing *Kaintuck'*, the composition Billy had dedicated to me. The orchestra was under the distinguished baton of Otto Klemperer. It was the culmination of years of hoping and the begin-

ning of new musical aspirations, and it was a memorable experience to
work with a conductor as thorough and inspired as Klemperer.

We were particularly interested in the reception *Kaintuck'* would
receive in Los Angeles, because Klemperer had placed it between compositions by Weber and Mozart. We wondered how the new music
would hold up in the company of two recognized masterpieces. To our
immense gratification, it seemed exactly right for the spot, and a tribute to Klemperer's instinctive flair for programming.

By this time, Still had developed a sure hand as a composer. He
had become an expert craftsman with a quiet mastery of his art.
He had learned how to extend his themes, how to use a little to make a
lot in an economy of thematic material. This was a far cry from the
early days of *Darker America*, when he had used so many themes that
the work (in his later opinion) became fragmentary. Now there was
none of the insecurity of the beginner.

He had also learned the art of the climax, and had taught himself
to build onto the accepted harmonic structure in a creative way, so
that exotic new harmonies emerged—but never by discarding the old
rules, as some ultra-modernists do.

His work began in the morning after breakfast, when the inspiration flowed. This was when he sketched his intentions in thin, spidery,
pencilled notes. Later he did the mechanical work, recording and putting into readable form what he had composed, reviewing and rewriting all the time (even many years after the completion and performance of a work; once, after a composition had been in print for
thirty years). He orchestrated everything immediately, and extracted
his own parts.

In later years, I heard other composers, some merely young hopefuls, lamenting the chore of copying their own music, thinking apparently that the Almighty owed them a copyist. Never once did I hear
Billy make such a complaint. It was not only the fact that we couldn't
afford to employ copyists, but also because he felt that going over his
own scores in this way helped him to ferret out mistakes—mistakes
which could later be costly if they were allowed to last over into rehearsal time.

Money was still not plentiful, but we were willing to make do because we felt we were working toward an ideal. We received royalties and rentals in small amounts from the published compositions, supplemented by modest payments from ASCAP, and as long as we had a roof over our heads, food, clothes and our integrity, we felt the luxuries could wait.

Someone, it appeared to us, had to be willing to fight it out and show that it can be done, not only for his own sake, but for the sakes of those to come. We decided that this was what we wanted. It wasn't lucrative work (in contrast to the fabulous sums supposedly earned by the Jazzists) but it turned out to be far from unrewarding or lonely. At last, a serious Negro composer had measured arms with his contemporaries and shown signs of being recognized permanently as a leading American creator in addition to being a leading Negro. We thought we would like to keep it that way. We had noted all too many examples of composers who thought they'd get themselves well-settled financially in commercial music first, and then invade the serious field, but it seldom worked like that. They almost never seemed to escape the early association.

Living in the same house, I soon discovered more of Billy's working habits. He would change everything around in his workroom and clean vigorously after finishing one composition and before starting another. Time after time, he would call me into the workroom to explain where the orchestra scores would be if I wanted them, where the master sheets and instrumental parts were, and so on. I would memorize it all, only to find—several weeks or months later—that a new cycle had changed the locations of everything. Now the scores were where the master sheets used to be, the parts where the scores used to be, and so on. After trying for a while to keep all this in my head, I gave up. Then neither of us could find anything.

The neighborhood in which we lived had started out to be all-white. We were the second colored family to move in. After that, it gradually became multi-racial. Those of our neighbors with whom we established friendships proved to be intelligent, warm and responsive.

We never ceased to be amazed at the way so many of our neighbors, all of us middle class, were constantly improving their homes and property, taking pride in their surroundings, and banding together to see that undesirables were kept out. Once a colored prostitute moved in and nightly played hostess to the owners of sleek cars.

Another time one of the bungalows was taken over by gamblers. Each time the decent neighbors got together, enlisted police help, and put a stop to the nuisances.

We did have one cross to bear in the neighborhood, but not for too long. This came in the form of a strange woman who moved next door and proceeded to make it her business to be ugly and annoying, particularly when she discovered that we were not planning to include her in any of our plans. We were not surprised when we learned from another neighbor that a man who roomed in her house (a postal worker) had found it necessary to move because his landlady was trying to convert him to communism. When she was unsuccessful, she devoted herself to making life miserable for those who had opposed her.

Most of the colored people we knew were selective about their associates, not socializing with people from the lower segments of life, but once in a while a dissenting voice could be heard. There was a particular person to whom both Billy and I had an aversion. I remarked once that I would not want him in my home as a guest. Zora Neale Hurston, the colored author, heard me and replied, "Well, now that you have married one of us, you have to take *all* of us." I replied, "No, I don't either have to take *all*. If I married a white man, would it be assumed that I would have to socialize with all the white riff-raff?"

There is always the hint of social ostracism when an interracial marriage is concerned. If we were ostracized, we certainly never became aware of it. We had more invitations from both white and colored people than we could accept. By choice, we preferred not to go out a great deal: if we had done everything we were asked to do, we could never have gotten any work done. When we entertained—never on a lavish scale, but always with love—it seemed to us that our guests enjoyed being with us and meeting our other guests.

How did we get along together, Billy and I? Well, we were both strong-minded people, so from time to time we fussed, just as every other married couple does, but probably not as much. We faced the difficult task of living and working together at home all day and all night for close to forty years, and we remained friends. Not many couples can boast of such a record.

He never criticized the way I made coffee (which, according to current TV ads, is the way many marriages fail). I'm still wondering how those wonderful Southern cooks he admired manage to cook mustard greens for days on end without any liquid in the pot and without burning them. I tried, but I couldn't quite make it. The art of his grandmother's Southern cooking escaped me, though I did learn how to make enchiladas and jambalaya.

Most of our friends, white and colored, seemed to be happy over our marriage. One of them, Allan, a white Southerner who had been raised in Little Rock on the opposite end of Billy's own street, raised a brief question mark in our minds. He and his wife, Helen, had been our dear friends for many years and yet we wondered how he, a white Southerner, would accept our marriage. We asked Helen to visit us and told her the news quite soon after it happened. "Oh, you must let me tell Allan!" she exclaimed. "He has always said you were so well-suited to each other that it's a shame society might frown on your getting together"! She went away then. The next night the doorbell rang and there they stood, the two of them, with their arms full of gifts. When our son was born, a year later, we named him Duncan Allan Still.

Some oddballs of both races misunderstood our marriage. It took a little doing to convince such people that we were normal and not of their kind. One of several weird encounters took place when some of our friends brought over a rather nice-looking, middle-aged woman who promptly sat on our floor, crossed her legs and looked Billy straight in the eye, saying, "You must come to visit me in my studio. I need *you*, possibly more than you need *me*." Everyone present blushed and fidgeted; while Billy and I changed the subject and kept it changed.

Another woman, an actress who had done neurotic bit-parts in films, used to sit with a cigarette dangling from her mouth, her eyes surveying me with intense curiosity. It made me nervous, until I discovered that she had gotten the idea that I was oversexed because I had married a Negro.

It goes without saying that, quite apart from racial considerations, there are certain things that must be faced by any woman who marries a prominent man. I have been through it all, but have been saved from embarrassment because my husband was staunch and loyal—in every sense of the word, a gentleman. There have been the panting females, the insistent Communists, the collaborator-seekers, and sometimes just people who—observing a mild-mannered individual—try to impose their will on him. All of them were sure that if they could just get me out of the way, they could take over. None of them was around during the lean years, when a helping hand and a word of encouragement meant so much—only when the rewards began to flow in. We had reason to know who our friends were.

Besides, the seekers woefully misjudged Billy's character. Because he appeared amiable, they imagined that he would be putty in the hands of anyone who wanted to start molding. Not so. Billy's outward amiability concealed forthright convictions, which he wasn't about to abandon. Furthermore, he was always honest enough to say exactly what he felt. Once several people proposed a new opera along lines they were sure would appeal to him. He listened with interest, his eyes sparkled and he said enthusiastically, "It's a great idea!" Encouraged, our friends wanted to know when he could get to work on it, whereupon he added hastily, "Oh, it *is* a great idea. But not for me."

Another suggested that Billy would improve his creative output if he would accept some suggestions. Billy asked what, precisely, would the suggestions be? The man exclaimed, "Why not write a ballet about Toussaint L'Ouverture of Haiti?" "But why?" responded Billy. "I've already done an opera about Jean Jacques Dessalines of Haiti. I'd only be repeating myself." The man hadn't even known about the previous opera and its production. He had no suggestions after that.

Out-of-the-ordinary, pleasant events took place at our house, aside from our musical and social life. We enjoyed having Adrian Tucker and Tom Craig paint Billy's portraits, and were especially pleased when Joseph Portanova came repeatedly to make the William Grant Still bust which has been shown in so many exhibits. And then Alain Locke persuaded Katherin Garrison Chapin that Billy would be the ideal composer to set her long ballad, *And They Lynched Him on a Tree* to music, so she visited us too. This was before her husband, Francis Biddle, became Solicitor General of the United States, and long before he was appointed Attorney General. Billy had completed a set of seven piano pieces (a companion suite to his earlier *Three Visions*) for which he needed an overall title. Mrs. Biddle suggested *Traceries*, so they were published under that title.

The *Lynching* piece, as we called it for brevity's sake, turned out to be of sizable proportions. To perform it, two choruses (one white, one colored, Mrs. Biddle's idea) were required, in addition to a narrator, contralto soloist and symphony orchestra. When it was finished and a suitable outlet was needed for its presentation, it was clear that its demands were going to make for difficulties. Mrs. Biddle did not have a solution to the problem, so we wrote to Artur Rodzinski, who had previously asked if he might give a "first" performance of a Still work and, to our delight, his response was favorable. He made only one suggestion: that the text in the final chorus be changed so that it would speak of brotherhood. His native country had only recently been taken over by Nazis, so he felt that the world needed every possible constructive affirmation. His point was well taken. Mrs. Biddle accordingly devised the lines, "O trust your brother and take his hand" which appear at that point in the music.

About a year later, when Rodzinski's plan to introduce the work at New York Lewisohn Stadium on June 24th was made public, we ran into another of those astonishing situations involving another composer. Roy Harris read the announcement in the papers early in June, and apparently decided that this was something he would like to share. He thereupon wrote a new composition in four days, according to the newspapers: begun on June 10th, finished on June 14th. It was scored for—you guessed it—Negro chorus, white chorus and orchestra. He persuaded Rodzinski to open the evening's program with it, so that his use of the two choruses would precede Billy's, and he would appear to be the innovator.

Mrs. Biddle was photographed at rehearsal with a smiling Roy Harris. Billy was not there, nor was he able to attend certain other premieres, because traveling such distances so frequently was a luxury not provided for in our slender budget. Rodzinski wrote later that he and the musicians were thrilled to have presented the work, and that the audience received it warmly. Indeed, an aircheck we received of the broadcast ended with the announcer's remark that the applause "knew no bounds" and was continuing for minutes on end. He added that "it is not given to many people to witness such a beautiful performance of such a beautiful work." Some of the participants later reported that many of the women in the choir were weeping unashamedly after hearing the song of the lynching victim's mother.

The *Lynching* piece presented a dark picture of the United States. Around the time of its creation another composition about the South was coming into being, a happy, humourous work. This was the ballet, *Miss Sally's Party*, on which Billy and I collaborated and which we dedicated to Thelma Biracree, who afterward choreographed it and presented it in Rochester under Howard Hanson's direction. This was real Americana with a Cakewalk as is climax; it too was applauded enthusiastically, but with smiles rather than tears.

All the while (1939–40) the William Grant Still Theme Music was grinding away in the New York World's Fair Perisphere, performance after performance daily, until at the Fair's end it was estimated to have been played about fifty or sixty thousand times.

Artie Shaw's entry into our lives came at about this time. He wanted to record six sides of a new album, and asked Billy to make the orchestrations. Of the six arrangements, more than one became famous, and one—*Frenesi*— is still heard today from time to time. Shaw called it the second or third best selling record he ever made. When *Frenesi* was first issued, enthusiasm ran so high that when we tuned in to a new radio program one day we heard the announcer comparing Billy's new arrangement with what had gone before, so that everyone could hear the improvement. Gerald Strang told us that he had played the recording for his college music classes to demonstrate the skill of popular orchestrators; he was surprised to learn later that it was a Still orchestration. He hadn't known before.

There were two ASCAP orchestral concerts in connection with the two World's Fairs, one on the east coast and one on the west, in which Billy was one of several leading American composers conducting their own works. These were welcome outings for us; we enjoyed every opportunity to help make serious American music better known to the American public. We also enjoyed our contacts with other ASCAP members, a group of professionals, all accomplished in their fields, sometimes disagreeing but in the end working together toward a common goal. It was always inspiring to watch them in action, from the era of dynamic Gene Buck to the expert and farsighted Stanley Adams.

ASCAP and its activities were to become an important part of our lives in the years to come, but more important to us was our son, Duncan, born approximately a year after our marriage. When he was

Billy and Verna with young son Duncan (and dog Shep), 1940. Photo by Loyd Rathbun.

two and a half, his little sister, Judith Anne, came to join us. We felt that our lives had truly been fulfilled. We supervised their early training, drove them around to the many places of interest in southern California (there were lots of those, even before Disneyland, and always the color and flavor of the old Spanish days abounded) and glowed with pride when they showed signs (unmistakable to us!) of brilliance. No children were ever more thoroughly loved, unless it could be the grandchildren who came along much later.

We were still driving our old 1936 Ford; our house was still furnished with odds and ends (including furniture Billy had made and the rag rugs I had crocheted); we still budgeted carefully on food and clothing; and we still faced opposition. But we also had some of the most wonderful gifts God can bestow, so we never ceased to be grateful.

—I3—

More busy years lay ahead, for the Forties brought us the kind of decade every composer dreams about. Conductors were asking for new works because their audiences were applauding those already written, the press was generous with its attention, our children were growing, our home life was happy, and our friends were multiplying.

After the success of *And They Lynched Him on a Tree*, John Barbirolli visited us to request a new composition for an important anniversary concert of the New York Philharmonic Orchestra. This began our friendship with him and his gifted wife, an oboist, which lasted through the years. They became Sir John and Lady Barbirolli after we had known them for some time, so we had the new experience of addressing them in that fashion instead of "Mr. and Mrs." To us they were always gracious colleagues, according to us the same respect we gave to them. During their stay in southern California, I requested and was given an interview with Sir John for *Etude*, and now remember that interview as one of the most uplifting experiences of my life.

As I now recall, Billy asked the questions while I took notes. Once Billy remarked, "I have never had a patron," to which Sir John replied quickly, "Neither have I—and we are both fortunate in that respect. When you have a patron, you are subject to that patron's likes and dislikes and, in some measure, you are bound to conform to his wishes. It's better for an artist to be free to follow his own convictions."

The composition Sir John was requesting was an Overture, but Mrs. Biddle had previously sent some additional poems which she hoped would find musical settings. Among them Billy found the "Plain-Chant for America," a strong and timely affirmation. This he proposed to set for baritone and orchestra. Sir John agreed. He also suggested, as the composition took shape, that an organ part be added to the finale.

When performance time approached, we asked that Robert Weede be engaged to sing the baritone solo part. We had long been enthused over Weede's ability as a singer, actor and all-around good performer. We also knew that he was much in demand by the writers of lyrics, because his clear enunciation brought out every nuance in the poems. In addition, we felt personally indebted to him for many kindnesses. Weede had scheduled engagements outside of New York for the time in question, however, so the Philharmonic management suggested Wilbur Evans instead. We met him and liked him, and so it was he who sang *Plain-Chant* at its premiere.

When Sir John Barbirolli decided to perform *Plain-Chant for America* in Los Angeles with our Philharmonic Orchestra, we had acquired another baritone friend, Eugene Pearson, who, with his wife (a fine soprano) spent hours learning, rehearsing and performing new Still compositions for the fun of it. He was a good musician and the first to learn *Plain-Chant* so that he could sing it for Francis and Katherin Biddle and Francis' artist-brother, George, and his wife, Helene Sardeau, at a social gathering. Now we proposed that Pearson should sing it with the Philharmonic. We felt that we owed him that opportunity for his devotion. But Mrs. Irish, the orchestra's manager, called and said, "Verna, I'm sending a young baritone to your house. I want you and Billy to listen to him. If you can honestly tell me you don't like him, then we will use your baritone."

Her baritone turned out to be Jerome Hines. Even at nineteen, his talent and skill were evident. What could we say, except that we agreed? So it happened that young Jerry Hines was given one of his first appearances of note in a William Grant Still work, a fact which his devoted mother never failed to remember in the years to follow, when she became and remained one of our dearest friends. We were then faced with the problem of explaining to Eugene Pearson, which we did, as we always tried to do such things, with complete honesty. When we had finished our story, Pearson said, "Tell me just one thing: what is the name of the baritone?" When we said that it was Jerome Hines, he replied, "Well, it's all right then. I know him and his work and I know you're telling me the truth."

In succeeding years, we were never willing to ask our artist-friends (not even Pearl Whitelow, the soprano who worked so hard to sing the music exactly as Billy wanted it) to perform for us for nothing. If other people asked them and they agreed, we usually went along gratefully. We didn't ask for ourselves, since we felt so keenly our inability to compensate for kindnesses of this sort.

Jerry Hines sang the baritone role in *Plain-Chant for America* on a Standard Oil broadcast after his Los Angeles Philharmonic appearance. These Standard broadcasts, under the imaginative and capable direction of Adrian Michaelis, and the musical leadership of Carmen Dragon, were also to be a part of our lives for many years. At one time they were designed solely for classroom listening, so Billy was accustomed to scores of letters from schoolchildren whose teachers had asked them to comment on the music.

One such letter found its way into one of our scrapbooks. It was from an eighth grader who had been assigned to write a report on William Grant Still and who needed a picture to go with it. "If it's possible," she asked, "can you sent me a picture of yourself? Please send it the day you receive this letter. My deadline is Thursday and I want this to be my best project." She signed it, "An unknown friend, Vicki," and on the opposite page added: "P.S. If he is not alive, still send me it."

She wasn't the only who thought William Grant Still could be dead. I was constantly meeting people who had read about him in textbooks so long before that they were positive he couldn't still be alive.

As time went on, we came to know other patriotic American composers with whom we had much in common. George Frederick McKay, on leave from the University of Southern California, started a long and staunch friendship when he and his wife visited us in the Forties. He and I had an extensive discussion on American music. He felt (at that time) that when American music is presented it should be carefully screened, so that the very best examples could reach the listening public, thus building a sympathetic audience for our native output as a whole. Then he added, "I know, I know. You'll tell me that everything should be performed, and let the public decide. But I think it's wiser to do a little screening beforehand." He was right. That was exactly what I did think: I let the public decide.

Twenty years later, McKay and I were still having the same discussion and were still on opposite sides of the fence. But now it was he who advocated playing everything, and I who wanted to be selective, after noting that some foreign laymen had become violently anti–American-music after hearing some particularly inept compositions, to the point of trying to persuade conductors and impresarios not to put American music on their programs. The years had made me realize that George McKay was right in the first place, but they had convinced him that my original feelings had merit.

George McKay also discussed audience reactions with us. In their entirety, he said, audiences are usually correct in their verdicts. Not so with individuals in those audiences, the latter are fallible.

With Meredith Willson we used to talk about the so-called "avant-garde" music. We didn't like it and neither did he—with one reservation. We all agreed that the ugly idiom could be useful momentarily to express certain things. As Willson remarked, if someone writes a piece of music and calls it "storm" or "quarrel" or "dispepsia," then perhaps the ultramodern idiom would be appropriate. But not if the composition is supposed to depict a sunset or something else of beauty.

We had a great deal in common with Paul Creston and his wife, for their experiences had paralleled ours in many ways. They too had encountered both friendship and jealousy among their colleagues, one incident struck us as being typical of our common experiences. It was after a performance of one of Creston's compositions by Arturo Toscanini (the unapproachable conductor whom all composers wanted to reach, but usually couldn't) that one of our aggressive American colleagues walked over to Creston with a sneer on his face. "And how," he inquired sarcastically, "did *you* get that performance?"

In southern California, one of the most beloved of American composers was Charles Wakefield Cadman, a man who made it his business to be nice to people. Charlie Cadman was on our side politically—that is, the American side. He told us how all of his colleagues in the McDowell Colony had gone in for communism, and when he made a speech on politics in music one of the New York composers told him he should not have done it.

The popularity of his songs pleased Charlie, but he had his eye on other goals. He wanted to be recognized as a composer of serious works. This eluded him. No matter how hard he importuned symphonic conductors, they listened only rarely. At his funeral, however, the conductor of our Los Angeles Philharmonic and a friend arrived to take their places among the mourners, even though in life the conductor had kept his distance.

When he happened to go into music offices in the Forties, Billy was often greeted with this statement. "Oh, Russell Bennett was here a few days ago. He spoke very highly of you and your work." This would have been appreciated in any event, but it was doubly important to us because we had such great admiration for Russell Bennett and his accomplishments. Billy decided to write to him in gratitude. "I hear you have been going around saying nice things about me!" he said. Russell Bennett's friendship was another which never wavered throughout the years.

We also enjoyed the story told about him by Louis and Annette Kaufman, who inspired and introduced Billy's and his works for the violin. Bennett, they said, was once in an audience of composers, listening to a fellow composer's work which was pleasant, but not overly intellectual. Some of the avante-gardists rose and attacked the music and the composer whereupon Bennett remarked that whether they or he approved of the music didn't matter. All that mattered was the composer's right to write as his conscience dictated, and that right, he insisted, should be defended above all else.

When W. C. Handy and Louise (then his nurse and later his wife) came to southern California, we thoroughly enjoyed entertaining

(*Clockwise from top left*) William Grant Still, W. C. Handy,
L. Wolfe Gilbert. Courtesy William Grant Still Estate.

them. We gave a party for them, our cousins Norman and Corinne and the League of Allied Arts feted them, Billy took him to Jefferson High School to speak to the students, and then we drove them to Baja California for a day's outing. On the way, we were involved in an incident which demonstrated Handy's perception. He had said there was an old friend in San Diego whom he would like to visit. We took him there, after first phoning to make sure the lady would be home. As the four of us walked up the stairs, me carrying our baby son, Duncan, our hostess burst out of a doorway completely nude. She saw all of us, said "Oh, excuse me," went back inside and returned fully clothed. During the course of an uneventful conversation, she remarked that her sister was in a mental institution. Handy was blind by that time and had seen nothing; certainly we had said nothing. Later, as we drove away, he remarked drily, "If you ask me, I think she's a little off too."

Afterward, in Tijuana, we were seated at a table in a little restaurant when a strolling musician came and asked if he could sing for us. Handy was delighted. He said that Langston Hughes had told him that everywhere he went outside of the United States, the "St. Louis Blues" was like an American theme song. Now was the time for testing. Because I knew Spanish, Handy asked me to request the "St. Louis Blues" from the Mexican troubadour, which I did. To our astonishment, he said he was very sorry, but this song he did not know. Would we settle for "Mexicali Rose"? Rather frantically, because this was all in Spanish and Mr. Handy hadn't yet gotten the gist of the conversation, I explained that this distinguished gentleman was the composer of this distinguished and very famous North American song, and it would please him so much to hear it sung in Mexico. "I am sorry, Señora," replied our man with finality. "Please take 'Mexicali Rose,' por favor?" So we settled for "Mexicali Rose" and it's anybody's guess as to what Handy said to Hughes the next time they met.

A different story came from Europe. Ivan Browning, one of the Americans who used to entertain abroad, told us of the love the Duke of Windsor (then the Prince of Wales) had for the "blues." All the entertainers knew this, so when the Prince entered a room where they were performing, they would break off whatever they were singing and begin the "St. Louis Blues."

Very often in our conversations, Handy would accuse colored people of snubbing him, not including him in their reports of Negro achievement, but always anxious to make use of his assets if they could. He spoke of receiving requests for donations from performances and of looking down their programs and seeing music by Bach, Beethoven and Mozart listed—but no Handy. So he would write right back and suggest that perhaps they should ask Mr. Bach, Mr. Beethoven or Mr. Mozart for contributions.

This reminded us of R. Nathaniel Dett's strong plea, when he visited groups of Negro musicians in Los Angeles, for Negroes to buy and perform works by Negro composers. At the time we thought he was being a little chauvinistic, but later we realized that the more people buy and perform music, the more it is publicized and the better it is for everyone. We knew what he meant when we tried so hard to reach Marian Anderson, to ask if she would be willing to examine some of Billy's songs, with a view to including a Still work on her concerts. We were not able to get near her—nor indeed, to any of the top Negro singers of the day, when their attention would have helped so much.

Times have changed, of course, to the extent that most far-seeing members of the National Association of Negro Musicians are loyally and eagerly promoting works by Negroes whenever possible. In the end, their vision and their support will have played a great part in the recognition of Negro cultural achievement.

From time to time, opportunities that might have seemed golden to some people came along and were passed by. In later years, we had reason to be thankful in every instance. It happened, for example, that Howard University's director of music was retiring. We learned about it when, out of the blue, a man we had never known before (Sgt. Brice, bandmaster) determined that William Grant Still should be the new director of music. He worked to get Billy to agree to accept the post if it should be offered, and to get the University to make the offer.

His skill in planning amazed us. He had a list of distinguished, internationally known musicians from whom he solicited endorsements. Some of them had never even bothered to acknowledge letters we had written to them, but now—according to Sgt. Brice—they all wrote with great enthusiasm, with the highest praise for William Grant Still.

The campaign went on and on, and Billy was at a loss to know what to say or do, for it was a position he did not want. He did not consider himself qualified for administrative work; he had no wish to spend his days conducting a choir; most importantly, he realized that such a post would leave him no time for his own creative work, so that the career which was spiralling upward at a great rate would be sharply curtailed. The project had reached the point where the University was on the spot and would probably have had to offer the position if Billy had actually displayed an interest in it. Finally, Dr. Embree of the Rosenwald Foundation came to our assistance and said he thought Still would be stifled in such a position. After that all of us breathed a little easier. The University offered Billy an honorary degree *in absentia* as compensation.

Then Brice let slip the fact that all of this wasn't his idea in the beginning—it was Olin Downes' idea and Olin Downes' planning. We understood then why so many prominent musicians were so eager to send their endorsements, but we did not understand why Downes seemed to want Billy stowed away in a University post. We found it hard to believe that his motive was kindly. By the time this happened, we had sensed that Downes was no longer a champion of Still's music. We did not know why.

In his reviews, instead of writing reasonably as he had in the past, Downes was now ignoring Still completely (much of the time he was giving forecasts of coming musical events and failed to mention the Still works which were scheduled) or hedging (neither praising nor condemning). When Billy's *Poem for Orchestra* (which had been commissioned by the Kulas Fund for the Cleveland Orchestra at the suggestion of Erich Leinsdorf and Arthur Judson) was performed by Rodzinski in New York, Downes lamented the fact that the composer had become sophisticated, and hoped he would return to a truer indication of his racial origin.

A somewhat different reaction to *Poem for Orchestra* came our way and produced a little shock. A theatrical agent in Cleveland had heard the composition when it was broadcast by the Cleveland Orchestra and was (she said) thrilled by it. She promptly wrote to ask whether its composer would write the music for a play she contemplated producing in New York. Billy said he would consider it, so she sent the script. Well, the *Poem for Orchestra* is a serious symphonic poem, dealing with a desolate world and with man's eventual rebirth and emergence from darkness as he draws closer to God. The play script, on the other hand, was one of the very lowest sort of Negro life: sensual, promiscuous and ignorant. How the agent could have imagined that the composer of *Poem for Orchestra* could descend to that level was beyond us. Billy, of course, declined to write the music and added the admonition that the production of such a play would be bad for race relations in America.

We thought of this incident when Countee Cullen was adapting an early novel by Arna Bontemps for the stage and was trying to get financial backing for it. Arna's story dealt with the race track, and with Negroes who belonged to that milieu. It was nowhere near as low and depraved as the script which had been submitted by the agent from Cleveland, but we wondered if it were the sort of thing that should be presented in a crucial era.

Countee Cullen made a trip to the west coast to discuss it. We drove him to the beach near Palos Verdes one night, and there as we talked, the three of us walked near the ocean under the stars. Cullen wānted Billy to write a letter to the producers assuring them that colored people would not be offended if the play were to be produced, for one colored actress had already announced that she would not appear in it. "I have never had very much money," he said plaintively. "If this were to go through, I might be able to make a living, and relax and do some of the things I want to do."

This posed a dilemma for Billy, because we counted Arna and Cullen as friends, and it was true that the book did present an authentic picture of what it purported to be. Yet how could he endorse a project which, to say the least, seemed to be so badly timed? We ourselves had never had much money either. We were even then continuing to make personal sacrifices in order to stay true to our ideals. Why should we sacrifice ours because someone else wasn't willing to keep on sacrificing? As I recall it now, Billy did write a letter, saying only that he did not believe that either Arna or Countee Cullen would knowingly do anything to hurt colored people. He did not endorse the play.

When the play was finally produced in New York, it proved to be entertaining, but not remarkable. This was in 1946. One colored reviewer hit the nail on the head when he commented: "Every time someone decides to spend a half-million dollars on a Negro stage show, they present a wench as a central character. I cannot keep telling myself it's purely accident. It looks like a plan and I can't say I like it."

Billy found himself in a number of similar situations throughout the years, some of them most uncomfortable. Once, in the days before there were so many qualified Negro teachers, a very good friend of ours decided that he would like to teach in college. He took an examination and flunked both the oral and written sections, whereupon he claimed that he had been excluded because of his color. The Board set up another examination, the judges to be brought in from some of the local colleges. There had to be at least one colored judge, so Billy was invited to sit in. He was delighted because we had always had a great deal of respect for our friend, and now it appeared that Billy would have a chance to crusade for him.

To our immense chagrin, our friend again flunked the tests. At the end of the examination, the other judges all looked inquiringly at Billy. In that instant, Billy realized that if our friend were hired, he would prove to be less than the best, and that fact alone would eventually work to the detriment of future Negro teachers who really would be qualified. Reluctantly, he had to vote "no."

There came the inevitable problem of explaining to our friend, who telephoned us later in the day, exuberant and hopeful. Billy sat at the phone and told him in detail every mistake he had made during the examination, in the belief that the truth might be of service. Unfortunately, he is no longer our friend, by his own wish. He felt that Billy was an Uncle Tom.

In some respects, having to act as a judge makes for a lonely life, but we tried not to waver in our feeling that it was not our task simply to put Negroes into jobs, whether or not they were qualified. It was our task to try to open the way for qualified *people*, and whenever they happened to be Negroes, we were overjoyed and did our best to recommend and to help. Instead of feeling loyal to individuals, we preferred to be loyal to the generations to come.

This feeling was intensified by yet another distressing incident. One year the manager of the Hollywood Bowl phoned to ask Billy whether he would like to conduct at the Bowl during the coming summer season. Billy, who naturally would have enjoyed conducting at the Bowl at any time (he had done it before and was to do it again many years later) unfortunately chose that moment to be generous. He suggested that instead they invite another Negro conductor who had been successful in Europe, a man to whom he was grateful because he had conducted Billy's music in Europe, and who had been deluging us with glowing press notices, an aircheck of his BBC performance which seemed quite acceptable, and many letters indicating that it was the dream of his life to conduct in America. Billy wanted to give him his chance, and felt safe in recommending him because of the good reports of his work. He was to discover that generosity can have its drawbacks.

From start to finish the project was a disaster, even though some of our friends of the Los Angeles press tried their best to help everyone save face. It taught us a lesson: when God opens a way, one must not throw the opportunity out the window.

It is one of the saddest of all experiences to deliberately try to make opportunities for other people and then discover that they don't qualify. This doesn't mean that we should stop trying, only that we should exercise more care and better judgment, and that we should emphasize more strongly the need for better preparation, more education, and more understanding of the work to which people aspire.

Wanting Billy's recommendations to mean something, we were not pleased when we discovered that some people had used his name without permission to gain access to various people or institutions. Whenever such instances came to our attention, we were careful to write and explain that any endorsement from William Grant Still would come only over his own signature. A choir director once requested an endorsement to be printed in her brochures, and got it. When the brochures came out, an entirely different statement, one she had concocted as suitable, appeared over the name of William Grant Still.

The widely publicized *Stormy Weather* affair involved another film studio intrigue, though it is doubtful that the people concerned intended it to turn out as it did. It was reported to us later that questions were raised as to why Mr. Still was treated so poorly, when Mrs. Still was so highly respected?

The whole thing started happily enough, when a film was to be made around the highly successful popular song, "Stormy Weather." Irving Mills, the publisher, was discussing it with Leopold Stokowski, who agreed to conduct a chorus and symphony orchestra in a grand finale, provided that William Grant Still would compose an original work for the spot. At the time, the film was planned as a cavalcade of the Negro in the theatre. That, at least, was the way all of us understood it.

Irving Mills was pleased with the suggestion, as was Billy, who accepted the post of Supervisor of Music on the picture. When he arrived at the studio on the first working day, he discovered that it wasn't a cavalcade of the Negro in the theatre at all. It was a film biography of Bojangles Robinson. To make matters worse, the initial publicity releases stated that William Grant Still had been persuaded to work on the film by virtue of his lifelong friendship with Bill Robinson. It wasn't true, for though Billy had many wonderful friends in show business, Bill Robinson was one whose path had seldom crossed it. They had very little in common, and were speaking acquaintances only. From that day on, Stokowski's name was never mentioned. He was, no doubt, as surprised as we.

Since he had promised to work on the picture, Billy decided to make the best of the situation and to cooperate as much as possible. Then he discovered what it is to be a supervisor who is supervised by everyone else. Everything he did was thrown out with some disparaging comment. It was "too polite" for Negro music. It was "not erotic enough." "Negro bands didn't play that well in the Twenties," he was told. Billy protested that he had been a member of Negro bands in the Twenties, and that they had played better then in many respects. When the Negro bands came to audition, Billy was for Noble Sissle's group, which had been going since the Twenties and was therefore as authentic as could be. This was turned down, because the musicians were said to be just like white musicians. The supervisors of the Supervisor selected a more animated band.

At last there was nothing left for Billy to do except to sit around the studio and wait for them to put his name on something that had no connection with his work or his ideas. Then the Music Director informed him that the studio would not approve of his bringing his own work to the studio and doing it on studio time. He was simply to sit and collect his paycheck.

With four weeks to go on the picture and four weeks of salary uncollected, Billy resigned. To clarify his situation, I wrote an explanatory article and sent it to Dolores Calvin, who, with her mother and sister, ran a syndicate serving more than one hundred Negro newspapers. The story broke a few weeks later, under a dramatic headline Dolores had added. There was quite a bit of shouting back and forth. One of the most interesting comments was made by a studio spokesman to one of the reporters who called to inquire. He said the whole thing happened because Mrs. Still wanted more money for her husband, though I had never once said a word to anyone at the studio during the turmoil and the question of money had never come up.

We had lots of support from colored people, but some or our own relatives said later, "Why didn't Billy do what Paul Robeson does: take the money and *then* make his protest?"

Once in succeeding years we tried again in Hollywood, this time not even getting to first base because we did not care to recommend a colored nightclub singer for a concert of serious music at the Hollywood Bowl. Her management thought she would fit in nicely.

In Hollywood, whenever a serious film came along, it was said that William Grant Still was "too popular," so white composers were employed, even when the film dealt with racial matters. When a popular film of any kind, employing Negroes or not, was in progress, then it was said that William Grant Still was "too symphonic" and, again, other composers were hired. Even when the government sponsored a film dealing with the Negro soldiers in the war, the Hollywood people in charge had to put a Beethoven Symphony under the footage depicting the soldier's tomb, because they knew of no Negro music that was suitable—no one, evidently, had heard of the *Afro-American Symphony*.

The thought crossed my mind that this (despite some of the statements that had been made) could be more professional than racial; that those who were entrenched were determined not to admit anyone who might conceivably be a threat. Not even, as we had observed, to give him a reasonable chance to learn the business.

At any rate, while we were annoyed by such things momentarily, there came a time when we were enormously grateful and relieved that it had all happened the way it did. We could finally see that we were more fortunate not to have been a part of Hollywood. For one thing, William Grant Still retained his distinction as a composer for the concert hall. For another, all the music he composed in those golden years now belongs to us—that is to say, to his estate. If he had been under contract to a studio, it would have belonged to the studio, and chances are that he would not have had the time or the energy to do a lot of creative work on his own. What amount of money could have compensated for that?

The *Stormy Weather* experience had one extra dividend. For several years thereafter, I wrote articles which the Calvins distributed to their clients. My feeling was that I wanted to see more attention paid to Negro achievement and much more attention to the good things that emerged from Negro-white or white-Negro relationships. For too long we had had only one side of the picture, complaining about how badly people treated each other. It appeared to me that a positive viewpoint would help to turn more people's thoughts in a positive direction. Those were the sort of articles I tried to turn out. They were welcomed and printed by responsible members of the Negro press. I hoped that some of them helped to create a better feeling.

Among the many things I did for and with the Calvins was to request and receive a statement from George Bernard Shaw, in his own handwriting, and to solicit from all the film studios opinions on the Negro in films. At least one of those interviews had a tangible result, for Walter Lantz, then President of the Film Cartoonists' Association and creator of the impudent Woody Woodpecker, had a little colored boy as the only human character among the animals in his cartoon magazine which was circulated nationally. He and I discussed racial matters on a friendly basis, and when I left his office he gave my children a subscription to his magazine.

The magazine began to arrive regularly. After a short while, I noticed that his colored character, Li'l Eight Ball, had stopped talking in dialect and was using good English. Later, Li'l Eight Ball himself disappeared, evidently because it had become apparent that it was incongruous to present him alone among animals, as if he were one of them. I asked Lantz how this happened. He said he just began thinking of the situation after our interview and wanted to do something to advance good interracial feeling. This was one thing he could do, so he did it. It must have had an effect on the millions of small fry who bought and read comic books during their impressionable years. These are the unsolicited gestures for which medals should be awarded, the cogs in the mechanism of better human understanding.

Lest I be thought to have a Pollyanna attitude it must be added that I also wrote of some of the more sombre matters that came to my attention, such as the murders of a family of four colored people (a handsome, intelligent family whom we knew and whose father was a refrigeration engineer) who had been forced to settle in nearby Fontana when there was a housing shortage in Los Angeles. They were burned up by white citizens who resented their presence, one of the most tragic events in the history of California's race relations.

It was possible to look on the bright side in many instances, but it was not possible to overlook the fact that ugly events were taking place in so-called enlightened communities.

—14—

Several times we invited our friends to give interviews to members of the Negro press at our home. Ted LeBerthon, a Los Angeles journalist whose columns in the daily paper were often devoted to colored people, was one, Leopold Stokowski was another. The night Elsie Houston came to be interviewed for *Etude* had a party-like atmosphere, because Loyd and Betty Rathbun and Kenneth and Adelaide Winstead brought her to our house. Loyd (the oboist) and Kenneth (the bass player) had been in Karl Krueger's Kansas City Philharmonic Orchestra when Miss Houston was soloist there. They had a recording made during her performance. Miss Houston (who, incidentally, was one of the most sensitive and professional performers we had ever met) didn't seem to be particularly interested as this recording was playing away in the backroom. But when she heard herself speaking (announcing an encore) her mood changed. She stopped talking, jumped up, ran down the hall and paid close attention from then on.

She had known in advance how the rehearsal part of the program would sound, but she had no way of knowing how the unrehearsed part would come out. It was a novelty to her to hear it as the audience had heard it on the night of the performance.

It was tragic that an artist who had so much to give should have wanted to take her own life, but she did. She was too sympathetic and impressionable; she took to heart everything that happened in the world. Shortly before her death she wrote to us of "The mess we are in—all of us."

Then there was the party that wasn't a party, because nobody was invited, but everybody came. It happened on a Sunday afternoon when we weren't expecting guests, so we weren't dressed for the occasion and had no refreshments on hand. Each person who arrived came in looking guilty, thinking he was crashing our party. When they understood that everyone had dropped in unexpectedly, interesting things began to happen. During the afternoon, Prince Madupe of Nigeria organized the guests into little groups and was teaching them African songs, complicated and contrapuntal.

Loyd Rathbun, excited over the fact that he was in a gathering with two American composers, was inspired to tell us about the new oboe d'amour he had just bought, and to suggest that both of the composers write something for him to play on it. He then disappeared for an hour or so. When he returned, we found that he had driven across town to his home to get the oboe d'amour so that he could demonstrate its potential. Henry Cowell, the other composer, was impressed enough to say that he just might go into the back room and write something for it.

Billy was impressed too, so that he remembered it when Werner Janssen called not long afterward, to ask him to write a composition honoring the birthday of the City of Los Angeles, which Janssen would premiere on the Standard Hour a few days hence. Loyd was Janssen's first oboist at the time. He was quick to inquire whether Billy would please write something special for the oboe d'amour to play in the new composition. Billy had already planned to do so, but thought he would first play a little joke on Loyd. He wanted me to call Betty and ask her to tell Loyd that he was very sorry indeed, but he could find absolutely no place for the oboe d'amour in the new piece. She was to make sure though that Loyd would carry the instrument with him when he went to the first rehearsal. She did it, though she later confessed that she felt badly over deceiving him so. At the first rehearsal, of course, Loyd discovered that he and his oboe were featured in the opening measures. He was such a fine sight reader that he had no problems; Billy had known that in advance.

This composition was *Old California*, later played by many famous conductors in many noteworthy concerts. (The oboe d'amour part then had to be played by a regular oboe, since not all oboists have this unusual instrument). The piece was dedicated to George Fischer, our dear friend and publisher. It portrayed in music three significant periods in California's history: the Indian, the Spanish and the American. After the first performance, Billy revised it because it had been written so hastily, smoothing out all the rough edges.

Applause and lots of performances served as spurs to inspiration. During the second World War, Claire Reis and the League of Composers commissioned seventeen new works on patriotic themes to be performed by Rodzinski and the New York Philharmonic Orchestra over the CBS Network. As soon as Mrs. Reis' letter arrived, Billy realized that he must use this opportunity to pay tribute to the colored soldiers all over the world who were fighting and dying for a democratic way of life that some of them had never known. As a matter of fact, the first American soldier to be killed in that war happened to be a Negro. We felt that the loyalty and patriotism of these men should not go unnoticed, and that feeling was the basis for Billy's poignant requiem, *In Memoriam: The Colored Soldiers Who Died for Democracy*. It was finished, broadcast in 1944, and immediately published.

Warmly received by audiences and critics, this little piece was destined to live long after its initial performance. Typical of its reviews was this by Henry Simon in *PM*: "Perhaps the most effective of the League of Composers commissioned series to date. Its basis is a beautiful Spiritual-like melody, simply and effectively orchestrated and contrasted with a mournful motif played mostly by the brasses. It says what it has to say directly and tellingly, and remains within the five-minute strain as the other works in the series have not done." Other critics, including Olin Downes, agreed that it was one of the best in the series.

George Szell, then beginning his brilliant American career, took the composition up after its initial success and played it in concerts all over the country, even in Boston where, despite the oft-repeated claim that the Boston Symphony was championing American composers, it marked the first and only time a William Grant Still work had appeared on the regular concert series.

Then, recalling the fact that Sir John Barbirolli had spoken of the need for good overtures in the symphonic repertoire, Billy decided to write one. He was well along in the composition when I came into the workroom one day and asked if he knew that the Cincinnati Symphony Orchestra had announced a contest for an overture to celebrate its Jubilee season. "No, I didn't," he answered, "But maybe that's why I'm writing this Overture."

On the day he completed it, he put the finished score on the piano. Szell, then visiting the west coast, came to visit us. To our amazement, he sat down at the piano and played the piece, reading at sight from the conductor's score! We had never seen anyone do anything like that before and we told him so. He shrugged it off, assuring us that where he was educated, a conductor had to be able to read and play scores as a matter of course. Then he said, "What are you going to do with this?" Billy replied that he had thought of entering it in the Cincinnati contest. "Well, if it doesn't win," declared Szell, "You send it to me. *I'll* play it!"

It did win the contest, entered anonymously, as were all the compositions. The three distinguished judges (Eugene Goossens, Deems Taylor, and Pierre Monteux) were in unanimous agreement on the winning work. This was Billy's *Festive Overture*, a composition which continues to be performed from time to time today, a fact that has meant a great deal to us, as many competition winners are played once and never heard again.

On more than one occasion, William Grant Still's music was performed auspiciously abroad, on official government functions. Once Sir John himself conducted *Plain-Chant for America* as part of a Thanksgiving celebration in London's Royal Albert Hall, a dramatic tribute to Anglo-American friendship attended by Sir Winston Churchill and by our ambassador to Britain.

Several years later George Fischer's son Joseph received from our State Department the translations of glowing press reports from Helsinki, when the Municipal Orchestra played the *Afro-American Symphony* at a concert attended by the wife of Finland's president, Finnish government officials and American dignitaries. We were a little surprised, as it seemed somewhat unusual for the State Department to go out of its way to advise us of this. One of our friends who had worked in a government agency during the war said it was indeed out of the ordinary. He ventured the opinion that they were probably so delighted to have good reviews from other countries that they wanted to share them immediately. The Finnish critics had commented mainly on the characteristically American flavor of the music. We had been hearing similar comments elsewhere for many years—once in a while from critics, very often from listeners: "I never knew before that an American composer could write this sort of music" or, "Your music made me proud to be an American."

On request, Billy composed several works in different forms. Lady Evelyn Barbirolli asked for something for her Zephyr Trio (flute, oboe and piano) which resulted in the *Miniatures*. Some years later, she requested another work for her Camden Trio (oboe, bassoon, piano), so the *Vignettes* were composed. These were two suites based on folksongs of the Americas. For Louis Kaufman he composed his *Suite for Violin* and *Pastorela*. For Cantor David J. Putterman of New York's Park Avenue Synagogue he made a setting of the 29th Psalm which he called *The Voice of the Lord* and which was performed in the Synagogue at the 44th Annual Sabbath Eve Service of Liturgical Music by Contemporary Composers. There were the *Danzas de Panama* for Elisabeth Waldo's string quartet, and there were also the *Songs of Separation*, a suite of five songs based on poems by Negro poets, which Herta Glaz introduced in New York. There were new orchestral works, such as *Wood Notes*, inspired by the work of the white Southern poet, J. Mitchell Pilcher, as well as three new symphonies and the *Archaic Ritual*.

Archaic Ritual had been in the making for months before it was completed. It was always mentioned in Billy's notes as a primitive suite. Primitive in tone, perhaps, but it was informed by a high craftsmanship in its development and intermingling of themes. It was comprised of three movements: "Chant," "Dance before the Altar," and "Possession" (when the participants in the ceremony are supposed to be possessed by spirits).

When we checked the orchestral parts which are returned to us after each performance, we were often interested in the notes some of the players wrote on their parts. Sometimes the European musicians would write their names and the dates on which they played a particular work. The Americans were more inclined toward humor. One of the latter, coming to the third movement of the *Archaic Ritual*, had pencilled this under the title: "Re-possession: regards from the finance company."

All through these years—in fact, ever since he had begun to compose serious music—Billy had had two ambitions which seemed impossible to realize. One was to have an opera produced by a major company, the other was to have competent commercial recordings of his music. Everywhere we went, after people had heard the music in concert, they came backstage and asked where they could buy recordings. Unfortunately for us, the large companies were adamant in their refusal to do any of Billy's work on a big scale, despite the fact that when Howard Hanson, Karl Krueger, Leopold Stokowski, Louis Kaufman, Morton Gould and Arthur Lange did make a few recordings, they sold out and then they were no longer available.

Werner Janssen reported that the Victor people objected to his recording *Old California*. Artie Shaw encountered the same opposition when he suggested recording *Lenox Avenue* in its entirety. When Karl Krueger finally did record the entire *Afro-American Symphony* abroad, brought the recording back to the United States and contracted for it to be professionally processed here, he wrote us that he had had a great deal of bad luck because "RCA has had repeated breakage of the matrixes."

Opposition from the opera companies was even worse. The big dream of Billy's life had been to compose operas, the one form in which all other musical forms are combined, and the one form which offered full expression to his love for the theatre. As I have said, he often felt that he had turned to writing symphonic works merely as a substitute for operas, in which form he couldn't get a hearing. We approached everyone we could think of and finally had to come to a most painful conclusion: that there really did exist people who considered this too much for a colored man. We had always been uncomfortable when some colored people blamed their failures on racial considerations, because this had been the stock excuse for years. It was generally the first refuge of the incompetent, so we had been careful not to use it, but now in the matter of opera, we could not escape the suspicion.

We recalled what we had read on page 222 of Ilka Chase's book, *Past Imperfect*, published by Doubleday in 1943: "At one time I was most anxious to have Dorothy Maynor, the famous Negro soprano, sing on my program, but I was refused permission to ask her, on the grounds that she sang like a cultivated white singer. If she sang Spirituals or Boogie-Woogie, or otherwise showed that she knew her place, that was all right. But this raising oneself above the ruck is not to be encouraged. Many and strange are the ways of censorship in the land of the free."

A ray of sunlight flashed across our horizon when Leopold Stokowski was engaged by New York City Center's Opera Company. We asked him if he would conduct one of Billy's operas there, and he said he would. He invited us to his home, high above Sunset Boulevard, for a conference one afternoon. Here it began to look as if Fate itself had stepped in to thwart us. We started off in our car, only to have it break down . We changed to a taxi. In Beverly Hills, the taxi broke down and we had to change to another one. That one managed to deliver us to Stokowski's door and then as we were going home, Stokowski himself having driven us to the bus stop, the bus broke down. Eventually we got home safely and the plans to launch the opera had been made.

Stokowski had decided to ask for public contributions to produce the work, so he and Mayor LaGuardia, backed by Eleanor Roosevelt, along with other people of distinction, informed the press. Contributions began to come in, not in huge amounts, but every dollar (we liked to believe) from people who shared our aspirations. Before the project could be completed, Stokowski wrote to advise us that he had decided to resign from City Center.

Nothing at all was done about producing the opera. Some of our friends who had sent money began to ask us what had become of their contributions. We asked the City Center to return the donations. When this wasn't done, we suggested that it might be necessary for us to make a statement to the press. That must have been unsettling for Billy began to receive letters begging him not to do it. Even so, the money was not returned. So we sent special delivery letters to every newspaper that Billy had requested that the donations be returned. After that appeared in print, the contributors got back their donations.

Some time later, the City Center decided to produce the opera *Troubled Island* after all. Everyone at the Center was most cooperative, even agreeing to Billy's stipulation that there should be a clause in the contract forbidding any changes without the composer's permission. This, as we were later to discover, was a wise precaution.

There was some indecision about the date. Someone had suggested a date which had already been set for the premiere of a new Rodgers and Hammerstein show. When another was finally settled on, the same date happened to be selected for the big Cultural and Scientific Conference for World Peace, to be held at the Waldorf Astoria, Dmitri Shostakovich was expected to appear. *Life* magazine called him the "star" of that show, and also ran a series of photographs of "Dupes and Fellow Travelers" coincidentally. Among them were Olin Downes, Aaron Copland, Leonard Bernstein, Dean Dixon and Langston Hughes.

Troubled Island, however, went into rehearsal as scheduled. Again, we asked for Robert Weede in the leading role of Jean Jacques Dessalines, and he gave up a far more lucrative engagement in New Orleans in order to create the role. Our second choice was Lawrence Whisonant, who sang at the second performance. Eugene Bryden, an imaginative and creative stage director, was also engaged, as was Marie Powers, when Carol Brice turned down the leading contralto role.

As soon as Billy arrived in New York for rehearsals, he learned Laszlo Halasz, the conductor, lived in the same apartment house as Olin Downes, whose opinions Halasz eagerly sought. Downes had seen the opera score and had made up his mind that the end of the first scene in the second act would have to be rewritten. "The audience won't take it," Halasz told Billy, as he insisted that he would have to compose a new ending for the scene in the three weeks before the opening. Billy invoked the "no changes without the composer's consent" clause in his contract and refused. The audiences loved it as it had been written. In the light of what happened later, we couldn't help but wonder whether Downes had anticipated the success of that crucial spot, and had tried to block it.

At rehearsal, one of our friends (a critic on one of the other New York papers) came out with a startling statement. He warned Billy that plans were then afoot for "the boys" to pan the opera, even before they heard it. They must have been surprised when a Blue Ribbon audience gave it a tremendous ovation, with many curtain calls on opening night. Surprised enough, apparently, to make them pull in their horns. *Time* magazine reported it as a triumph; the *Boston Post* placed it well above other American operas; the National Association for American Composers and Conductors gave Billy a citation for outstanding service to American music. But the New York critics sat on the fence. An odd word—"partisan"—crept into one of the reviews. For us, this word had a curious connotation. I had heard it used previously only in connection with the people (partisans) who were fighting for the communists. That made me wonder what was meant when a critic wrote that a partisan audience had found very little to be partisan about. Some hidden meaning, clear only to the initiate? Carl Van Vechten made haste to tell us, by airmail: "The critics always hedge a little at first, rather than have to eat crow later. The principal thing to notice is the way the audience ate it up. It is never a bore. Of how many other operas can this be said?"

Laszlo Halasz was so excited at the evening's end that he asked for another opera right away. Bryden left New York late that night, secure in the knowledge that he had participated in a huge triumph. When he arrived back in Los Angeles, he found that he had not. "It never happened that way before in all my years in the theatre," he said, in complete mystification.

A colored singer, Helen Thigpen, told us later that she had discussed the opera with another of the New York critics and had asked him why he and the others were so determined to go against the enthusiastic public reaction. "Well," he said flatly, "we are only going to let just so many Negroes through."

After three performances, *Troubled Island* was scrapped, but it was not to end there. The United States government had recorded the second *Troubled Island* performance in its entirety, and after some months of processing, had sent the recordings to our information offices overseas, to be made available to broadcasters in other parts of the world.

In Paris, they were heard also by the man who was then director of the famed Theatre de la Monnaie, who wrote that he liked the work but that his company would find the idiom strange and therefore could not attempt it. But why wouldn't Still consider bringing a *Troubled Island* company of his own to Europe? Naturally, we were delighted with the idea. Since Billy had no company of his own, we thought that perhaps Laszlo Halasz might consider traveling with the City Center company, so we sent him a copy of the letter.

To whom did he show it? We never found out. All we knew was that a few days after our letter to him arrived in New York, the United States information offices overseas were instructed to recall copies of the *Troubled Island* recordings on the grounds that they were "mauvais" and, in at least one instance, to suggest that the foreign radio stations substitute one of Menotti's operas.

Europeans are much more sensitive to politics than we, so naturally some of them assumed that there was something political about the withdrawal. One friend wrote that it was undoubtedly a "cabal" and urged us to investigate. Immediately, I wrote letter after letter, usually getting the runaround, particularly from a man who later resigned his government post during a senatorial investigation.

Finally one of my letters reached a conscientious man in government. He agreed that my charges were serious and promised to investigate, which he did. In a few weeks he wrote to tell me he had ordered the recordings reinstated. In the meantime, some of our friends abroad didn't know what to think. Were we under suspicion for some unexplained reason? Did they dare associate with us?

Incredibly, rumormongers here in the United States were busy telling people that Laszlo Halasz had been fired from the New York City Center because he had produced *Troubled Island*.

All of this was shattering to Billy. He had had the success of which he had dreamed all his life, and it had been taken from him. He had honestly believed in the goodwill and decency of the American people and had thought that if a product were proven worthy it would automatically be acclaimed. Now we knew that this was not always true.

Where now were all the people who proclaimed so smugly, "When the Negro is ready, he be given his rights!"?

Success, success, success! If anyone else had done but a fraction of what Billy had done, he would have risen to the top, with prestige and money. With us, they seemed to come and then be absorbed into the vast caverns of time.

During all the stress and the heartache, Billy reacted as he always had: he kept on writing music. Sometimes he would wake up in the morning saying he had been composing all night in his sleep. Now that he knew how well his operatic work could be received, he wrote more and more operas, some of them still unproduced.

There was a revealing passage in one of his diaries of this time: "A strange period through which we are now passing. It is as though we await something and the waiting is a heavy burden. But we must not forget to thank God for sparing us suffering, want or sorrow. Our lot would be unbearable were it not for Him."

— 15 —

Many times we had reason to recall a letter written to Billy by George Fischer on May 29, 1940: "Dear Friend Still: Methinks you will be making a number of our New York composers envious. I am enclosing a clipping from the New York *Times*, Sunday, and another item which appeared in this morning's paper." Both clippings mentioned Billy's name.

Later events gave credence to his statement, but the *good* composers were never jealous; men like Deems Taylor, Howard Hanson and others went out of their way to be friendly. Only the aggressive ones who must have felt insecure displayed their venom. Also, we noted that our detractors (the people who busily spread rumors that Billy was "difficult" and that we were "crackpots") were found on official un-American lists, with increasing regularity.

It may be possible that a statement by Ilya Ehrenburg, the Soviet's well-publicized literary figure, had something to do with it. He said, when interviewed on a visit to the United States, that America's *great* composer would be a Negro composer. A rather far-fetched conclusion, yet it seemed that suddenly quite a few people banded together to see that it couldn't possibly happen.

Others of our friends were having experiences similar to ours. What happened to Deems Taylor, for example, was incredible, but we had seen it happening over the years. Here was a man at the very top, a man who did well at everything he attempted: writing both music and books; commenting over the radio; serving as president of ASCAP, and so on. He also happened to be a patriotic, forthright American who was never afraid to express his views. The early whispering campaign grew bigger and bigger. His music was played less and less—a terrible fall for a man who had held so important a place in our nation's music!

At one time Taylor considered going to live in Europe to avoid the persecution. He wrote us, "I no longer bother even to try to get my own stuff played by organizations such as the Philadelphia, Boston or New York Philharmonic. The performances I do get are by the smaller fry. They don't feel that they are doing me a favor, and they haven't signed up with the Inner Circle boys. It may interest you to know that my wife is apartment hunting in Paris. If she finds one, we're going to get out of here—maybe for good." At another time, when Billy wrote to tell him how well his music had sounded when it had been revived after many years of silence, he replied: "I want to thank you from the heart for the letter you wrote me. I am keeping it in my scrapbook, along with a letter Rachmaninoff wrote to me years ago—and I shall look at them both the next time someone tells me that he never missed listening to me narrate the Metropolitan Opera Broadcasts!"

Our troubles went beyond the "whispering" stage. We discovered that we could not tell anyone in advance what Billy was working on, or whether some big event was scheduled to take place, lest it be suddenly snatched from us. Other composers could send out little postcards, announcing a forthcoming concert. We never could, because when we tried it, it served only to let our hidden enemies know what was going on. Our one experience resulted in delay after delay, and finally in a complete cancellation of the performance. Advance newspaper announcements were not any more satisfactory. Once a conduc-

tor gave the list of American works he intended to play abroad to one
the New York dailies. On his list was the *Afro-American Symphony*.
He didn't play it abroad, and we never quite understood why, except
that our publisher later mentioned that the conductor's music had
been impounded in customs when he reached the foreign country, so
that he was not able to give the concert he had planned.

At the same time, we received several visitors who cautioned us
never, never even to hint that leftists might be responsible for these
shenanigans. Our troubles, they insisted, were personal—not political.
They also told us not to do or say anything; not to ask questions; not
to investigate—just let things take their course. One even said point-
blank that the communists were going to win in the end, so we should
not oppose them or any use they might wish to make of Billy's music.
Needless to say, we had our suspicions as to the political leanings of
these people. Most of them asked specific questions about what Billy
was working on, what was in the wind, and so on. Since we were never
quite sure who was and who wasn't displaying a sincere interest, we
said nothing.

Even a few of those who were not leftists joined the chorus. One
man who was exceedingly powerful in the United States musical circles
wrote to me to the effect that if I knew what was good for my husband's music, I would remain silent on the subject of leftists in music.
Today that man has been stripped of his power. We don't know why or
how, but rumor has it that it was done by the conniving of a man
whose name appears on un-American lists. The exact wording of his
letter to me was that I should not "enter into controversial matters" as
long as I had the interests of my husband and his work at heart. "After
all," he added, "in the course of time, these things solve themselves."
How accurate he was, though not exactly in the way he thought.

Years later, we were to read an intriguing paragraph taken from
Arnold Shoenberg's published correspondence, revealing his own bit-
terness: "There is great activity on the part of American composers, Le
Boulanger's pupils, the imitators of Stravinsky, Hindemith and now
Bartok as well. The only person who can get an appointment in a university music department is one who has taken his degree from one
of them."

This was evident in other areas also. Our friends, Frederic Balasz of Tucson and Fabien Sevitzky of the Miami Philharmonic were subjected to several years of whispering campaigns before they finally gave up.

After we had endured our cross for several years, we happened to see on television a film called "The Mozart Story," bringing out facts of his persecution which we had not known before. We went back to our research files and discovered that everything in the film was based on fact: three powerful individuals opposed Mozart in all his undertakings until he died in poverty while one of his known enemies was accused of having poisoned him. The thought that today Mozart is recognized as a master, while his enemies are seldom mentioned, was somewhat consoling. But we felt we wanted to live now, not in the unforeseeable future.

We also came across an account of Beethoven's last hours which had been contributed to the Boston *Folio* for May, 1877; we discovered that he, too, had been treated with disdain by many of his contemporaries, among them Haydn, who could say of him no more than that "he was a clever pianist." The result of such treatment was that the great Beethoven came to doubt his own ability to compose music. Only a single touching incident toward the end of his life restored his faith and self-confidence. Even so, he died poor, ill, and virtually friendless.

The long range effects of such situations were graphically illustrated by two quotations from the New York papers, several years apart. In an article for the New York *Times* for October 2, 1949, Lazare Saminsky quoted Robert Bernard, editor of *La Revue Musicale* in Paris, as saying, "Those musicians who do not listen to the voice of politics . . . who do not use the fine art of maneuver and pull, have no voice in their country's musical life. They lead, of course, a noble life of culture and creation, but beyond walls."

Then, sixteen years later, an article in the New York *Herald-Tribune*, reprinted in the Los Angeles *Times* for June 6, 1965, said: "France's music situation is nothing short of desperate. . . . Serious music could not exist there at all without massive subsidy, and the reason is a massive lack of public interest."

In Soviet Russia the serious composers have also had their difficulties. In 1978, Mstislav Rostropovich, a Russian exile who became conductor of our National Symphony Orchestra, said: "Composers are always jealous of each other, and at the top of the Soviet musical hierarchy there are some very mediocre composers. They're good organizers, but they think they are good composers and therefore they don't always help the truly talented composers. . . . Khrennikov has been the general secretary of the Composers' Union since 1948—almost thirty years. He writes very banal music, and he likes only that kind of music. He has his school, and only supports those who belong to it. Since he's head of the organization, that's the official guidance."

In the United States, the situation could also be considered political, in many aspects, but it was not always possible to put a finger on this or that culprit. What was mystifying to us was that among the brethren themselves, their right hands usually didn't seem to know what their left hands were doing. One segment would be enthusiastically involved in persecuting anyone who could be labelled "opposition," while another segment would be just as busily trying to make use of the same person in one way or another. Despite the continuing rebuffs we continued to have, documents were sent for Billy's signature; people asked him to participate in all kinds of projects, and strangers came to our house to instruct us on how to think and how to vote.

We had to be careful, because at the outset, we didn't know who was who or what was what. It was a while before we realized that we had to screen new proposals on the basis of the names on the advisory committee, as well as on the proposals themselves. One day a man called to invite Billy to join one of the organizations we considered suspect. Tactfully (I hoped) I told him that we could afford to give neither time nor money to any organizations, particularly political ones. He said that we wouldn't have to pay dues to take an active part. All they wanted was to have Billy's name, and they would do the rest. I left the telephone and reported this to Billy. He said, "Go back and tell him that I said 'no.' Whenever my name is used, I want to be in on what is done with it."

This same organization had another member call a short time afterward, with the same invitation. I gave the same answer, but the new caller (whom we knew personally) argued at great and boring length. At last, when he understood that the decision was final, he said, "Well, if Billy doesn't want to join, then I will call you every few days to see if he will let us sign his name to telegrams, such as to Truman regarding the F.E.P.C. and so on." I then called the telephone company and asked for a new, unlisted number.

This man supplied us with a revealing anecdote. At one election, when Franklin Roosevelt was running for the presidency, our persistent caller and his wife asked us whom we intended to vote for. "Roosevelt," I replied. Both of us always voted for the individual rather than the party; sometimes it happened it happened to be a Republican in whom we believed, sometimes a Democrat. This time it was F.D.R. The wife wagged her finger in my face sternly. "You can't do that," she said. "He belongs to one class and you belong to another. He will never be able to understand your problems!"

"Well then," I asked, "Who do you suggest?"

"There's a good guy running," she replied, referring to the Socialist candidate.

Some years afterward, her husband phoned to tell me that he had just quit his job and wanted to let us know why he had done it. He had heard his employer talking to some friends and, oh! the terrible things they had said about FDR! "And Verna," he added, with a real sob in his voice, "*You* know how *I* feel about Mr. Roosevelt. There was nothing for me to do but quit." Between the two incidents, the Party line had changed on Roosevelt. He had gone from ogre to hero.

One night I had a disturbing dream. A hearse came up to our door to call for Billy. The following day was a quiet one; Billy was perfectly well. By late afternoon, I had convinced myself that I had been foolishly alarmed over a nightmare. Then a colored woman who lived on our street, two blocks away, came up to our gate. She hadn't even bothered to change her soiled apron. She demanded to see William Grant Still personally. It was an urgent matter which she could not confide to me. So I called him to the gate.

Her story was that a Jewish man and a white girl were driving to Los Angeles from New York. In New Mexico they had been involved in an auto accident. The Jewish fellow whose name Billy did not recognize and who was, she said, one of "that bunch" in New York, was in an apartment recuperating and wanted Billy to phone him at a certain telephone number. Billy was to come to this woman's house to make the phone call. And guess who was recuperating in bed, at this woman's house? The white girl.

With visions of concealed photographers popping out of closets and an unclad white girl jumping out of bed to embrace him, Billy declined. Later one of our friends remarked, when we related the incident, "They don't want Billy to be a leader. They're trying to frame him." We couldn't help but remember that the destruction of all opposition by invective, slander, smear and blackmail is one of the techniques of Communism.

So one day I went to the local F.B.I. office. I sat there and simply related our experiences, without ascribing them to any particular origin. When I finished, the agent commented, "Excuse me, Mrs. Still, but this is the first instance that has come to my attention in which the persecution has lasted so long. Do you know why? What would be your guess?"

I didn't know, and neither did he. It was not until the Sixties, when the terrifying race riots erupted in so many large cities, that we could discern the long-range plan back of our experiences. For when the riots came, there wasn't a single solid Negro voice prominent enough to be recognized and listened to by all the people. The leftists had carefully built up the people who would speak for them in a time of crisis. The decent Americans, through apathy, hadn't bothered. And the news media, though giving a measure of attention to the solid Negro citizens, were still so hungry for colorful features that they too helped the phonies by bringing them to public attention and keeping them there. The result was that we had Negro leaders who weren't leaders at all, the destructive element speaking instead of the constructive, the ignorant in many instances trying to dictate to the informed.

When George Schuyler's autobiography was published, we realized that our suspicions through the years had been well-founded, for Schuyler had been a target of communists and had been in a position to know of their activities, especially concerning Negroes. He wrote of the fierce communist efforts to "capture" Negroes; to divide, disrupt and indoctrinate Negro leadership, and to crush any Negro who opposed them. He also documented communist efforts to control and direct the creative output of writers in America. Many years before, Billy had received in the mail an unsolicited magazine in an unmarked wrapper: the April 23, 1946 issue of *New Masses* in which William Z. Foster, then chairman of the Communist Party, discussed using art as a weapon in an article entitled "Elements of the People's Cultural Policy," so we knew that Schuyler's story had a solid basis in fact.

Some European sources corroborated all of this when they wrote of "The Attack on America," not as a nuclear attack from without, but a racial attack from within, initiated by foreign leftists and by people who have no notion of what it is all about. They felt that responsible Americans weren't aware of it, yet these same responsible Americans had been living through the symptoms and the preparations, and apparently had dedicated themselves to ignoring the warnings.

During the Congressional investigations of communists spanning many years, the suspected ones were given an opportunity to clear themselves publicly, and were repeatedly exposed when they were guilty. Nothing happened to them afterward, except that they somehow retained their power and managed to exclude others as before. They usually started protesting, claiming that they had been blacklisted because of their beliefs. But those of us who had disclaimed such beliefs in favor of patriotism were hounded in a far more subtle way. They were able to enlist public sympathy; we were simply considered nutty and ignored as much as possible, particularly where jobs and money were concerned.

In other fields, the same influence was at work. Orson Bean, reviewing his own case for the February 23, 1971 issue of *National Review* concluded that "all the blacklisting in the communications media has always been done by the liberals." And in literature, there was the case of John Dos Passos who (when he openly sympathized with the Left) was called "the greatest novelist of the century," but after he became disillusioned with communism and spoke out as a conservative, was lightly passed by by the critics and lived the rest of his life in a sort of isolation.

It was a frustrating and nagging period. We suffered, we worried and we griped constantly, always upset. So many powerful forces seemed to be arrayed against us! The leftists made themselves the most obvious, yet we were warned not to call anyone a communist. It appeared that the real communists could call anyone anything and get away with it, while the patriots didn't dare open their mouths for fear of being dragged into court in a lawsuit, or worse, for fear of physical violence to themselves or their families. The myterious deaths of many ex- and anti-communists were all too well known.

Amid the complaints and the uncertainty, we turned instinctively to our family and to our friends; by "friends," I mean the wonderful friends here on earth as well as our invisible friends who worked so hard to keep our spirits up and to give us the assurance that we would eventually triumph. We were told that this would happen because we had never turned our faces and our faith away from God.

Our nomadic crystal-gazers had long since stopped visiting our neighborhood, but we found solace elsewhere. Southern California had been known to be the center for all sorts of crazy cults, fraudulent fortune tellers and false philosophers. We knew this, and yet along with the inept many, we were fortunate enough to find a few, from time to time, whom we could consider genuine.

Among those few, we were often startled and gratified to find that frequently several of them (unknown to each other) would duplicate each other's predictions, sometimes in the same words. It was consoling to be told in the middle of the Thirties that a long, dark tunnel lay ahead, but that we would eventually emerge unscathed; to have the troubles begin and then to be told repeatedly in the Forties, Fifties and Sixties that we would still come out victorious. All of this, of course, was interspersed with information which we knew to be true at the time, and quite often from psychics who were not personally acquainted with us.

Several of the California psychics had mentioned to me over the years that Billy was the reincarnation of Saint John, who was greatly loved by Jesus, and that he had been the one chosen to take over when the Master wanted to go into the wilderness alone. Later I discovered that this same revelation had been made by a psychic in New York, long before Billy and I had met.

We did learn, though, not to accept everything we were told, and never to trust the time concepts given us through psychics, because it quickly became evident that in the spirit world, time does not exist as it exists on earth. For example, "soon" to us means tomorrow, or next month, or even next year. To them it means anytime in the near future.

We simply had to accustom ourselves to having patience and to doing the best we could every minute of every day. It wasn't easy.

In 1953 we embarked on an entirely different experience which, continuing through succeeding years, gave us a feeling of being a real part of God's plan for brotherhood. It happened this way: Arthur Lange, one of the greats in the field of orchestration and a composer-conductor in his own right, had used his retirement from the Hollywood musical scene to enter the field of serious music, to found the Santa Monica Symphony Orchestra and to establish Co-Art, a small record company, where I recorded some of Billy's piano music. While in the studio, I noticed on the bookshelves numerous books on occult subjects.

Several years later, we met the Langes at a party. When I mentioned the occult books to Marjorie Lange, it was as if I had given her a signal which illuminated her whole being. She told us then of having been contacted by spirits who said they had never been in human bodies, and who were active all over the world. When she visited us a few days after that, we were formally introduced to her invisibles who, in an instant, seemed to us to have been old friends. It did not surprise us to be informed that they had been our constant companions, for we had felt all along that we had been sustained by unseen forces.

Marjorie herself was a unique instrument, or channel, for communication with these spirits, or invisibles. Modest, sensitive and sympathetic, she was a former national beauty contest winner and stage personality. In the past, she had of necessity subordinated herself to her husband's career. Often she doubted her own mediumship, and yet information came through which could not possibly have come from her own mind. She had started on the Ouija Board. One day, the little leg on the pointer broke off and, to her amazement, her finger kept on going around by itself. That led to automatic writing and ultimately to a system in which her fingers continued to doodle, though the words were spelled out in her own brain and she spoke them, instead of writing them.

The Beings who came through would not give themselves a name, but they usually began their sessions by making the little wave-like lines (through Marjorie's pencil) similar to those used to designate the astrological sign of Aquarius (perhaps conveying their association with the coming Aquarian age), something like a string of *w*'s. Accordingly, Marjorie called them her WW's. They said they were bringers of the love-force, the helpers of the democracies in the war. They made it very clear that they would not tell fortunes. Once they remarked that spirits who help humans are forever sacrificing in order to do it. "And," they added sternly, "they are not your servants."

In explaining themselves, they would write paragraphs such as these: "We are indeed operating through many channels, all over the world. And we have done this from time to time as the need arose during the world's development. The critical times bring us into closer contact insofar as your awareness grows. We have an ever-increasing love for earth people who are striving for continuity of life and for the good of humanity, and it becomes our duty to act as teachers and advisors for those who show a readiness to fall in with the plan outlined for such constructive growth.

"There are many WW factors involved in the ushering in of the new era, and much activity is taking place on the psychic side as well as on the physical side. In fact, even more, we might say. And so, from the world of thought activity comes transference to the world of physical activity."

They said they wished to comfort us in these strenuous days, for if we were to be too apprehensive over what lay ahead, our power would be lessened or lost. "Optimism is one of the forces that leads onward and outward constructively, whereas apprehension is similar to the emotions that tend toward panic, paralysis of activity, and so on. You see, you do have to deal with a physical world and you do have a certain amount of power over this physical world. By augmenting your power, you also help us to do our work. Our work is to bring about a true concept of the brotherhood of man, in practice as well as in theory. You are also helping us, for in order to act in the physical world, we need your physical force.

The WW's spoke always of the New Era fast-approaching for all of us. "You will see a flowering of the free world such as has never existed before on this planet. The way in which people will live will be astonishing, for the inventions which have been held in abeyance will have a chance to be furnished to the people in general. Travel will be cheaper; money will be easier and people will really enjoy life again."

Although we were warned not to expect personal predictions from the WW's, the teachings they gave us made us feel quite special, as if we had been privileged to share a lofty vantage point and a look in on the destiny of the world. Once in a while, they would electrify us with a startling statement which would be borne out by the news media a long time afterward. For instance, on February 16, 1956, they suddenly said that they felt there might be a contest between the Russians and the Red Chinese. If such a split did exist at that time on a physical plane, not one of us present knew anything about it. We had thought, as did everyone else of our acquaintance, that Russia and China were very close, so we were incredulous. Yet months later, the press informed the world of the Sino-Russian split.

In answer to direct questions as to who they are and why they come to earth as they do, the WW's said, "We are forces of what is commonly known as Light, or Intelligence which is not embodied. We come to acquaint earth people with our work, with the fact that the seen world is only a small part of existence, and that life-force can exist without human form."

Then in 1964 there came a big, slow writing which said, "Please do not hesitate to ask for WW help when you feel the need, for this will be a promise which we make to you, William Grant Still."

It was not until 1967 that we were told the source of the new big writing. It came again, and this time the WW's introduced it as belonging to the "Great Ones" whose forerunners they had been privileged to be, and who have in their keeping the destiny of our planet. The WW's congratulated Marjorie and all of us who were present, because of the "beautiful beings of light" who had come. They said the new forces were similar to what the ancients called the Gods, and that they were the particular forces which were entitled to take a hand in earth's affairs.

What, we once asked, was the real purpose of music, to which we had devoted so much of our lives? The WW's replied that it was "to raise the vibration and the level of purposeful goals for humanity," somewhat as the composer Cyril Scott, himself an occultist, expressed it. "The Higher Powers wish to help through the medium of music to mold the desirable characteristics of the future, not merely to express the characteristics of the present," he said.

This, then, was the source of whatever inner strength we possessed. While some will undoubtedly label it "superstition" and sneer at it, we found that we had lots of distinguished company. Some of the world's finest minds, past and present, have not hesitated to admit their interest in (and in some cases, dependence on) extra-terrestrial forces. We did, and we do, feel privileged, inspired and grateful. And it is only fitting that we acknowledge the help we continue to receive.

16

When we were first married, the most common comment was, "Well, it's all right for you if you want to do it. But" (in horrified tones) "think of the children!"

We did think of the children and it didn't seem to us that they would be any worse off than the millions of children who had already been born of mixed parentage, legitimate or illegitimate. Some of these had risen to positions of greatness in the world. We had every confidence that our children would be sources of pride and joy to us, and that confidence was fully justified.

Our son, Duncan, was born in 1940, our daughter Judith in 1942. From then on, we lived for them and with them. We learned from them and their friends, as they learned from us. Principally, we discovered that if children are unencumbered by preconceived notions, the matter of race prejudice doesn't exist. People prejudice maybe, but racial prejudice, no. Children tend to gravitate toward other children

Still and his family at the piano, 1944. (*Left to right*) Billy, Duncan, Verna, Judith Anne. Photo by R. M. Decker.

with whom they have something in common, regardless of race. It was only when their parents' misconceptions entered the picture that they reflected racial bias. Even so, incidents reflecting bias were isolated. When they did occur, the children didn't seem to be deeply affected. They let them pass, just as we did. There weren't any scars, real or fancied, engraved on our hearts.

In our home, we seldom identified any visitor as to race. The result was that among all our visitors (white, colored, oriental) the children accepted those they liked best for their personal, not their external qualities. Judith was thirteen before she knew that our beloved friend,

Backstage at the Hollywood Bowl, concert on August 25, 1949. (*Left to right*)
Billy, Duncan, Judith, Verna. Courtesy William Grant Still Estate.

Bessie Lawson Blackman, was colored. Mrs. Blackman had been
Duncan's nurse in his babyhood and had even delivered Judith when
the doctor didn't arrive on time, so the children had known her all
their lives. They didn't realize she was colored because no one had
thought to mention it.

This approach allowed our children to grow up completely un-
selfconscious as far as color was concerned. They knew what they

were because none of us denied it, but they didn't go around all the time thinking, "I am this color" or "I am that color." They seemed, however, to be conscious of having come into life with a mission and to be aware of God as a part of their very existence. "Mommy," announced Duncan one morning, "There isn't any white and there isn't any colored. We all belong together." I said, "Yes, that's what your Mommy and Daddy came to show people." He corrected me. "No, you came to teach me and Judith. Then *we* will teach people." Then I heard Judith ask, "Duncan, can God talk to you?" and Duncan replied, "No, but he makes you think. That's how he talks to you."

Another day Judith colored a hand in her coloring book brown, saying, "Oh look, Mommy, here's a Southerner's hand." I asked, "How do you know? All Southerners don't have brown hands." She had a quick answer: "Well, some people have brown skins, Mommy, and this is one of them."

As to parental rules and discipline, our children didn't have the freedom others had. They objected, of course, but it appears to me now that that course was a wise one for us. They weren't permitted to run all over the neighborhood without supervision. They were driven to and from school (which was a distance away from our home) and they weren't left to babysitters, with only the two exceptions of my mother and a close friend. Usually, when there was babysitting to be done, I did it. When both of us had to go out together, we would take the children along. That way, they had to learn to behave in public.

Nor were our children able to have money to waste (on soda pop, candy bars and the like) as some others did. As a result, they grew up thinking we were poor indeed. When he was very small, Duncan asked me what his Daddy did to earn money. I told him that Daddy was a great composer. "Well, I don't want him to be a composer," he argued, "I want him to be a gardener and earn lots of money so he can buy Duncan lots of Christmas presents."

I asked whether Daddy really would earn more money being a gardener. He thought for a moment and then said, "Well, all right. Daddy can be a great composer again, but not till after Christmas. First I want him to be a gardener so he can buy the presents." He had seen the gardeners in the neighborhood being paid for their work, but had never witnessed his Daddy in such a transaction.

We were criticized by amateur child psychologists for being overly protective and we were under even greater fire when we decided to keep the children out of school until they were eight, teaching them at home from the same textbooks approved by the Board of Education. Yet when our children did get into school they were found to have excellent backgrounds and to be reading fluently texts which were far in advance of their grade-levels.

We lived in an integrated neighborhood, so the children attended integrated schools: elementary, junior high and high school. There they did receive instruction in racial matters, not by teachers, but usually by the dark-skinned colored students whose consciousness of race (no doubt acquired in their homes) seemed uppermost in their minds. There came the inevitable day when Judith came home from school and inquired, "Mom, are we white or colored?"

"We are colored people. We are a colored family," I replied firmly. The next day she came home and said, "Mom, you're wrong about this color business. We're white. The other kids told me." It developed that one of her friends, a dark little girl, had paraded her before a line of youngsters sitting on a bench, asking each one, "Is she white or colored?" Her skin was fair, so all the youngsters said she was white. As far as they were concerned, that was it.

This was like young David, the son of some white friends who came from San Francisco to visit us. Billy showed him around the yard and, just as they were looking over the back fence, some of the neighborhood children ran by, simulating a track meet. "Look, there are some colored people," exclaimed David. "You have quite a lot of them around here, haven't you?" He was oblivious to the fact that his host, standing beside him, was a colored man.

Twice, but only twice, as I recall it, did the matter of intermarriage come up unpleasantly during the children's school years. Most of the colored children accepted us without question, as did the whites. But in high school, a few who came from lower class homes said ugly things to Duncan when they learned that he had a white mother.

My mother was fond of our children, and they of her. We visited frequently, particularly since she lived alone after my parents' divorce in 1927. One day she left our house, boarded a streetcar and took the seat next to a colored woman. The two of them struck up a conversation during which my mother asked if she had ever heard of William Grant Still. She had indeed heard of William Grant Still, she said with a touch of venom. He had an excellent reputation in the community she said, but he could have done better than that horrible woman he married. "Why, even her own mother doesn't come to see her."

On the amusing side was another incident. When our Los Angeles County Museum had a showing of the Berlin Masterpieces, I took our children and four other youngsters to see it. Two of the others were colored, two were Oriental. It was a little discouraging to find that they all seemed to be more interested in the huge skeleton of a whale that hung from the Museum's ceiling than they were in seeing the famous paintings, but the seven of us dutifully trudged through most of the rooms and studied nearly every item. Near the end of the tour, I became aware that we were being followed. As we left the exhibit, a breathless white lady came up and grasped my arm. "I can't let you go," she exclaimed, "without telling you what a *magnificent* thing you're doing, bringing all these children to this exhibit. They'll never forget it!"

Of course I was surprised. Those children were all friends, in and out of our house frequently, so to me there was no special virtue in entertaining them. The next day, I mentioned the incident to one of the teachers at school, who remarked, "You should have floored her. You should have said, 'That's nothing. They're all mine!'"

Judith and Duncan were quite different in many of their habits. Judith was the one who taught us that a punch bowl was one of life's necessities. She filled the house with her friends of all racial groups for parties, parties, parties. We entertained the young people, sometimes their parents, too, and sometimes some of the teachers. Judith engaged in all sorts of activities in and out of school and took care to see that her grades were the highest. In college, she was elected to Phi Beta Kappa and Phi Kappa Phi, and won many awards. As the years passed, she became more and more the sort of dedicated daughter of whom every parent dreams: loyal, loving and trustworthy. She was both extroverted and introverted.

There was little of the extrovert about Duncan. He had a high I.Q. and was usually in the advanced study groups, but he learned so quickly that it was hard for him to find mental challenges. As a result, he did not always work up to his full capacity.

It was only after leaving high school, after finishing an enlistment in the Air Force Reserve and then entering college, that Duncan was inspired to do his real work. He plunged into the new, more demanding tasks with enthusiasm, and graduated from UCLA with honors in the School of Engineering. He won his Ph.D. after graduate school in Berkeley and became a nuclear engineer.

Judith's college was USC, which she attended on a scholarship, majoring in English, as Billy's mother had done long years before. She was versatile enough to do well everything she set out to do. In college she came in contact with several psychoanalysts, some real, some pretending. All of them, of course, had their own theories about race. One morning in the cafeteria several students were discussing racial matters from a psychological standpoint. Judith listened quietly while they explored every aspect of the subject, rounding the discussion off with their views on intermarriage, and closing with the usual question, "What about the children? What a tragedy for them!"

At that point Judith opened her wallet. She showed them a picture of her father and told them who he was. Then she displayed my picture and told them who I was. There were deep, in-drawn sighs of astonishment. Finally, one of the students ventured, "But have you really had a happy life?" "Absolutely," replied Judith. "I've always been happy."

Midway through Judith's college years, she met a young geologist with whom she—and all the rest of us—fell in love. They eloped and were married, and then we discovered that he came from a wonderful family, a white family, from Texas. When their son took Judith to northern California to meet them, she liked them at once, and they liked her, but they didn't know about us. When we made plans for them to spend Christmas with us in Los Angeles, they still did not know. One by one, we all begged Larry to tell them before they arrived, so they wouldn't be shocked. He refused. Instead, he growled, "Now, don't you worry about my folks. They're all right!" And so they were. They walked into our house with never a hint that anything was unusual. We have been friends ever since; we have often felt that we belong to the same family.

Our grandson was born between semesters as Judith had predicted. We babysat little Daniel while Judith returned to classes and Larry worked. Then along came another pregnancy in Judith's senior

Billy and the Headlee grandchildren. (*Left to right*) Lisa, Celeste, Billy, Daniel, Colleen. Courtesy William Grant Still Estate.

year. Until the night before graduation she didn't know whether she would make it or not, but she did, Magna Cum Laude. Within a week, our granddaughter Lisa was born, to be followed in later years by Coleen and Celeste. Judith, meanwhile, began a career in creative writing which seemed (to us!) to reflect a brillant and constructive mind. Motherhood and the care of a home went side by side with the goal she had promised herself she would reach.

The four beautiful babies returned to us—and to Larry's parents—our youth and our enthusiasm. My parents, too, though old and ill, enjoyed them. We all competed to see who could dote the most.

We told the story of Judith's wonderful husband and in-laws to some of our longtime friends who happened to be of the same religious faith. They said it gave them renewed hope, because they had never dreamed it would happen this way in their lifetimes! Now, they said, a world of brotherhood didn't seem so far away.

This was Larry's legacy of love to all who were fortunate enough to know him. When, at age thirty-two, his gallant life ended in a tragic undersea misadventure off the coast of Catalina Island, not one, but two families mourned the loss of a beloved son. He belonged to all of us.

— 17 —

While the children were growing up, Billy used his creative ability in many ways. He built toys for them out of wood—big toys and little toys—culminating in the scenery, miniature cars and buildings for a model railroad outfit which we were never able to enjoy fully because we never had room to set it up properly. He made papier-mache dolls and jigsaw puzzles and—just as mental exercise—experimented in developing his own system of numerology. In a few years he forgot it, though at the time it often was uncannily accurate. He set up charts for the new-born babies of our friends which, when reviewed in later years, contained much information that had become apparent only as the children grew.

In my own lifetime in southern California, I had seen huge fields of tall grass within the Los Angeles city limits give way to heavily populated areas, for Los Angeles had long since ceased to be a sleepy little Spanish town. Yet there were still reminders of that early California life which fascinated all of us so much, and there were always good things to see and do in the area. We enjoyed driving around the countryside; that was our relaxation and our pleasure. I have to admit, though, that the majority of our trips were to places where Duncan wanted to go: train yards, Model Railroad clubs, or the harbor where the big ships were anchored.

We welcomed the opportunity to do all these things for those we loved so much, especially since we were then maintaining a cheerful demeanor while acknowledging to ourselves in private that a melancholy regarding our work had engulfed us. Billy used to whistle softly a little plaintive motif, over and over and over, as he worked on the toys, and as he went from one chore to another. Still, there was a good deal of excitement, musical and otherwise, and encouragement, even in the dark hours.

Along with several other American composers, Billy was invited to compose a piece for the Sesquicentennial Celebration of West Point, which was to take place in 1952. He decided that for this special occasion the most appropriate gesture would be a simple affirmation of faith in and loyalty to America. So, for the USMA Band, he wrote *To You, America*. Musical inspiration for this was slow in coming. He had received the invitation on April 30, 1951. It was not until September 16th that he began work, but by October 16th he had completed the creative aspect and had begun to score the music. The following year, in February, he conducted it in its initial performance at West Point. The composition was to win a Freedom Foundation Award medal.

Since it was intended for band, he wrote it for band as he had been hearing bands play over the years. It was not until he reached West Point and heard the magnificent group developed by Lt. Col. Francis E. Resta that he realized that a band could be the equivalent of symphony orchestras. So when he wrote his *Folk Suite for Band* some years later, he gave it a more intricate instrumentation, remembering the band at West Point. At its first performance, I had an uncomfortable reaction. There were spots in the music that sounded thin. Could this really be a William Grant Still orchestration, I wondered? Had the Old Maestro lost his touch? After the concert, backstage, the explanation came. The conductor told us that at a later date he would return to us the parts—and there were quite a few of them—which he had left at home. He hadn't been able to use them because he didn't have the instruments to play them! Then I understood why so many composers write so solidly for bands, as if most of the instruments are playing the same thing all the time. Later, we heard Clarence Sawhill and the UCLA Band play the *Folk Suite* with all the instruments called for and it turned out very well.

West Point also provided another sort of experience. Billy was deeply impressed on seeing so many mementos of events which had played significant parts in our country's history: the gun that killed Abraham Lincoln, the series of plaques devoted to famous Americans (on one of which the name Benedict Arnold had been chiseled out), and so on. It was a most moving experience.

Meanwhile, Los Angeles, as usual, continued to be a Mecca for distinguished artists. One we met there was the Brazilian composer, Heitor Villa-Lobos, about whom Elsie Houston had reminisced when we interviewed her. We became friends by mail with the Belgian composer, Christian Dupriez, and with the Danish composer, Knudage Riisager. Some of the American composers resident in Los Angeles whom we saw frequently were Elliot Griffis, Vernon Leftwich, Eugene Hemmer, Louis Gruenberg, Grant Beglarian and Castelnuovo-Tedesco. Among the visiting Americans were Theodore Fitch and his wife, Lorraine Noel Finley, and many others, particularly Paul Creston and his wife.

There was also our continuing friendship with Wolfe Gilbert, the songwriter, and his gifted wife, Rose, who always insisted that she was "married to ASCAP" since Wolfe, as one of ASCAP's directors, was such a vital part of the Society. Rose gave birthday parties for Wolfe, at which the turnout of America's top songwriters always brought a touch of nostalgia into the evenings. Probably for no one but Wolfe would they all come out. Each would get up and sing a medley of his own best-loved songs in voices no vocal teacher could love, but their presentations were so authentic and so full of enthusiasm that professional singers couldn't match them.

During those days honors were being bestowed on Billy by northern whites and northern Negroes, and by southern whites and southern Negroes. When Billy received the honorary degree of Doctor of Letters at Bates College, two of the other distinguished recipients were the author, John P. Marquand, and Sherman Adams, then President Eisenhower's assistant. Warmed by the knowledge that Mr. and Mrs. Adams were music lovers, we corresponded with them from time to time through the years. A few days after the Bates Commencement, Billy delivered the keynote address to the American Symphony Orchestra League Convention, again with our familiar theme: "It is time to re-assert ourselves as Americans."

In Jackson, Missisippi, the symphony orchestra proudly presented the first performance of our *The Little Song That Wanted to Be a Symphony*" (music by Billy, narration by me), advertising it as the work of a native son of the state. Billy had been composing this one over a period of years and had usually referred to it in his notes as a fable. The basic idea had occurred to him many years before. Mississippi received the work with enthusiasm, recalling to my mind the surprised words of one of our white musician-friends who had performed in the South, including Billy's music on her programs: "Do you know," she exclaimed to me in amazement, "that your husband is *beloved* throughout the south?"

I was amazed that she was amazed. After all, Billy was southern by birth, and he had achieved something in the world. Southerners who would be aware of such achievement would necessarily be cultured and intelligent people, the sort to feel pride as well as goodwill.

Not long after the Jackson performance, Southern University in Baton Rouge decided to celebrate the completion of its new music building with a series of recitals, the last of which was to feature William Grant Still conducting the New Orleans Philharmonic-Symphony (a project conceived by our old friend, Tourgee deBose). No Negro had ever conducted a major symphony orchestra in the deep South before, but it proved to be a harmonious and mutually satisfying achievement. Billy remarked later that he had never had more cooperation than those musicians gave. It had been a joy to work with them. It was a mixed and unsegregated audience and there were no complaints.

Serenade, for cello, was written about this time as a result of Billy being asked to join Artur Rubinstein and Gregor Piatigorsky in judging a young artists' competition for the Santa Monica Symphony Orchestra. After it was over, Piatigorsky buttonholed Billy backstage and asked if he would write something for him to play. Billy agreed, went home and started work on a romantic, melodic piece. Midway through the composition, he received a commission from the Great Falls, Montana, High School. As a result, Piatigorsky's piece quickly became a *Serenade* for the Great Falls High School Orchestra. This and two subsequent commissions from the American Accordionists' Association were the only ones completed during this period. It was dedicated to our friends, LeRoy and Ruth Brant, who had honored Billy with an official William Grant Still Day (by order of the Mayor) in San Jose, California, presenting his music in concert, presenting him as a lecturer for the Chamber of Commerce, and arranging for him to be given the key to the city.

So, in case Gregor Piatigorsky ever wondered what happened to his composition, it went to Great Falls. And in case anyone wonders why that composition features the cello, it's because it was originally intended for one of the world's great cellists.

Following the composition of *Serenade*, Billy wrote his first and only piece for harp, called *Ennanga*. Our dear friend, the fine harp virtuoso Lois Adele Craft, helped with the development of the work and premiered it at one of Landau's composers' workshop concerts in Los Angeles.

It was inevitable that we would wonder how Still music would stand the test of time. With the passing of the years, we were reassured on this matter many times over. Once, when *In Memoriam: The Colored Soldiers Who Died for Democracy* was revived in New York City, fifteen years after it was first performed, Winthrop Sargeant wrote that it was "an essay in pure lyricism—a very difficult thing for a contemporary composer to achieve, since it lays upon him the allegation of having something to say and deprives him of the technical devices with which most composers nowadays tend to obscure their personalities from their listeners. On the whole, I thought Mr. Still's work the finest on the program."

Similar reactions followed the programming of the same composition by Szell in 1965 for his Cleveland Orchestra concerts, and again when the Cleveland Orchestra made its triumphant tour of Europe sponsored by the State Department.

Several times Billy had participated in UNESCO conferences, so when a contest for an orchestral work dedicated to the United Nations was announced, he was eager to participate. When his tone poem, *The Peaceful Land*, won the prize offered jointly by the National Federation of Music and the Aeolian Music Foundation, our old and dear friend, Fabien Sevitzky, was chosen to give it its first performance with the University of Miami Symphony Orchestra. After the concert, Sevitzky asked for a short opera which he could produce with the University's facilities. An opera? Could we have understood correctly? Yes, an *opera*.

For Sevitzky we developed an idea that we had had long before, and had tentatively begun. The music was Billy's, the text mine, and the plot our own. We wrote about ordinary people with a reasonable problem, people who live in the America of today, who love each other, and who share the aspirations of most American families. It was a simple plot, but a dramatic one. It exemplified our feeling that the most direct approach is usually the best, whatever one does. We called it *Highway 1, U.S.A.*

The opera was a notable success. The premiere fell on the night of Billy's 66th birthday, so it was converted into a birthday party. The University of Miami audience gave him a standing ovation, sang "Happy Birthday to You," and greeted him at a most enjoyable social affair following the production. The critics then, as at subsequent performances, described the music as truly American, original, free in spirit, unmistakably modern without being dissonant just for the sake of dissonance.

Now, when newspapers all over the world had been spreading the news of lynchings and other horrors which occurred in our south, here was an artistic triumph in the south by a Negro collaborating with his non-Negro wife, sponsored by a leading white institution and acclaimed wholeheartedly by the white community.

Among all the leading white periodicals outside of Miami, only the New York *Times* chose to notice it. Fabien Sevitzky was deeply grieved, and surely the other white sponsors must have wondered about the silence.

Highway 1, U.S.A. was only one of the new operas on which we worked after *Troubled Island*. There were also *A Bayou Legend*, *The Pillar*, *Costaso*, *Mota* and *Minette Fontaine*—all full-length works, based on plots original with us. That is to say, we did not adapt them from literary works already known. As we wrote the operas and tried without success to get them produced, we were curious to see and hear the operas of our contemporaries which *were* being produced.

What we witnessed in the following years was disappointing. Gian Carlo Menotti had established a style of his own: mostly declamatory with few melodic passages, and had been able to promote performances of his works. Accordingly, most of the other operatic composers seemed to feel that they must conform to the Menotti style. They did, and were often performed, but we felt in no way obliged to change our style or our basic approach. We felt then, as now, that creators must be individuals, not copyists. The Menotti style was fine for Menotti, but not for us nor for anyone else, in our opinion.

Despite the good things that continued to come our way, we had begun to feel the real pinch of opposition, and to understand something of what Deems Taylor must have felt with the passing of the years and the calumny that had been thrown at him. When, in the mid-Fifties, thirty-three prominent songwriters (of whom Billy was one) banded together to sue Broadcast Music Incorporated, we heard with some astonishment the evidence the lawyers had dug up. A BMI campaign of denigration had been felt by Billy (only more subtly) for years. Now we understood that it had not been a figment of our imaginations and that other people had been targets, just as we had been.

It was no longer so easy for us to get performances by the major groups, to reach the top conductors, or to be given the publicity we had in the old days. The big foundations still gave commissions for new works, but overlooked William Grant Still in doing so. Meanwhile, his printed music and his few commercial recordings were out of print. The publishers were reluctant to reprint them.

The sinister force behind this is exemplified in the junk turned out nowadays to replace what we once knew as music. Plato's *Republic* warns us that, "the introduction of a new kind of music must be shunned as imperiling a whole state, for styles of music are never disturbed without effecting the most important political institutions." This type of music was for years not permitted at all in Russia, but here it is encouraged, subsidized and once in a while people even pretend to enjoy it.

Its promoters take refuge in the fact that composers like Wagner and Debussy were said to be too revolutionary for their days, yet now they are accepted as part of our musical repertoire. But Wagner and Debussy didn't discard everything that had gone before, as some of the modernists do; they retained what was good and built on that. The so-called "avant-gardists" of today can't claim that sort of distinction. In many instances, we suspect, they are the composers who can't quite make the grade by legitimate means, so they settle on stunts to bring themselves to people's attention. This would be all right, if they didn't go out of their way to scuttle other people's boats. If their products are truly worthwhile, they should be able to coexist with the products of other people and other epochs.

Billy had left the so-called "avant-garde" fold in the Twenties and had had the courage to develop an idiom of his own. In the Fifties, when the avant-garde movement had been trying and failing to win public approval for so long that it could no longer be considered truly avant-garde, some who were not aware of his background said that "time had passed Mr. Still by." Nothing that is basically good can be altered by the passage of time.

As late as 1967, Billy received a request to compose a short piano piece for an anthology. He did, only to have it returned to him with the note that the evaluation committee felt that the few broken chords it contained were a nineteenth-century device. He was asked to delete the broken chords and return the piece immediately, to meet a deadline. He tried the piece their way; it was terrible. So he refused to make the changes. The fact that broken chords had been used a century ago, didn't mean that they had to be discarded today, particularly when there was an artistic reason for their inclusion. All through the years, I found caustic references in Billy's diaries to this supposedly new music. In 1951 a recording of a contemporary symphony made him feel physically ill. "If," as he noted, "one may call disjointed sounds 'music.'" In 1957 he came home from a boring concert, noted the audience's apathy, and wrote: "There is today a great need for music that reaches beyond the intellect into the listeners' hearts." He spoke often of the exhibitionism of the avant-gardists; of the wide gap between the merely new and the worthwhile; of mediocrity trying to distinguish itself by the use of big words; of the failure to make a distinction between music and sound. "Sound," he wrote, "is merely a component of music." Then he added, "If they (the avant-gardists) could write music, they would." After an afternoon in which we listened to some of the most discordant composers trying to justify their position, Billy asked, "When are they going to stop arguing and start writing music?"

More than a score of years earlier, when I was interviewing Sir Hamilton Harty at the Hollywood Bowl, he remarked: "People don't really like that sort of music. The just endure it and pretend to like it."

In 1957, one of the New York critics who remained a friend through the years wrote to us in this fashion: "These are discouraging times for anyone who has to listen to so much allegedly new music as we do. Actually, what we hear is for the most part a rehash of stuff already beginning to be faded in the Twenties and Thirties. Most composers of any intelligence will admit, in private conversations, that atonality is played out and that they are up a blind alley, but what is to be done? The propoganda campaign on behalf of modern music has been carried on so relentlessly and successfully for the past thirty or fifty years that it's their story and they are stuck with it."

Quite aside from music, there were other discouragements. Our ideas on racial matters (particularly that the making of friends rather than enemies is the only solution to our problems) were all too often brushed aside in favor of the hastily-conceived slogans and actions of people whose backgrounds did not qualify them for leadership. We also tried desperately to convey to people the thought that there are different groupings in Negro society as in white. People had listened so long to the demagogues that they didn't want to open their minds. Some considered us traitors for speaking as we did. Traitors to whom, or to what? White people have always discriminated among themselves. Why should it be so hard to believe that Negroes do too? Integration should only mean an alliance between people who are attracted to each other, regardless of color, instead of a forced mingling of one or the other group.

When we tried to clarify the subject of intermarriage, we also met disbelief, even though this was a topic on which we felt we could speak with authority, after so many years together. One editor, in rejecting an article I wrote on this subject, told me he was doing so because he couldn't bring himself to believe that what I said was true. He evidently thought that I should have had a negative, instead of a positive approach. This made me wonder how many other truthful accounts have been suppressed or altered in order to conform to someone else's preconceived ideas.

And aren't the so-called "liberals" just as biased in their own way as the acknowledged bigots? The bigots are open in their dislike and disapproval, but some of the "liberals" will approve of you only so long as they can feel themselves big and generous just to be associating with you. The minute you begin to measure arms, they withdraw their "friendship." We learned to like the people who were liberal in their hearts, but not those who made such a fetish of being "liberal" and "broadminded."

Once in a while, it was a shock to discover that a few of the people whom we had considered friends weren't friendly at all. One well-known Negro choir director, for instance, was twice engaged to have his choir perform Billy's compositions, and each time allowed the choir to come to dress rehearsal without having looked at the music. The resulting performances were something less than perfect. Then there was the Negro composer who refused to permit Billy to make an arrangement of a Negro spiritual (presumably in the public domain) which had appeared in his own collection, on his own assertion that Billy's arrangement would be so much better than his own that the latter would no longer sell. At the time this happened, his arrangement had been in print for thirty-one years. Yet another Negro composer, a younger man who hoped to climb from the popular field to the serious, deliberately (with the connivance of his manager) set out to take over a series of concerts which had been intended for Billy alone.

During those years our government was beginning to bring leading citizens from other countries to visit the United States to see how we live, and many of the people we knew personally here were sent abroad as goodwill emissaries. No one thought of sending Billy, and yet some of the visitors, (especially those from countries where the people have dark skins) confided that he was the only colored American to whom they had talked whose views coincided with their own. We were even told, unofficially, that at least one and possibly two of the African nations had requested him as a visitor, but the request, or requests, had been denied, on the grounds that a jazz band would be more suitable.

We had clear evidence of this slight when we met the internationally-known poet, President Leopold Senghor of Senegal. When he met Billy, the President indicated that he had already heard of him and asked if he would like to visit Senegal. Billy said he would. We then mentioned it to the State Department attaché who accompanied the visitors, whereupon the attaché said very pleasantly, but with finality, "Oh, they would not accept anyone like you in Africa. They would only accept someone like Duke Ellington or Louis Armstrong."

It was President Senghor who later warned of the danger of the cultural chauvinism which subtly relegates all black culture to the status of folklore.

It did appear to us that we were living in an incredible era—we and the rest of the world—an era in which disloyalty seemed to be rewarded with the plums of one's profession, when it became nasty to speak of loving one's country and when humility before God became something naive. Adherence to beauty in art made one a "square," and if one were not addicted to sick comedy, subversion, musicless "music," dirty "literature," and meaningless daubs which purported to be art, he was out of the stream of life.

We watched in horror as mobs here and abroad flaunted their hatred for our country and our flag, and as characters whom no decent people would invite into their homes paraded before television cameras, sneered and shouted that they would take over. We knew as well as anyone that all Negroes are not on the highest rung of the ladder anymore than all white people are, and that all are not equal in accomplishment or even in potential, no matter how much they would like to think they are. It would be tragic if some of the very ignorant were to be given power which they claim they deserve. The resultant world would be intolerable.

The mobs never expressed the sentiments of decent people, but expressed the rantings of anarchists. To those of us who were and are loyal Americans, and to our many friends abroad who still consider America a land of freedom and opportunity and who hunger to be able to live here, the racists on both sides and the politically motivated represent the incarnation of evil.

A few white people (some highly placed in American life) suggested that the better class of Negroes should now go down and work with and for the lower classes. Others mouthed the old slander that "the Negro intellectuals aren't doing their share," as if every Negro should be a social worker. Do all white people descend to the dregs to work with and for the lower classes of white people? And as if every lower class Negro would be willing to listen to his betters and accept their advice.

To live in such an era was in itself an ordeal, and to try to keep one's light shining meanwhile an even greater one. This, we realized at the time, was the long, dark tunnel of the dream. A lonely tunnel but, thank God, not an endless one.

_18_

I t must have been happening gradually, but to us it seemed as though it came in a flash, our personal miracle. We had travelled through the long darkness of our tunnel, complaining, griping and protesting all the way; and we suddenly emerged into the bright sunlight. There were no trumpets sounding, no banners flying, no unexpected bequests—but all of a sudden, it was there.

We went out among people and encountered new respect. We discovered that the things we had been saying and believing about music were what the solid musicians believed, and what they had been waiting to hear. ASCAP asked Billy to run for the Board of Directors, knowing that all the incumbents would be re-elected, as always. But to our surprise, when the votes were counted, Billy received the largest number of any non-incumbent. This, despite the fact that he hadn't lifted a finger to campaign for himself. Such a tribute from one's colleagues is tribute indeed, as was the one given Billy later the same year by the National Association of Negro Musicians.

We had always been sensitive because we had never been able to make a big showing with money. Now we found out that people understood this, and they also understood why. They seemed grateful that we had done as we did. There were times when we felt that many were going out of their way to be pleasant and to do nice things for us, it gave us a feeling of real humility and gratitude.

We found, too, that thinking people agreed with us on racial matters. Deems Taylor had once said that the only way to handle the race problem is to ignore race, and to treat every person as a person rather than as a members of any particular group. We agreed. There should be no such thing as "race" relations, we thought, only human relationships. We all should be associating only with those people who are on our own mental level, regardless of their color.

We found that people in general no longer stared at us, as they had in the old days. We no longer encountered patronizing white people who asked us whether we knew their cook or their maid.

Billy's constant prayer had been that God would make it possible for the music he had written to be heard and that the music, in turn, would bless all who heard it. His prayers were answered in a most remarkable way. There came a time when, at the major performances, there would seem to be a spiritual bond between the music and the audiences. It seemed to be a living, tangible thing. Billy, conducting, felt it. When sometimes I played the piano part, I felt it. The audiences certainly felt it, for often there would be a hushed silence and a huge ovation, of a different quality than we had known before.

This occurred also during the year of Billy's seventieth birthday, when the league of Allied Arts in Los Angeles, guided by Dorothy Vena Johnson and Ursula Murrell, gave him a testimonial banquet at Los Angeles' then-new Music Center. The feeling of love that permeated the room was so strong that we felt we could reach out and touch it. It was impossible to describe in words. The feeling of love was there again when Delta Sigma Theta's Dannellen Joseph arranged for us to appear with the Coppin String Quartet and Lois Adele Craft played *Ennanga* during the 1965 Convention.

It was a happy co-incidence that this convention was held in Los Angeles precisely at the time of our race riots, so that large numbers of intelligent, beautifully dressed colored women from all over the country were in the city. The convention didn't get as much publicity as the riots did, but it helped to establish a balance.

Among the others who helped to make Billy's seventieth birthday year a memorable one were the conductors Izler Solomon, Joseph Wincenc, Leo Scheer, Paul White, George Szell, Richard Bales, Maurice Bonney, Fabien Sevitzky and Richard Franko Goldman—all of whom performed William Grant Still compositions specifically at that time with their respective organizations. In Los Angeles the Bureau of Music, under the direction of Lloyd Stone and Richard Robinson, sponsored a city-wide production of the ballet, *Sahdji*, just recorded and published by Howard Hanson and the Eastman School of Music. A different sort of tribute came from Miriam Matthews, whose outstanding article about Billy in *Phylon* magazine had been a highlight of our lives. She commissioned a local artist, Alice Gafford, to paint the portrait of Billy which now hangs on our wall, together with the portrait painted by Ted Phillips, Jr. after he returned from service in Vietnam. The Los Angeles City Council and the Los Angeles Board of Supervisors both awarded citations of honor, and finally, three young men completed their requirements for degrees by writing theses on Billy's life and works. We found new friends, such as the conductor James Guthrie, Dr. Robert Bartlett Haas of UCLA, the Arthur Bennett Lipkins, Albert Dominguez, and John and Emelie Haugh of Tucson, as well as new considerations from old friends like Carl Princi, Tom Cassidy and Howard Rhines at KFAC, Mary Sevitzky Portanova (the brilliant harpist), Harry Ruby and his wife, actress Eileen Percy, Florence Cadrez of the local Chapter of the American Federation of Musicians (the musicians' union), Lilian Kaufman, widow of the pianist Harry Kaufman, journalist Charles White McGehee, and too many more to mention here.

We thought it fitting at this time that our choral work, *A Psalm for the Living*, (re-affirming our belief that God is among us on earth as well as in Heaven) should be published and performed. It had been written some time before. The new *Christmas in the Western World* or *Las Pascuas*, based on folksongs of ten countries of the Western Hemisphere also came out, our tribute to the Prince of Peace. In both cases, the texts were mine, the music Billy's.

When Sevitzky asked Billy to compose a piece dedicated to Jean Sibelius, he wrote his short *Threnody, in Memory of Jean Sibelius* with a grateful heart, for the Finnish master, before his death, had been given a copy of Karl Krueger's first recording of the *Afro-American Symphony* by our mutual friends, the Brants of San Jose, and had remarked of Billy, "He has something to say." So it was a pleasure to honor him, and to have the little piece played magnificently and later broadcast over the Finnish National Radio. There followed a series of songs for various music textbooks and, last, the incidental music for Carol Stone's charming children's play, *The Prince and the Mermaid*, which was staged imaginatively by Mary Jane Evans at San Fernando State College.

In 1968 we had travelled together to the Pacific Northwest for a concert with Werner Torkanowsky, the New Orleans Philharmonic-Symphony Orchestra and the Dillard University Choir, an event conceived by Frederick Hall and Albert Dent, as Dillard's contribution to the celebration of New Orleans' 250th anniversary, and later broadcast over the Voice of America. We stayed for several days in each place and always we found the same warm, friendly atmosphere—not only from our colleagues, but from strangers on the streets, in the shops, hotels and restaurants. We felt that this was truly America, and we were proud to be a part of it.

One of the New Orleans reviews seemed to sum up what we had been working for throughout the years. In the *Times-Picayune* dated April 19, 1968, Frank Gagnard wrote: "Dr. Still faced his professional challenge a long time ago, and by winning it he also secured a place in musical history and American history. He broke barriers of race in symphonic music, not through revolution, but by gentle, attractive persuasion."

In 1973, after Billy was awarded an honorary degree by the New England Conservatory of Music, we traveled to Washington D.C., where we met President and Mrs. Nixon. In his last active years, Billy served on various committees having to do with music, one being Mayor Yorty's Advisory Committee in Los Angeles, others in the field of education. He lectured at universities, conducted orchestras and

William Grant Still was awarded an honorary doctorate from the University of
Arkansas in 1971. (*Left to right*) Still, Verna Arvey Still, David Mullins
(then president of the University of Arkansas). Courtesy of the Division of
Information, University of Arkansas.

chamber groups in his own compositions, visited many schools, some
in what are termed our "culturally deprived areas," composed new
work when he felt like it, revised old ones when he saw a need for
revision.

He enjoyed going from honor to honor, such as Oberlin's two-day
celebration of his 75th birthday, receiving the honor plaque from the
Association for the Presentation and Preservation of the Arts in Washington D.C., and the honorary Doctor of Laws from the University of
Arkansas. Our home was designated as one of Los Angeles' cultural
monuments and the William Grant Still Community Arts Center was
dedicated by Mayor Bradley and Councilman Cunningham. Pepper-
dine University and the Peabody Conservatory of Music also gave Billy
honorary degrees, as Wilberforce, Howard University and Bates College had done years earlier. He received the Richard Henry Lee patriotism award from Walter Knott, of Knott's Berry Farm.

University of Southern California Testimonial Banquet for Still's birthday, 1975. (*Left to right*) composer Howard Hanson; Abram Chassins, director of the USC School of Music; Howard Rarig; William Grant Still. Courtesy University of Southern California.

When USC's "Friends of Music" sponsored a banquet in Billy's honor in 1975, prior to awarding him its honorary degree of Doctor of Laws, we were overwhelmed and honored to discover that our great and good friends, Dr. and Mrs. Howard Hanson, had been willing to make the trip to the west coast, to give the keynote address at the banquet. And then there was a very special pleasure when Opera/South in Jackson, Mississippi, undertook to give a premier performance of our opera, *A Bayou Legend*. Dolores Ardoyno and Donald Dorr, the skillful and creative directors of Opera/South, agreed to present it exactly as written. They were supported by Dollye Robinson and Jackson State University, and their efforts were brought to memorable fruition by conductor Leonard dePaur. (DePaur, recalling the days of his youth when he had studied orchestration by sitting in on William Grant Still rehearsals at the radio studio, said he would have "come for carfare!" to conduct the work. "This man was one of the giants," he said). Apparently Mississippi ETV agreed with Mr. dePaur, for under the able direction of Ed Van Cleef, they filmed the production and brought it to national television. All of us were delighted with this success and with the wonderful press coverage! Interesting that the success we had long coveted came in the deep south, when the "liberal" North was not open to us at all.

As we looked back over our lives we both agreed that although we wouldn't want to go through some of it again, we had enjoyed making a good fight. Though we had had to struggle and go without, we eventually found ourselves grateful to God for the experience. We considered ourselves both wiser and better than we had been at the beginning.

Money? We wanted it and needed it, but we didn't starve and we had a roof over our heads. We had the love of our family and friends. Money would be only the frosting on the cake, and who needs frosting when the cake is so good? We wouldn't have been willing to exchange what we had, not for a billion dollars.

Epilogue

The last three years of Billy's life were spent in a nursing home as a result of a series of strokes and heart attacks. Death came on December 3, 1978, at age 83.

An Afterthought

by Judith Anne Still

After my father died in 1978, my mother seemed to lose heart. She had long been plagued by diabetes and other serious illnesses, and now she appeared to give way to a chronic lethargy. In the summer of 1981 a stroke rendered her almost totally bedridden, and I felt it necessary to help with her business affairs.

I found WILLIAM GRANT STILL MUSIC to be in a state of suspended animation. Orders for parts and scores had not been filled. Copyrights were yet to be renewed. Taxes were owed. On Mother's desk, amid the unanswered mail, was a manuscript in a green folder entitled, *In One Lifetime*. I gathered it up with the rest of the records, wondering what, if anything, was to be done with it.

At first I knew little about musical affairs. But labor hones judgment, and I was encouraged by the favorable response of the artistic public to the revitalization of the Still business. People were visibly delighted to be able to order sheet music again. In addition, good things were beginning to happen. The California Arts Council sponsored conductor Frank Fetta's impressive "William Grant Still Festival." Our fine and able friends, Donald and Dolores Dorr, now of the Baton Rouge Opera, proposed a premiere of the opera *Minette Fontaine*, and Mr. Dorr was making long strides in his research for a book about William Grant Still's ancestry. An album of piano music recorded by Albert Dominguez was almost ready for public distribution. KCET, educational television, was looking for funds for a William Grant Still documentary, and the University of Arkansas at Fayetteville began preparation for a Still festival and a recording of the *Third Symphony*. The prestigious Mississippi Institute of Arts and Letters and the Governor of Mississippi, William Winter, honored William Grant Still for the ETV showing of *Bayou Legend*. (The latter honor was accepted by my seventeen-year-old daughter, Lisa, when she travelled to Jackson and was royally entertained by the warm and cultured Mississippi dignitaries.

Even so, amid a gathering tide of affirmation, there were some disturbing occurrences. Someone in New York had heard a rumor that William Grant Still had spurned his first wife and children, and had ignored them in their time of need. Strangely, at the same time, agents for the disinherited relatives were seeking to steal a share of the composer's royalties.

One day a man from the Library of Congress indicated that the Library would like to have all of the Still papers. Mother said that the papers had been promised to the University of Arkansas, but she offered him Still's collection of personal tape recordings. He talked about microfilming the scrapbooks and interviewing Mother for an oral history tape.

Later, as I was driving the librarian out to our place of business to look at the William Grant Still collection, he observed, "I think the most important thing about your parents is that they have known *everybody* in music over the years."

"Yes, they did have many, many friends," I replied. "But, really, it's not who they *knew*, but what they *did* that's important. My father was incredibly pioneering where orchestration was concerned, and he wrote music that will be enjoyed long after the tin-pan clangers have ceased to be recognized."

"Tin-pan clangers?"

"You know, the proponents of the atonal."

"Actually, I've had occasion to deal with the music of some of your tin-pan clangers." (He mentioned several composers of the dissonant idiom.) He talked of these men with animation, and then mentioned his association with Leonard Bernstein, of whose choral group he was a member.

"Oh," I brightened. "Do you ever get a chance to talk to Bernstein?"

"Yes . . . sometimes a group of us will get together after rehearsal."

"Marvelous," I said. "The next time you see him, please do me a favor and ask him why he has been so supportive of the Black Panthers, yet refuses to even look at William Grant Still's scores."

The librarian seemed surprised. At last he replied, "All right. I certainly will ask him."

The rest of the day was pleasant. The Library of Congress treated me to lunch, and took from me a priceless photograph of William Grant Still conducting the Black Swan Orchestra, in return for which their agent promised to send several copies of the photo for my own use.

After that, I waited. Months passed and no copies of the photograph arrived. My follow-up letters to the librarian were not answered. The Library of Congress made no move to send for the Still tapes, microfilm or recorded interview. What had happened? Had someone said, "You must not admit that composer?" I began to have visions of the William Grant Still files disappearing from the Library mysteriously. It appeared as if the old intrigue, professional jealousy and detraction continued to cast a shadow over our lives, ignoring and shutting us out.

However, my unsubstantiated fears were eased by the ongoing success of WILLIAM GRANT STILL MUSIC. My father's dear friend, Christian Dupriez, a commentator for Radio Belgium, indicated in a letter to me that the validity of my father's efforts had been borne out after all. "Your father," he said, "was one of the greats current in our grasp, something human, embracing race and culture in the music of a culture. For me, he was an unbelievable and radiating personality, representing a complete way of being—he was intellectually, morally and spiritually a synthesis of two good worlds."

With the confidence of Dupriez beside me, I thought of my mother's manuscript. Perhaps the best way to vindicate the music was to let the composer's story be heard. Since my mother's biography had not been written from a journalistic point of view, but as a personal memoir, readers would see in it the endearing humanness of William Grant Still and his wife. They were, after all, full of affability, gentleness, and intense compassion. They were guileless because they were idealistic, and loved because they were loving. I decided to release the book for publication.

Later, I found in my father's papers, many sets of predictions from various psychics over the years, in which the promise was clear: "The Big Break will come, and your enemies will be confounded. Publishers and recording companies will seek you out. Everything will be taken. Meanwhile, your story must be told."

Appendix 1

A GLOSSARY OF TERMS

Throughout the notes, members of the Negro race are referred to as Negroes, the term preferred by both Still and Verna Arvey.

Africa. An orchestral work written by Still in 1928. Its three sections are entitled "Land of Peace," "Land of Romance," and "Land of Superstition."

Afro-American Symphony. William Grant Still's first symphony and his most performed work. Written in 1930, it is the first major work by a Negro. In four movements, the work is noted for its blues idioms. Excerpts from the poems of Paul Laurence Dunbar precede each movement. Of interest is Still's use of the banjo in the third movement (so far as is known, this is the first use of the banjo in a major symphonic work. The banjo, with four or five strings, has long been an instrument associated with Negro music, having been brought to the U.S. by slaves from West Africa).

air-check. A tape or videotape recording made of a broadcast as it actually occurs on the air.

ASCAP (American Society of Composers, Authors, and Publishers) is a society founded in 1914 by Victor Herbert mainly to protect copyrights and performing rights.

Blues. Type of American popular music, both instrumental and vocal, with roots in Negro work songs and spirituals. Traceable history begins with the "Jelly Roll Blues" by Jelly Roll Morton in 1905, followed by the "Memphis Blues" by W. C. Handy in 1912. Basic features are: slow tempo; groups of 12 measures instead of the usual 8 or 16; frequent seventh chords; use of portamento and pitches which lie between major and minor; melodic qualities found in spirituals, especially the frequent use of the minor third; and the use of the "break," a brief improvised instrumental cadenza of about two measures and marked by syncopation.

Capital Hill School succeeded Union School in 1902 as Little Rock's School for Negroes. It was replaced by M. W. Gibbs School in 1907. It was located at 11th and Wolfe.

Cole and Johnson Shows. Those written and produced by Robert Cole (1863–1911), J. Rosamond Johnson (1873–1954), and James Weldon Johnson. In 1898, Cole presented New York with its first all-Negro full-length musical comedy, entitled *A Trip to Coontown*. In 1901, he teamed with the Johnson brothers to produce numerous shows, among which were *The Shoo-Fly Regiment* (1906) and *The Red Moon* (1908).

Composers' Guild. See International Composers' Guild.

Dinah. Broadway musical of 1923, produced by Irvin C. Miller, who also wrote the book. Lyrics and music are by Tim Brymn.

Dixie to Broadway. A New York show of 1924. The book was by Walter De Leon, Tom Howard, Lew Leslie, and Sidney Lazarus. Music by George W. Meyer and Arthur Johnston. Cast included Florence Mills, Sheldon Brooks, Hamtree Harrington, and Will Vodery. In the pit was the Plantation Orchestra.

The Etude. Music periodical, (Philadelphia, 1883–1957).

FEPC (The Fair Employment Practices Commission). The FEPC was created by President Franklin Roosevelt in 1941, but allowed to lie dormant because of World War II. When Truman became president, he showed great courage by openly seeking congressional support for the FEPC, which was the first federal commitment to a policy of racial equality in employment.

Gibbs School (M. W. Gibbs School). Replaced Capital Hill School in 1907 as Little Rock's school for Negroes. Located at 18th and

Ringo, it served until 1930, when Dunbar High School opened. M. W. Gibbs is now an intermediate school.

Hansel and Gretel. Opera in three acts by Engelbert Humperdinck.

International Composers' Guild. An organization formed in 1921 in New York by Edgar Várèse and Carlos Salzedo to promote contemporary music. Membership was open to composers who performed their own music. In 1923, some members broke away to form the League of Composers. The Guild disbanded in 1927.

La Guiablesse. Ballet written by William Grant Still in 1927. First performed at the Eastman School of Music in 1933. The ballet is based on a legend of Martinique. It tells of an evil spirit, La Guiablesse, appearing in the guise of a beautiful woman, who places Adon under a magic spell of exotic beauty and lures him to the mountains above the sea. On a high cliff the spirit reveals itself in its hideous form, and fear causes the man to leap to his death. The story includes the romance of the village maiden, Yzore, who attempts to save Adon from La Guiablesse in typical Martinique tradition.

La Revue Musicale. A music periodical published in Paris, France (1920–40, 1946–49, and 1952–   ).

League of Composers. An organization founded in 1923 in New York by members of the International Composers' Guild to promote contemporary music. Merged with the International Society for Contemporary Music in 1954. The league commissioned more than 110 works by American and European composers, including Aaron Copland, Bela Bartok, Samuel Barber, and William Grant Still.

Musical Courier. Music periodical (Philadelphia, 1880–   ).

Old California is a programmatic work written by William Grant Still in 1941 to commemorate the 160th birthday of the city of Los Angeles. It portrays Indian beginnings, the Spanish occupation, and the coming of the American.

Opera, Concert and Symphony (later *Counterpoint*). Music periodical (San Francisco, 1934–1953), 18 vols.

Phylon. Formerly the *Phylon Quarterly.* The Atlantic University review of race and culture (1940–   ).

PM. A New York City daily newspaper which existed from 1940–1949.

Poem for Orchestra. Written by William Grant Still in 1944. It was inspired by the concept of a world being reborn spiritually after a period of darkness and desolation.

Quadrille. A French dance of the early century which gained popularity in the United States. The music consisted of five figures with alternating 6/8 and 2/4 meters. Normally danced by two to four couples moving in a square.

Quick-step. A march very popular in 19th century America. It was heard regularly as a part of ballroom dances which began with a grand march played as couples promenaded around the room. In addition, the quick-step march was heard between dances and at intermissions.

Rhythm Boys. A quartet of 1928–29 which included Paul Whiteman, Harry Barris, Bing Crosby, and Al Rinker.

Sahdji. Ballet written by William Grant Still in 1930. The story is based on an African legend. There is a chorus which sings constantly, providing a text connoting incidents in the action. There is also a chanter who recites old African proverbs. Sahdji is the favorite wife of the Chieftain, Konumbju. She betrays the chief through infatuation for his nephew and heir, Mrabo. Konumbju is killed while on a hunting expedition. Mrabo, intimidated by the Medicine Man, repudiates Sahdji, who vows to die when the body of Konumbju is brought back to the village. The ballet closes with the death of Sahdji, who stabs herself with a sacrificial dagger.

"St. Louis Blues." Probably the best known of the blues written by W. C. Handy, who also wrote the "Memphis Blues," "Beale Street Blues," and others. In a letter to William Grant Still, dated August 31, 1927, Handy expressed his profound gratitude for the role Still and Don Vorhees had played in making "St. Louis Blues" a standard, and thanked Still also for being the first to arrange and record a fantasy or symphonic version of that tune.

Shuffle Along. Broadway musical of 1921. Produced by the Nikko Producing Company (John Scholl, Al Mayer, Flournoy E. Miller, Aubrey Lyles, Noble Sissle, and Eubie Blake). Book by Flournoy Miller and Aubrey Lyles. Music and lyrics by Noble Sissle and Eubie Blake. Stage director was Walter Brooks. Dances by Lawrence Deas and Charles Davis. Musical arrangements by William Vodery. Orchestra directed by Eubie Blake. For the 1930 edition, the music was written by James P. Johnson and Thomas "Fats" Waller. Staging by Irvin C. Miller.

Stormy Weather. Film produced in 1943, lightly based on the career of Bill Robinson. A fast moving revue, it starred Bill Robinson, Lena Horne, Fats Waller, Cab Calloway, Flournoy Miller, Eddie Anderson, Ada Brown, Dooley Wilson, and Dathering Dunham and her dancers.

The Woodville Massacres. Woodville, Mississippi. Woodville is located in Wilkinson County, in southwest Mississippi, approximately 40 miles south of Natchez. It is one of the oldest counties in Mississippi, dating from the French occupation of adjoining Adams County.

During the reconstruction period which followed the War Between the States, the black population of Wilkinson County outnumbered the white population by a ratio of more than three to one.

The massacres cited by the author occurred on May 12–13, 1875, during historic elections which ignited riots and countless allegations of fraud and denial of basic civil rights.

Owing to the many reports of widespread violence and fraud, the United States Senate, on March 31, 1876, ordered an inquiry into the 1875 election in Mississippi. The lengthy report of testimony from citizens of Woodville and Wilkinson County describes the brutal killings (some seven by hanging) of as many as 50 black citizens, along with a variety of fraudulent acts.

For more details, see Jones, J. H. "Reconstruction in Wilkinson County," in *Publications of the Mississippi Historical Society*, Vol. VIII, 1904; and *Reports of Committees of the Senate of the United States*, 1875–76, three volumes.

Union School. Built in 1877 as the first school for Negroes in Little Rock. Located at 6th and State, it was replaced by Capital Hill School in 1902.

USS *Kroonland*. Passenger ship built in 1902. The U.S. Navy equipped the *Kroonland* with guns in 1917 and pressed the ship into military duty. Although the ship was torpedoed by a German U-boat in May of 1917, the torpedo did not explode. In 1918, the *Kroonland* was taken over by the U.S. Army and converted to troop transport. After the war, *Kroonland* shuttled across the Atlantic returning American veterans.

Appendix 2

WHO'S WHO IN THE LIFE OF
WILLIAM GRANT STILL

Adams, Sherman (1899–   ). American political figure. Served in Congress. Speaker of the House in 1943–44. Governor of New Hampshire from 1949–1953. Assistant to President Dwight Eisenhower from 1953–58.

Adams, Stanley (1907–   ). American author and composer. Director of ASCAP, 1943–   , 1953–1956, and 1959–1980.

Anderson, Marian (1902–   ). American Negro contralto; In 1939 she became a center of national attention when she was forbidden to sing at Constitution Hall in Washington, D.C. As a protest against racial discrimination, a distinguished group of citizens headed by Eleanor Roosevelt sponsored her concert at the Lincoln Memorial (1939). It drew some 75,000 persons. She was the first Negro to be a permanent member of the Metropolitan Opera Company. On her 75th birthday Congress passed a resolution to strike a gold medal in her honor.

Andrews, George Whitfield (1861–1932). American organist. One of the founders of the American Guild of Organists.

Ardoyno, Dolores. American opera director. General Manager of Opera South in Jackson, Mississippi (1973–80). General Manager of Baton Rouge Opera (1980–   ).

Armstrong, Daniel Louis "Satchmo" (1900–1971). Negro American jazz trumpeter and singer. Studied music at the Colored Waifs' Home for Boys, and learned to play the trumpet by listening to jazz performers from the streets of New Orleans. Played in the bands of King Oliver, Kid Ory, Fate Marable and Fletcher Henderson. Led a series of his own bands, including the early groups Hot Five and

Hot Seven. Among the most recorded of all jazz artists; his auto-biography is entitled *Satchmo: My Life in New Orleans.*

Astor, Mary (1906–). American actress.

Baker, Josephine (1906–1975). American Negro singer and enter-tainer. Left home at the age of 13 to join a touring show. At 15 years of age, she became a member of the chorus of *Shuffle Along.* In 1958, she staged her musical biography as *Paris Mes Amours.* Two autobiographies are published: *Les Memoires de Josephine Baker* (1927) and *Voyages et Aventures de Josephine Baker* (1931).

Balasz, Frederic (1920–). Hungarian-American conductor.

Bales, Richard (1915–). American conductor.

Barbirolli, Lady Evelyn Rothwell (1911–). British oboe virtuoso. Wife of Sir John Barbirolli. Appeared as soloist in recitals and with symphony orchestras all over the world. Also known as an accom-plished chamber player. Her Zephyr Trio and Camden Trio were popular attractions. Many works for oboe were written or arranged for her.

Barbirolli, Sir John (1899–1970). English conductor. Studied at Trin-ity College and at the Royal Academy of Music. Made his debut in Queen's Hall as a cellist at the age of 11. Achieved recognition when he conducted the London Symphony Orchestra, substituting for Sir Thomas Beecham. Renowned for his performances of works by Elgar, Sibelius, Brahms, and Mahler. Made several transcriptions for orchestra, and wrote an oboe concerto on themes by Pergolesi (dedicated to his wife, Evelyn Rothwell, the oboist).

Barrere, Georges (1876–1944). French flute virtuoso. Founded the Barrere Little Symphony (1914).

Barthe, Richmond (1901–). American painter and sculptor. In the Harmon Exhibit of 1928. Works include "Booker T. Washington,"

"Paul Lawrence Dunbar," "The Blackberry Woman," "The Harmonica Player," and "The African Dancer," which hangs in the Whitney Museum of American Art (New York).

Bartok, Bela (1881–1945). Hungarian composer. His early works and orchestration throughout his life bear the marks of French impressionism. Became devoted to folk music with its primitive rhythms and melodies. He has been proclaimed a national hero in Hungary where there are numerous monuments including streets and boulevards named for him.

Bean, Orson. American actor and comedian. Born Dallas Frederick Burrows. Began as a nightclub performer. Made his stage debut in *The Spider*, summer stock. Panelist on *To Tell the Truth* and other panel shows. Founder-director of the Fifteenth St. School for Children.

Beglarian, Grant (1927–   ). American composer. Was for several years dean of the School of Performing Arts at the University of Southern California. Works include several compositions for orchestra, sonatas, and chamber music.

Benkert, George J. American violinist. Member of the first violin section of the Los Angeles Philharmonic (1920–1962).

Biddle, Francis (1886–1968). French born lawyer and governmental leader. Director of the Federal Reserve Bank. Judge, U.S. Circuit Court of Appeals. U.S. member of International Military Tribunal. Attorney General of the U.S.

Beiderbecke, Leon Bix (1903–1931). American jazz cornetist. Played cornet in various jazz groups in Chicago and St. Louis before joining the Paul Whiteman Band in 1928. Developed a distinct style of rhythmic lyricism. Wrote a number of piano pieces including "In a Mist." Was addicted to alcohol and died at the age of 28. Was the subject behind Dorothy Baker's semi-fictional biography *Young Man With a Horn*.

Bennett, Robert Russell (1894–1981). American composer and arranger. Premier orchestrator of musicals. Worked closely with George Gershwin, Jerome Kern, and Richard Rogers. Wrote operas, concerti, symphonies, and chamber music. He also reorchestrated Bizet's *Carmen* for the all-Negro production of *Carmen Jones* (1943).

Bernard, Robert (1900–1971). Swiss composer, writer and editor. Was for several years the editor of *La Revue Musicale*.

Bernstein, Leonard (1918–). American conductor, pianist, composer, and writer. He has conducted most of the world's major symphony orchestras, and was for years the conductor of the New York Philharmonic. He was the first American to conduct a regular performance at La Scala; his works include a mass, several symphonies (*Jeremiah Symphony*, *The Age of Anxiety*, etc.) ballets (*Fancy Free* and *Facsimile*), chamber works, a light one-act opera (*Trouble in Tahiti*), and the broadway musicals *On the Town*, *Wonderful Town*, *Candide*, and *West Side Story*.

Biracree, Thelma (1904–). American dancer and choreographer. Founded the Thelma Biracree School of Ballet in 1925. Affiliated with the Eastman School of Music for more than 20 years as a dancer and choreographer. Was premier dancer and choreographer for the first performances (at the Eastman School of Music) of three of William Grant Still's ballets: *La Guiablesse*, *Sahdji*, and *Miss Sally's Party*.

Blythe, Betty (1893–1972). American stage and screen actress. Was presented in 1938 with a special academy award for pioneering contributions to the motion picture industry. Appeared in such films as *Slander*, *Silver Horde*, *The Queen of Sheba*, *Disraeli*, *Tuxedo Junction*, *The Miracle Kid*, *The Chinese Cat*, *Abbott and Costello in Hollywood*, *Joe Palooka*, *The Undercover Woman*, and *My Fair Lady*.

Bolm, Adolf (1894–1951). Russian ballet dancer and choreographer.

Bontemps, Arna (1902–1973). American Negro playwright. Wrote, with Countee Cullen, the musical *The Saint Louis Woman*, an adaptation of *God Sends Sunday*. Wrote with Langston Hughes another musical entitled *When Jack Hollers*. Her play, *Free and Easy*, an adaptation of *Saint Louis Woman*, has been performed widely in the U.S. and Europe.

Boone, Charles S. Probably the father of the early childhood friend of William Grant Still. Mr. Boone was an engineer for the Iron Mountain Railway, and lived at 206 Ringo, Little Rock, Arkansas.

Borden, Olive (1906–1947). American actress; née Sybil Tinkle. Studied at a convent in Baltimore. Began in silent films as a Mack Sennett Bathing Beauty. Appeared in feature films as Tom Mix's leading lady. Starred in films directed by John Ford, Howard Hawks, and Allan Divan. Suffered problems from alcoholism, and died in a hotel for destitute women. Films include *The Happy Warrior*, *The Overland Limited*, *The Yankee Señor*, *Yellow Fingers*, *Three Bad Men*, *Fig Leaves*, *The Monkey Talks*, *Gang War*, *Pigeon*, *The Eternal Woman*, *Love in the Desert*, *Wedding Ring*, *The Social Lion*, and *Hotel Variety*.

Boulanger, Nadia (1887–1979). French music teacher. Won the *Prix de Rome* in 1908. She was guest conductor with the Boston Symphony Orchestra and the New York Philharmonic. Her pupils include Jean Francaix, Aaron Copland, Leonard Bernstein, Roy Harris, Walter Piston, Eliot Carter, Harrison Kerr, Bernard Rogers, and Virgil Thomson.

Bradley, Thomas (1917–   ). Negro American political leader. Served 21 years as a member of the Los Angeles Police Department. Los Angeles Councilman (1963–1971). Elected Mayor of Los Angeles in 1973.

Brant, LeRoy V. (1891–1969). American organist and pianist. Descendent of Mohawk Indian Chief Thayendenaga. Founded the San Jose Municipal Chorus. His 56 year career earned him the title of

"San Jose's Music Man." Composed numerous works for keyboard instruments.

Brently, Florence Cadrez (1910–   ). Recording secretary of the Los Angeles office of the American Federation of Musicians, Local 747 (1938–53) and Los Angeles A.F. of M., Local 47 (1953–61); past president of the Western conference of the A.F. of M.

Brice, Carol (1918–   ). American Negro contralto. Was the first Negro to receive the Walter Naumberg Award (1943). Made her debut at Town Hall (New York) in 1944. Appeared in several musicals, including *The Hot Mikado, Finian's Rainbow, Showboat,* and *Gentlemen Be Seated,* in Truman Capote's *The Grass Harp,* and in George Gershwin's *Porgy and Bess.* Her recordings include Manuel de Falla's "El Amor Brujo"; and Gustav Mahler's "Songs of a Wayfarer". In 1971 she joined the faculty of the University of Oklahoma. In 1977, she and her husband Thomas Carey were named Oklahoma Musicians of the Year.

Bronson, Betty (1906–1971). American actress. Gained stardom in 1924 when Sir James Barrie selected her to play the title role in the first film version of *Peter Pan.* Starred in many silent films and early talkies. Retired in the early 1930's to marry a wealthy southerner. Returned once in 1937 to appear in a western movie with Gene Autry. Reemerged in the 1960's to play character roles. Films include: *Not So Long Ago, The Golden Princess, Ben Hur, Paradise, Everybody's Acting, The Cat's Pajamas, Paradise for Two, Open Range, The Singing Fool, One Stolen Night,* and *The Locked Door.*

Brown, Hallie Q. (1849–1949). Negro American educator. Graduated from Wilberforce College in 1873. Taught elocution, English, and public speaking at Wilberforce College (1900–1922).

Browning, Ivan Harold. American Negro singer, actor, and entertainer. Member of the renowned Four Harmony Kings quartet which appeared in the original *Shuffle Along* (1921). Toured with various vaudeville shows on the Keith Circuit, and extensively in Europe. Played the romantic lead in *Shuffle Along* opposite Little Gee, with whom he sang the first love duet by a Negro man and woman on a U.S. stage. Appeared as the leading man in the Noble Sissle-Eubie Blake show, *Chocolate Dandies* (1924). Had a successful career in Europe for several years. Settled in Hollywood, where he appeared in numerous films, including *Sunrise at Campobello*. Made several appearances on the Amos and Andy television show of the 1950's.

Bryden, Eugene S. Opera director. Directed in Salzburg, Austria. Directed for New York City Opera, 1945–50, the following operas: *The Bartered Bride, I Pagliacci, Madame Butterfly, Cavalleria Rusticana, The Pirates of Penzance,* and the world premiere of William Grant Still's *The Troubled Island.*

Buck, Edward Eugene "Gene" (1885–1957). American lyricist, sketch writer, and director. Began writing lyrics for the *Ziegfeld Follies* in 1912. Became Florenz Ziegfeld's assistant. Served as president of ASCAP from 1924–1941. Collaborated with such noted songwriters as Jerome Kern, Victor Herbert, and Rudolf Friml. Wrote for the *Ziegfeld Follies* of 1916–1918, 1922–1924, 1926–1927; directed the *Follies* of 1931.

Bunche, Ralph Johnson (1904–1971). American Negro educator and governmental leader. Long and distinguished career in the Department of State and the United Nations. Served on special assignment to Paris, Dumbarton Oaks, London, Palestine, Republic of the Congo, and Yemen. Awarded the Nobel Peace Prize (1950).

Burleigh, Henry T. (1866–1949). American Negro singer and songwriter. Served as baritone soloist at Saint George's Church, NY, for 52 years. Songs included "Love's Garden," "Memory," "A Prayer," "Deep River," "Saracen Songs," "One Year," and "Little Mother of Mine." The NAACP awarded him the Spingarn Medal in 1916 for highest achievement by an American of African descent.

Cadman, Charles Wakefield (1881–1946). American composer. Was a recognized authority on American Indian music. Helped to found the Hollywood Bowl Concerts. His opera *Shawnewis* (*The Robin Woman*) was produced by the Metropolitan Opera Company in 1918. Wrote cantatas and radio plays, suites, works for piano and violin, and over 180 songs which include the popular "At Dawning."

Calvin, Dolores. Negro American journalist and publisher. Together with Willa Lee Calvin (her mother) and Bernice Calvin (her sister), she operated a syndicated news service for more than 100 Negro newspapers. The Calvin News Service was a strong advocate of William Grant Still.

Carpenter, John Alden (1876–1951). American composer. Studied with Edward Elgar in Rome; was made a Knight of the French Legion of Honor (1921). In 1947 he was awarded the Gold Medal of the National Institute of Arts and Letters. His works employ jazz idioms and impressionistic techniques. Compositions include a concertino for piano and orchestra, several symphonies, works for chorus and orchestra, and several suites, including *Adventures in a Perambulator*.

Carrillo, Julian (1875–1965). Mexican composer. Widely known for his experimentations and works using fractional tones. Constructed special instruments, including a harp-zither with 97 strings to the octave. His concertino for fractional tones was performed by Leopold Stokowski and the Philadelphia Orchestra. Works include operas, symphonies, a triple concerto and numerous chamber pieces.

Carroll, Earl (1893–1948). American producer, director, composer and lyricist. Produced the *Earl Carroll Vanities* which rivaled the *Ziegfeld Follies* from 1923–1928, 1930–1932, and 1940.

Casella, Alfredo (1883–1943). Italian composer, pianist, conductor, and writer. Wrote several operas, symphonies, concerti for piano, organ, and violin, chamber and vocal work. Conducted the Boston

Pops (1927–1929). Won the Coolidge Prize in 1934. Returned to Italy in 1938, where he remained until his death.

Cassidy, Tom. Staff member of Los Angeles station KFAC. Served for 40 years as host of the *Evening Concert*.

Castelnuovo-Tedesco, Mario (1895–1968). Italian composer. Left Italy because of political events and in 1939 settled in the U.S., living in Hollywood. His works include operas, concerti, overtures, chamber music, choral works, songs, and music for films.

Chadwick, George Whitefield (1854–1931). American composer. Wrote operas, operettas, symphonies, overtures, string quartets, works for soloists, choir and orchestra, piano, organ, choir and over 100 songs.

Chapin, Katherin Garrison. Wife of Francis Biddle, Attorney General of U.S.

Chase, Gilbert (1906–). American critic and musicologist. Books include *The Music of Spain* (1941) and *America's Music* (1955).

Chase, Ilka (1903–1978). American actress, novelist, and playwright. Known primarily as a society figure, columnist, and author of several novels, volumes of memoirs, and one play. Films include: *South Sea Rose, The Gay Diplomat, The Animal Kingdom, Stronger Than Desire, No Time For Love, It Should Happen to You, The Big Knife,* and *Ocean's Eleven*.

Chavez, Carlos (1899–1978). Mexican composer and conductor. Returned to Mexico after living in France. Organized the Orquesta Sinfónica. Was director of the National Conservatory of Mexico, and of the National Institute of Fine Arts. His *Xochipilli Macuilx-ochitl* is scored for traditional Indian instruments.

Cherokee Bill. Real name: Crawford Goldsby. He first killed a Negro man in a fight. Then killed a deputy sheriff, his sister's husband, a railroad agent, a train conductor, a bystander at a hold-up, and a prison guard during an escape. He was convicted of murder and, in spite of an appeal to the Arkansas Supreme Court, was hanged in Ft. Smith, Arkansas, on March 17, 1896.

Cleef, Edward Van (1944–   ). American broadcaster.

Copland, Aaron (1900–   ). American composer. He is best known for his ballets (*Rodeo, El Salón Mexico, Billy the Kid*, and *Appalachian Spring*, for which he received the Pulitzer Prize in 1945).

Costello, Maurice (1877–1950). American actor. A Broadway matinee idol for 15 years. Billed as "The Dimpled Darling". One of the first important stage actors to turn to the screen. Biggest triumph came in the film *A Tale of Two Cities* (1911).

Covarrubias, Miguel. Mexican artist. Illustrator in New York City before returning to Mexico in 1926.

Cowell, Henry (1897–1965). American composer. Founded the *New Music Quarterly* in 1927. Was an organizer of the Pan American Association of Composers. One of America's most prolific composers, Cowell's more than 1000 works include numerous symphonies and other works for orchestra, chamber music, choral works, and pieces for band. His *Hymn and Fuguing Tune*, based on fuguing tunes by Willian Billings, is highly successful. Among his several books is *Charles Ives and His Music* (1955).

Craft, Lois Adele. American composer, author, and harpist. Soloist and first harp with the Kansas City Philharmonic. Harpist with 20th Century Fox Motion Picture Co. Las Vegas entertainer. Played the world premiere of William Grant Still's harp concerto. Compositions include: *Contemporary Mary, Foralones*, and *So Obvious* (all for harp).

Craig, Tom (1909–   ). American painter. Works are represented in

Seattle Art Museum, Metropolitan Museum (New York), and Los Angeles Museum.

Creston, Paul (1906–). American composer. He was elected president of the National Association for American Composers and Conductors in 1956; his music has strong melodic lines and often dance-like rhythms and has been performed by most of the leading orchestras and ensembles in the U.S. Included are several symphonies, solo pieces for nearly every instrument, chamber and choral works.

Cullen, Countee (1903–1946). American Negro poet, novelist, and anthologist. Won numerous awards for his poetry, including the Harmon Foundation Literary Award.

Cunningham, David. American governmental leader. Los Angeles councilman from the 10th district. Recommended William Grant Still for several citations. Responsible for turning an old fire house into the William Grant Still Community Center in Los Angeles. Still's music was performed at the dedication.

Dalton Gang. Group of American desperados which was formed and led by Robert Renick Dalton (1870–92), and which included his brothers Emmett and Grattan, along with Bill Doolin and several others.

Dawson, William Levi (1898–). American Negro composer. His Folk Symphony was performed by Leopold Stokowski and the Philadelphia Orchestra in 1934.

De Bose, Tourgee (1893–1971). American Negro pianist and pedagog. Served as a member of the faculty at Bethune-Cookman College (Florida); and as chairman of the music departments at Talladega College (Ala.); and Southern University (La.).

Dent, Albert (1904–). Negro American educator. Served as president of Dillard University (1941–1969).

de Paur, Leonard (1918–). American composer and conductor. Conducted the Orchestra of America. Among his compositions is the song *Glory Manager*.

Dessalines, Jean Jacques (c.1758–1806). Negro emperor of Haiti (1804–1806). Born a slave. Served under Touissant L'Overture in wars of liberation. Named governor of Haiti in 1801. Crowned Emperor Jacques I. Was murdered because of his depotic rule.

Dett, Robert Nathanial (1882–1943). Canadian-American Negro composer and writer. Born in Quebec, Canada. Wrote two successful oratorios: *The Charist Jubilee* (1921), and *The Ordering of Moses* (1937), along with numerous choruses and works for piano. His *In the Bottoms Suite* (piano) contains the popular *Juba Dance*.

Dixon, Charles Dean (1915–1976). American Negro conductor. Was the first Negro to conduct the New York Philharmonic.

Dobbs, Mattiwilda (1925–). American Negro coloratura soprano. Made her debut at Town Hall (New York) in 1954. Sang at La Scala in Milan, at the Metropolitan Opera, and with the San Francisco Opera.

Dominguez, Albert. Pianist. Recorded the complete piano works of William Grant Still.

Dorr, Donald (1934–). American opera director. Artistic Director of Opera South in Jackson, Mississippi (1973–80). Artistic Director of Baton Rouge Opera (1980–).

Dos Passos, John Roderigo (1896–1970). American author. Works include: *One Man's Initiation*; *Three Soldiers*; *Manhattan Transfer*; two trilogies: *U.S.A.* and *District of Columbia*; *Most Likely to Succeed*; *The Great Days*; and *Midcentury*.

Downes, Olin (1886–1955). American music critic. Served as music critic of the Boson *Post* from 1906–1924, and of the New York

Times from 1924 until his death in 1955. Books include *The Lure of Music* (1918), and *Symphonic Broadcasts* (1935). Contributed several articles to the *Musical Quarterly*, the *Music Review*, and other journals. Compiled and annotated *Ten Operatic Masterpieces from Mozart to Prokofiev* (1952).

Dragon, Carmen (1914–   ). American conductor. Widely recognized for his arrangements of light music. Conducts regularly at the Hollywood Bowl.

Dreyfuss, Henry (1904–1972). American artist and designer. Served for five years as director of the Strand Theater (New York). Designed settings for *Hold Everything, Fine and Dandy, The Gang's All Here, The Cat and the Fiddle, This Is New York, Blind Mice, Sweet Stranger, An Affair of State*, and *Paths of Glory*.

Duncan, Todd (1903–   ). American Negro baritone. Created the role of Porgy in George Gershwin's opera *Porgy and Bess* (1935). Appeared with many major symphony orchestras and on stage in London and across the U.S. Was the first Negro male singer to appear with a major opera company when he performed in *Pagliacci* and *Carmen* with the New York City Opera in 1945. In 1931, he began a long-lived teaching career at Howard University.

Dunham, Katherine (1910–   ). American Negro dancer, choreographer, and songwriter. Called "the mother of Afro-American dance." Founded such dance companies as Ballet Negre and the Negro Dance Group. Pursued research in the West Indies and toured throughout the world with her dance groups. Appeared in Broadway musicals and on radio and television shows. Wrote songs for such films as *Mambo*. Her pupils include Marlon Brando, José Ferrer, and Eartha Kitt.

Dupriez, Christian (1922–   ). Belgian radio program writer, pianist, composer, and musicologist. Radio commentor for Radiodiffusion Nationale Belge. Championed the music of William Grant Still on Belgian radio. Works include: "Valse Pour la Grande Amie."

Ehrenburg, Ilya (1891–1967). Russian novelist and journalist. Among his translated works are *The Love of Jeanne Ney*, *The Tempering of Russia*, and many reports on World Wars I and II. Twice received the Stalin Prize (1942 and 1948).

Ellington, Edward Kennedy "Duke" (1899–1974). American jazz pianist and composer. He is known for his landmark recordings such as "Black and Tan Fantasy," "Mood Indigo," "Limehouse Blues," "Delta Serenade," "Echoes of Harlem," "Blue Goose," etc. Noteworthy among his more 2,000 compositions are "Mood Indigo," "Solitude," "Sophisticated Lady," "In a Sentimental Mood," "I Got It Bad and That Ain't Good," "Caravan," "Take the A Train," and "Black Brown and Beige." His 70th birthday was marked by a gala celebration at the White House at which time President Nixon presented him with the Presidential Medal of Freedom.

Evans, Mary Jane (1923–   ). American dramatic director and educator. Member of the faculty at California State University, Northridge, where she is professor and Departmental Chairperson.

Evans, Wilbur (1908–   ). American singer, actor, director and coach. Made his New York debut in Carnegie Hall in the *Merry Widow* (1942). Played in *The New Moon, Mexican Hayride, Up in Central Park, The Chocolate Soldier, South Pacific* (London), *The Beggars' Opera*, and *Man of La Mancha* (touring company). Appeared in two films: *Her First Romance*, and *Man with a Million*. Performed on radio in "Kent Sunday Evening Concerts," the "Original Show Boat Hour," "The Rudy Vallee Show," "Philco Hall of Fame" (all NBC), "Coca Cola Showtime" (CBS), on TV he appeared in "The Verdict Is Yours" (CBS), and "Sunday Night at the Palladium." Appeared at the Thunderbird Hotel in Las Vegas.

Fambro, Anna. Mother of Carrie Fambro and grandmother of William Grant Still. In the early 1900's, her Little Rock address was 912 W. 14th.

Fazenda, Louise (1889–1962). American actress. Married to film producer Hal Wallis. Played in vaudeville. Appeared in *The Cheese Special*, *The Summer Girls*, *His Precious Life*, *The Fog*, *The Gold Diggers*, *Hogan's Alley*, *The Red Mill*, *Alice in Wonderland*, *Ever Since Eve*, *First Lady*, *Swing Your Lady*, *Down on the Farm*, and *The Old Maid*.

Fetchit, Stepin (1892–   ). American Negro actor and comedian. Born Lincoln Theodore Perry. Began his film career in 1927. After years of retirement, he resumed his movie career with *Amazing Grace* (1974). Of the many roles he played on screen, he said, "Like Chaplin, I played the part of a simple, sincere, honest, and lovable character who won sympathy from an audience by being tolerant of those who hurt him so that he could do good for those he loved. Among his many films are: *In Old Kentucky*, *Showboat*, *Hearts in Dixie*, *Stand Up and Cheer*, *Carolina*, *Judge Priest*, *County Chairman*, *Helldorado*, *Charlie Chan in Egypt*, *Steamboat 'Round the Bend*, *Dimples*, *Love Is News*, *Miracle in Harlem*, *Zenobia*, *Bend of the River*, *The Sun Shines Bright*, and *Won Ton Ton, the Dog Who Saved Hollywood*.

Fetta, Frank. American conductor. Conducted the Los Angeles Chamber Ensemble, *Opera-a-la-Carte*, Marina Del Ray-Westchester Symphony, recordings of Igor Stravinsky for Columbia Records.

Fields, Lew (1867–1941). American actor, producer, and director. Known as the partner of Joe Weber in "Dutch" comics which were part of a series of burlesque musicals which they presented for eight years at the Weber and Fields Broadway Music Hall. From 1920–28, he produced six musicals with scores by Rodgers and Hart, with librettos by his son Herbert Fields. He was also the father of librettists Dorothy Fields and Joseph Fields. Among his productions were *Dearest Enemy*, *A Connecticut Yankee*, *Helter Skelter*, *About Town*, *Poor Little Ritz Girl*, *Hit the Deck*, and *Present Arms*.

Finley, Lorraine Noel (born 1899). Canadian composer and author. Work includes Symphony in D. Sonatas for violin, clarinet. *Voices of Freedom* (27 songs). *Birth of Beauty* (cantata). English translations of National Anthems of the United Nations and Associated Powers. *When I Love You Best, Herons, Questions, Bondage, Where Are the Years, Grey Veils,* and a ballet, *Persian Miniature.*

Fitch, Theodore F. American composer. Member of ASCAP. Served as chairman of the Awards Committee for the National Association for American Composers and Conductors (1950).

Flaig, Eleanore. American dancer and writer. Protege of Pavley and Oukrainsky. Soloist and premier dancer with the Chicago Civic Opera, San Francisco Grand Opera, and Los Angeles Grand Opera. Wrote the story to Mary Carr Moore's opera *Legende Provencial, World History of the Dance,* and poetry.

Ford, Harrison (1894–1957). American actor. Appeared in more than 50 films including *The Mysterious Mrs. M, A Pair of Silk Stockings, A Heart to Let, When Love Comes, Shadows, Vanity Fair, Maytime, Bright Lights of Broadway, Proud Flesh, That Royal Girl, The Girl in the Pullman, A Woman Against the World, Three Week Ends, The Flattering Word,* and *Advice to Husbands.*

Foster, William Zebulon (1881–1961). Labor organizer and political leader. Leading figure in American Communism. Involved in his early years in labor issues. Became a "Wobbly" organizer, and leader of the American Federation of Labor (AFL). Served as secretary-general of the American Communist Party from c. 1921–1930. Was the Communist Party candidate for president in 1924, 1928, and 1932. Chairman of the American Communist Party (1945–56). Writings include many pamphlets and essays. Books: *The Great Steel Strike and Its Lessons, The Russian Revolution, Misleaders of Labor, Towards Soviet America, From Bryan to Stalin,* and *Pages from a Worker's Life.*

Gagnard, Frank (1929–). American journalist. Studied at North Texas State University. Music Critic of the New Orleans *Times Picayune* (1959–).

Gilbert, L. Wolfe (1886–1970). Russian born composer, writer and publisher. Began career singing in amateur nights before becoming a vaudeville entertainer. Toured with John L. Sullivan. Wrote for films and Eddie Cantor's radio show. Many appearances on radio and television. Songs include *Waiting for the Robert E. Lee, Lucky Lindy, Mama Inez, Oh Katharina, I Miss My Swiss, Marta, Green Eyes, The Peanut Vendor, Down Yonder, Maria My Own, Lily of the Valley,* and *Chiquita.* His autobiography is entitled *Without Rhyme or Reason.*

Glaz, Herta (1914–). Austrian contralto. Made her debut with the Metropolitan Opera Co. in 1942. She is known especially for her appearances in Wagnerian roles.

Goldman, Richard Franko (1910–). American bandmaster and composer; succeeded his father, Edwin Franko Golfman, as conductor of the Goldman Band; he has written numerous works for band and chamber music for winds, has published books *The Band's Music* and *The Concert Band.* For many years he was editor of the *Juilliard Revue.*

Gomezanda, Antonio (1894–). Mexican pianist and composer. His works include an "Aztec ballet," *Xiuhtzitzquilo, Fantasia Mexicana* for piano and orchestra, and numerous piano pieces.

Goossens, Eugene (1893–1962). English conductor and composer. He composed prolifically in many genres (opera, ballet, theater, symphony, concerti, solo works, and chamber music). He was knighted in 1955.

Gould, Morton (1913–). American composer. His music, much of which employs American themes, includes several symphonies, concerti, works for band, and sonatas. Especially noteworthy are *Cowboy Rhapsody, Spirituals* (for orchestra), *Symphony on Marching Tunes,* and concerti for piano and for violin.

Gould, Norma. American dancer and choreographer. Appeared in Dance Theater Ceremonials in the 1930's. First choreographer to present a complete ballet at the Hollywood Bowl (1929). In 1932 she founded a dance theater to assist young dancers from various countries. Operated a dance studio in Los Angeles.

Graham, Martha (1900–   ). American dancer and choreographer. Devised a technique of modern dance that could be taught as the basis for the dancer's own personal use in different styles. Founded the Graham School (of dance) in New York in 1941. Produced many successful ballets and dance programs often based on mythological or psychological subjects. Many of her pupils gained renown and formed their own companies.

Griffis, Elliot (c. 1890–   ). American composer. Brother of American ambassador Stanton Griffis. Wrote piano pieces and operettas. His *Ostinato* was performed over CBS.

Gruenberg, Louis (1884–1964). American composer. His works often embrace jazz idioms. His opera, *The Emperor Jones* (after Eugene O'Neill's play), was produced by the Metropolitan Opera in 1933 and won the David Bispham medal.

Grunn, Homer. California composer of children's music.

Guthrie, James K. American conductor. Conducted Young Audiences concerts in Los Angeles. Conductor of the San Jose Symphony. Instrumental in William Grant Still serving on the Board of Directors for Young Audiences in Los Angeles.

Haas, Robert Bartlett. American educator. Editor of *William Grant Still and the Fusion of Cultures in American Music*. Publications include *A Primer for the Gradual Understanding of Gertrude Stein*, translations from the German on Kurt Schwitters, and books and articles about Psychodrama.

Hackely, E. Azalia (1867–1922). American Negro soprano. Following her retirement from a concert career, she traveled extensively throughout the U.S. conducting "Folksong Festivals" where she taught black communities to sing and appreciate Negro folksongs.

Hairston, Jester (1901–). American Negro choral conductor. Worked on the film *The Green Pastures* and later arranged choral music for more than 40 films, including *Lost Horizons* and *Duel in the Sun*. The U.S. Department of State sent him as a goodwill ambassador to Europe, Africa, Scandinavia, and Mexico. Prolific arranger of African and Japanese folksongs.

Halasz, Laszio (1905–). Hungarian conductor. Became an American citizen in 1943; conducted the St. Louis Grand Opera (1939–42); after conducting the New York City Opera Co. (1943–51), served as conductor of the Eastman Philharmonic Orchestra (1965–68). Was appointed program director of music at the State University of New York, Stony Brook, in 1971.

Hall, Frederick Douglas (1898–). American Negro organist and music educator. He composed works for voice, chorus and chorus with orchestra; founded the "Delta Rhythm Boys."

Handy, William Christopher (1873–1957). American Negro composer, father of the blues. Father and grandfather were ministers. Graduated from Alabama A&M in 1892. Learned to play the cornet and was soloist at the Chicago World's Fair in 1893. Wrote "Memphis," "St. Louis," "Yellow Dog," "Beale Street," and "Joe Turner Blues." His *Evolution of the Blues* was performed in the Metropolitan Opera House in 1924. Published anthologies include *Negro Spirituals and Songs: A Treasury of the Blues* (1926 and 1949), *Book of Negro Spirituals* (1938), *Negro Music and Musicians* (1944), *Negro Authors and Composers of the U.S.* (1936). Wrote an autobiography entitled *Father of the Blues* (1941).

Hanson, Howard (1896–1981). American composer, conductor, and educator. Won the American *Prix de Rome* in 1921. Became director of the Eastman School of Music in 1925. Initiated and conducted several significant series of concerts which introduced American works to audiences in the U.S. and Europe. Awarded the Pulitzer Prize for his Fourth Symphony (1944). Elected a member of the National Institute of Arts and Letters (1935). Compositions include several symphonies, concerti, choral works, chamber works, songs, a ballet, and the opera *Merry Mount*, commissioned by the Metropolitan Opera (1933–34).

Harris, Roy (1898–1979). American composer. Studied philosophy and economics at the University of California. Later studied composition with Nadia Boulanger of Paris. His works embrace virtually every genre except opera. There are numerous symphonies, ballets, concerti, choral and chamber works, pieces for band, and music for films.

Harrison, Richard Berry "De Lawd" (1864–1935). Canadian born Negro actor and educator. His parents had moved to Canada to escape slavery. Trained in elocution. Recited professionally on both the Behymer and Chautauqua circuits. Repertoire included recitations from Shakespeare, Poe, Kipling, and Dunbar. Taught at North Carolina A&T State University, where an auditorium is named in his honor. Selected in 1929 to play "De Lawd" in Marc Connelly's *Green Pastures*, a role he played some 2,000 times.

Harty, Sir Hamilton (1879–1941). Irish conductor and composer. Received his music education from his father. Was conductor of the Halle Orchestra for 13 seasons. Made his American debut in 1931. Was knighted in 1925. Works include *Irish Symphony*, *With the Wild Geese*, *Concerto for Violin and Orchestra*, and transcriptions of Handel's *Water Music* and *Fireworks Music*.

Haugh, John "Doc" (1910–   ). American governmental leader. Served many years in the Arizona Legislature where he was Speaker of the House. He and his wife Emily are leading patrons of the arts in Tucson.

Hemmer, Eugene (1929–   ). American composer and educator. Works include *The School Bus* (commissioned by Thor Johnson for the Cincinnati Symphony), *Introduction and Dance* for two pianos, *Remembrance of Things Past* for two pianos, *American Miniatures* for piano.

Hertz, Alfred (1872–1941). German conductor. Held positions as an opera conductor in Altenburg, Barmen-Elberfeld, and Breslau. Joined the Metropolitan Opera Co. as a conductor in 1902. Conducted the first American performance of Wagner. *Parsifal* (1903). Served as conductor of the San Francisco Symphony Orchestra from 1915–30. After 1930, he conducted concerts broadcast over radio (the Standard Symphony Hour) for another ten years. Initiated the Hollywood Bowl concerts in 1922. Was affectionately known as the "Father of the Hollywood Bowl."

Hindemith, Paul (1895–1963). German composer. Studied at the Hoch Conservatory in Frankfurt. Became concertmaster of the Frankfurt Opera (1915–23). Owing to conflict with Hitler's regime, he left Germany for Turkey where he taught at the conservatory in Ankara. Came to the U.S. in 1937. Joined the faculty at Yale University in 1940. Lectured at Harvard University in 1950–51. Returned to Germany in 1949 to conduct the Berlin Philharmonic in a program of his works. Received the Sibelius Award of $35,000 in 1954. As a master eclectic, he drew upon archaic, Baroque, classical and romantic materials which he mixed with atonality and a rebellious spirit. He championed *Gabrauchsmusik* and *Hausmusik*. Writing prolifically in nearly every genre, his works include operas, ballets, concerti, symphonies, soli, chamber and choral music, especially renowned is his opera *Mathis der Maler*.

Hines, Jerome (1921–). American bass. Studied chemistry at U.C.L.A. Made his debut at the Metropolitan Opera House in 1946. Scored a triumph when he sang the title role in *Boris Godunov* in Russia at the Bolshoi Theatre (Moscow) in 1962. Has played concerts and performed in opera houses and with major orchestras all over the world.

Houston, Elsie. Brazilian-American singer. Great grand niece of Sam Houston. Studied voice in Germany. Made her debut in Paris in 1927. Appeared in numerous recitals with Heitor Villa-Lobos. Came to the U.S. in 1938. Wrote a book entitled *Popular Songs of Brazil*.

Hughes, Langston (1902–67); American Negro poet. Wrote librettos or plays before librettos such as *Troubled Island* for William Grant Still, *The Barrier*, *De Organizer*, *Soul Gone Home*, and *Street Scene* (music by Kurt Weill). Musicals to which he contributed include *The Ballad of the Brown King*, *Black Nativity*, *Simply Heavenly*, and *Tambourines to Glory*. His books include *Famous Negro Music Makers*, and *The First Book of Jazz*.

Huizar, Candelario (1883–1970). Mexican composer. Served as librarian of the National Conservatory (Mexico City). His compositions feature Mexican folklore and themes.

Hurston, Zora Neale (1903–1960). American Negro playwright. Plays include *Color Struck*, *A Play in Four Scenes*, *The First One*, *Great Day* (with Langston Hughes), *Mule Bone: A Comedy of Negro Life in Three Acts*, *Polk Country*, *Spears*. Also collaborated with Clinton Fletcher and Tim Moore to write a musical entitled *Fast and Furious*.

Irish, Mrs. Leiland Atherton (Florence) (–1971). Affiliated with the Hollywood Bowl from its beginning in 1922. General Chairman (1926–29, 1934). Executive Vice-President and Chairman (1934–44). Leading patroness of the arts in Los Angeles.

Jackson, Howard M. (1900–). American composer. Songs include "Lazy Rhapsody," "Let's Be Frivolous," "He's Mine," "Hearts in Dixie," and "The First Spring Day."

Janssen, Werner (1899–1965). American composer and conductor. His concert of music by Sibelius won praise from Sibelius. Received the Finnish Order of the White Rose First Class, for contributions to Finnish music. Made his American debut with the New York Philharmonic (1934). Served as conductor of the Baltimore, Utah, Portland, San Diego, and Janssen Symphony Orchestras. His compositions include *New Years Eve in New York*, *Louisiana Suite*, *Foster Suite* (on tunes by Stephen Foster), chamber music, popular music, and music for film.

Jarboro, Caterina (1903–   ). American Negro soprano; made her debut in 1930, as *Aida*, at the Puccini Opera House in Milan. In 1933 she became the first Negro to perform with a major opera company in the United States when she sang the title role of *Aida* with the Opera of Chicago.

Johnson, Dorothy Vena (–1970). Negro American teacher and administrator. Principal of Garden Gate High School in Los Angeles. Founder and first president of the League of Allied Arts in Los Angeles.

Johnson, Hall (1888–1970). American Negro conductor and composer. Played violin and viola in *Shuffle Along*. Gained wide recognition with the Hall Johnson Choir, which toured widely and recorded for RCA. Was appointed choral director for the production of *The Green Pastures*, including both Broadway and film performances. Wrote a folk play entitled *Run Little Children*, which ran on Broadway for 126 performances and was later revived. Works include an Easter cantata, an operetta, and many arrangements of art songs and spirituals.

Johnson, James P. "Jimmy" (1891–1955). American Negro pianist, composer, and entertainer. Early ragtime pianist who later pioneered the Harlem stride style. Influenced later musicians such as "Fats" Waller. Toured in vaudeville shows. Accompanist for blues singer Bessie Smith. Began recording in the early 1920's. Wrote the music for all-Negro Broadway shows *Running Wild* and *Messin' Around*. Later played with Wild Bill Davison and Eddie Condon. Wrote tunes such as "Charleston," "Old Fashioned Love," and "If I Could Be With You." Compositions include: *African Dreams, Symphonie Harlem, Symphony in Brown, Piano Concerto in A Flat, Mississippi Moon, Symphonic Suite on St. Louis Blues, City of Steel, Improvisation on Deep River, Manhattan Street Scene* (ballet), and *Kitchen Opera*.

Johnson, Sargent Claude (1889–1967). American sculptor.

Jones, Isabel Morse (1892–1951). American writer. Music critic of the Los Angeles *Daily News* and the Los Angeles *Times* (1928–47). Author of numerous articles and one book.

Joseph, Danellen. Music teacher in the Los Angeles schools. Led a string quartet during the race riots of the 1960's.

Judson, Arthur (1891–1975). American concert manager. Served as dean of the Conservatory of Music at Denison University.

Kaufman, Lilian. Wife of American pianist Harry Kaufman (1894–1961). Widely known as an accompanist and performer of chamber music.

Kaufman, Louis (1905–). American violinist.

Kay, Ulysses Simpson (1917–). American Negro composer. Works include two operas, an oboe concerto, *Dance Calinda* (ballet), *Of New Horizons*, *Six Dances* for strings, *Song of Jeremiah* (cantata), *Three Pieces After Blake* for soprano and orchestra, and the film score for *The Quiet One*.

Kenyon, Doris (1897–). American actress. Played leads in numerous silent films opposite such stars as Rudolph Valentino, Thomas Meighan, Lewis Stone, and Milton Stills, who became the first of her four husbands.

Kessler, Maurice P. (1889–1970). Alsatian-American violinist.

Khrennikov, Tikhon (1913–). Russian composer. General Secretary of the Soviet Composers' Union since 1948. Works include several symphonies, the operas *Brothers* (renamed *In the Storm*), *Frol Skobeyev*, and *Mother*, a piano concerto, and many songs.

Knott, Walter (1889–1981). American businessman. Intense patriot and philanthropist. Established the Richard Henry Lee Award for Patriotism.

Korngold, Erich Wolfgang (1897–1957). Austrian composer. His youthful achievements as a composer and pianist created a sensation throughout Europe. He wrote and published a piano trio at the age of 12, moved to Hollywood in 1934, and became an American citizen in 1943. Works include several operas, sonatas for piano and violin, three string quartets, a piano concerto for the left hand alone, and a violin concerto. His opera *Die Tote Stadt* was produced at the Metropolitan Opera Company (1921).

Krueger, Karl (1894–   ). American conductor. Was conductor of the Seattle, Kansas City, and Detroit Symphony Orchestra.

La Guardia, Fiorello Henry (1882–1947). U.S. Congressman (1917–19, 1923–33). Mayor of New York City (1934–45). Fought for labor reforms in Congress. Executed vast programs for municipal improvements. Because of his first name, he was often called "the little flower."

Lange, Arthur (1889–1956). American composer, arranger, and author. Studied music privately. Arranged for several Broadway shows. Head of the department of music for MGM in 1929. Wrote several books including *Arranging for the Modern Dance Orchestra*, *Harmony and Harmonics*, and *Spectrotone Chart*. Won Academy Awards for "The Great Victor Herbert" and "The Great Ziegfeld." Among his songs are "America Here's My Boy," "We're Going Over," "In a Boat," and "In the Valley of the Moon," instrumental works include *Atoms for Peace*; *Antelope Valley*; Symphony No. 1; *Four Symphonic Murals*; *Divertimento for Strings*; *Big Trees*; *Mount Whitney*; and *Symphonette Spirituelle*.

Lange, Haus (1884–1960). German violinist and conductor. Served as assistant and associate conductor of the New York Philharmonic and Chicago Symphony Orchestras. Was conductor of the Albuquerque Civic Symphony.

Lantz, Walter (1900–   ). American animated cartoon producer. Began with Katzenjamer Kids in 1916. Produced the first Technicolor cartoons. Creator of Woody Woodpecker. Won an Academy Award in 1979. President of Walter Lantz Productions, Inc.

Laster, Georgia Ann (–1961). Negro American singer. Born in Little Rock, Arkansas. Won the Atwater Kent Foundation Prize in 1948. Appeared regularly in recitals and in radio programs in the U.S., Germany, South America, and the Carribean. Known for her performances of William Grant Still's *Songs of Separation*.

LeBerthan, Ted. American journalist. President of the Los Angeles Newspaper Guild. Wrote for several dailies including the Los Angeles Daily News. His writings often followed a theme of racial and religious tolerance. Wrote articles for many magazines, including *Opportunity*.

Lee, Richard Henry (1732–94). American patriot. Served in the Continental Congress (1774–80, 1784–87). Signed the Declaration of Independence.

Leftwich, Vernon (1881–1977). English composer and arranger. Composed and arranged for films. Among his many songs are "When You Are Near," "Autumn Leaves," "Little Ranchero," "How Softly the Rain Falls," and "Beside the Sea of Galilee." Instrumental works include *Reverie* (for strings), *Elegy*, Concerto for Cello and Orchestra, *Septet* (string quartet and winds), *Festival Overture*, Symphony No. 1, *Lion and the Mouse* (tone poem), *String Quartet*, *String Quintet*, and several marches.

Lehmann, Friedrich J. (1866–1950). Professor at the Oberlin Conservatory from 1902–1932. Published *A Treatise on Simple Counterpoint in 40 Lessons* (1907), *Harmonic Analysis* (1910), *The Analysis of Form in Music* (1919).

Leinsdorf, Erich (1912–   ). Austrian-American conductor. In addition to his enduring association with the Metropolitan Opera Company, he has guest conducted all over the world.

Lert, Richard Johannes (1885–). Austrian conductor. Held posts as a conductor in Dusseldorf, Darmstadt, Frankfurt, Hanover, and Paris. Came to the U.S. in 1938 and settled in Pasadena. Married the novelist Vicki Baum.

Lipkin, Arthur Bennett (d. 1974). American conductor and violinist. Joined the Philadelphia Orchestra at the age of 18. Was for 10 years first violinist with the Philadelphia String Quartet. Elected three times as president of the American Symphony Orchestra League. Served as conductor of the Birmingham (Ala.) Symphony (1962–74). Guest conducted many orchestras in the U.S. and abroad.

Locke, Alain Leroy (1886–1954). American Negro writer. Studied at Harvard University (Ph.D. 1918), Oxford University where he was a Rhodes Scholar, and at the University of Berlin. Wrote books such as *The New Negro* and *The Negro and His Music.*

Love, Josephine Harreld (1914–). American Negro pianist and teacher. Toured widely as a solo and chamber pianist.

MacDonald, Jeannette (1903–1965). American singer, actress, and dancer. Most renowned for her films with Nelson Eddy.

MacDowell, Edward Alexander (1861–1908). American composer. After several successes with the Boston Symphony, he was appointed to Columbia University's first chair of music. Resigned from Columbia University in considerable controversy in 1904, after which his health began to fail and his life ended in insanity. His wife deeded their summer home at Peterborough, N.H., to the MacDowell Memorial Association, where it became known as the MacDowell Colony, a retreat for composers and writers. His works include several suites, two piano concerti, numerous works for chorus, chamber pieces, and many works for piano.

Mack, Cecil (Richard McPherson) (1883–1944). American Negro songwriter. Founded the Gotham-Attucks music publishing company, which issued such songs as "Nobody" and "The Right Church but the Wrong Pew." Wrote scores for Broadway musicals, including *Running Wild* and *Swing It* (with Eubie Blake). From his Broadway show came such songs as "Charleston" and "Old Fashioned Love." His Cecil Mack Choir was active on Broadway during the 1920's and 30's.

Maganini, Quinto (1897–1974). American flutist, conductor, arranger, and composer. Conducted the New York Sinfonietta, and founded the Maganini Chamber Symphony. In 1953 wrote an opera entitled *Tennessee's Partner* and numerous works for orchestra. *A Suite of Music by Royalty* embraces pieces by Frederick the Great, Henry VIII, etc., and *The Royal Ladies* is an orchestra suite based on airs by Marie Antoinette and others. He won the Pulitzer Prize in 1927.

Mansfield, Richard (1854–1907). British-American actor. Played in Gilbert and Sullivan shows before emigrating to New York in 1882. Noted for playing romantic parts as the title roles in *Cyrano de Bergerac* and *Beau Brummel*, a play written for him by William Clyde Fitch. Introduced the works of G. B. Shaw to the U.S. Played leading roles in *Dr. Jekyll and Mr. Hyde*, *Don Juan*, *Arms and the Man*, *The Devil's Disciple*, and Shakespearian roles.

Marquand, John Phillips (1893–1960). American author. Editor of the *Harvard Lampoon*. Works include *Unspeakable Gentlemen*; *Four of a Kind*; *Black Cargo*; *No Hero*; *The Late George Apley*; *Thank You Mr. Moto*; *H. M. Pulham, Esquire*; *Repent in Haste*; *Point of No Return*; *Thirty Years*; *Stopover: Tokyo*; and *Women and Thomas Harrow*. Won a Pulitzer Prize for the *Late George Apley*.

Martinez, Alfredo Ramos. Mexican painter. Known for his murals. Founded open air art schools as part of the Fine Arts Academy attracting over 11,000 Mexican young people as students.

Matthews, Miriam (1905–   ). California's first Negro librarian. First person to stimulate interest in Negro History Week (1929). Led movement to revise the American Library Association's Bill of Rights in 1948. Defender of textbooks against censorship. Owns one of the largest private collections of Negro art.

Maynard, Rezin A. "Daddy." American journalist and educator. Ordained minister. Toured the U.S. to promote Yellowstone Park. Taught journalism at Manual Arts High School in Los Angeles.

McBride, Rogert Guyn (1911–   ). American composer, clarinetist and saxophonist. Created works which are often programmatic, include jazz materials. Many of his compositions are written for woodwinds, e.g., *Workout* for oboe and piano; *Oboe Quintet*; *Swing Stuff*, for clarinet and piano; *Popover*, for clarinet and piano; *Jam Session*, for woodwind quintet. Other works include ballets, a violin concierto, a violin sonata, *Mexican Rhapsody*, and *Fugato on a Well-Known Theme* for orchestra.

McDonald, Harl (1899–1955). American composer. Wrote several symphonies, concerti, other orchestral works, and chamber music.

McEvoy, J. P. (1894–1958). American playwright and librettist. Author of *The Potters*, *The Comic Supplements*, *The Ziegfeld Follies*, *Americana*, *God Loves Us*, *No Foolin'*, *Allez-Oop*, *Show Girl*, *Mr. Noodle*, and *Are You Listening?*

McKay, George Frederick (1899–1970). American composer. Works include several compositions for orchestra, chamber works for wind instruments, two organ sonatas, a cello concerto, and a suite on Negro folksongs for strings entitled *Port Royal, 1861*.

Menotti, Gian Carlo (1911–   ). Italian composer. Although he has written ballets, concerti for violin and piano, chamber music and pieces for piano, he is best known for his operas: *Amelia Goes to the Ball*, *The Old Maid and the Thief*, *The Island God*, *The Medium*, *The Telephone*, *The Consul*, *Amahl and the Night Visitors*, *The Saint of Bleeker Street*, and *Maria Golovin*.

Michael, Adrian. Director of Standard Oil Broadcasts ("Standard Hour," an hour long program of music and educational commentary on Sunday evenings).

Miller, Flournoy "Honey" (1887–1971). American Negro singer and entertainer. With Aubrey Fyles as a partner, Miller wrote several plays and musicals, including *The Man from Bam*, *The Husband*, *The Mayor of Dixie*, and *The Oyster Man*. They also wrote the book for *Shuffle Along* (based on *The Mayor of Dixie*), *Keep Shufflin'*, and *Running Wild*. They were featured in such shows as *In Darkeydoon*, *Way Down South*, *Rang Tang*, and *Sugar Hill*. Their Sam Peck and Amos Brown characters were the direct inspiration for the radio and television show *Amos and Andy*. The duo also appeared in the white musicals *The Charity Girl* and *Great Day*.

Mills, Florence (1895–1927). American Negro singer and entertainer. Began as performer in *A Trip to Coontown* at the age of four. Toured with her sisters in a vaudeville act called "The Mills Trio" or "The Three Mills Sisters." Sang as a member of "The Panama Trio." Appeared in *Shuffle Along*, *Plantation Review*, *Dover Street to Dixie*, *Dixie to Broadway*, and *Blackbirds of 1926*. William Grant Still wrote *Levee Land* for her.

Molinari, Bernardino (1880–1952). Italian conductor. Made his American debut with the N.Y. Philharmonic in 1928. Conducted the N.Y. Philharmonic during the 1931–1932 season. Championed works by modern Italian composers, especially those of Respighi and Malipiero.

Molino, Carlos. American dance band leader during the 1930's and 1940's. Came out of retirement to play a nonmusical character role in the movie, *The Gumball Rally* (1976).

Monteux, Pierre (1875–1964). French conductor. Became conductor of the Diaghilev's Ballets Russes and there conducted the world premieres of Stravinsky's *Petrouchka*, *La Sacre du Printemps*, and *Rossignol*; Ravel's *Daphnis and Chloe*; and Debussy's *Jeux*. In

1917–18, he conducted at the Metropolitan Opera Company. From 1919–24, he was conductor of the Boston Symphony. Until his death, he remained one of the most sought after guest conductors, performing all over the world.

Moreno, Antonio (1886–1967). Spanish actor. Settled in Hollywood, where he played numerous romantic roles in silent films. Movies included *Voice of the Million, House of Hate, The Trail of the Lonesome Pine, One Mad Kiss, Storm Over the Andes,* and *Rose of the Rio Grande.*

Murrell, Ursula. Negro American cultural and civic leader in Los Angeles.

Maynor, Dorothy (1910–   ). American Negro soprano.

Nickerson, Camille Lucie (1888–   ). American Negro singer and college professor. Became an authority on Creole folk songs, publishing and performing many of them. Made her debut as a mezzo-soprano at Times Hall (New York) in 1944. Served as president of the National Association of Negro Musicians. Was a founding member of the Advisory Committee for the John F. Kennedy Center for the Performing Arts (D.C.).

Novarro, Ramon (1899–1968). Mexican actor. Studied singing, violin, and dancing. Began as a dancer before becoming a romantic lead. Starred in both the silent and sound versions of *Ben Hur, The Prisoner of Zenda, The Midshipman, The Student Prince, Mata Hari, The Big Steal, Crisis,* and *Heller in Pink Tights.*

Page, Ruth. American choreographer and dancer. Appeared with Diaghilav's *Ballet Russe,* the Metropolitan Opera Company. Choreographed and staged *The Bells, Billy Sunday, Frankie and Johnny,* and *Les Petits Riens.*

Patricola, Tom (1893–1950). American tap dancer. Reared in Italy. Toured as an adolescent with his father's band. Spent 15 years on the Keith-Orpheum circuit. Appeared in *George White Scandals*. Made two feature films: *Married in Hollywood* and *One Mad Kiss*. Worked at Billy Rose nightclubs.

Patterson, Franklin Peale (1871–1966). American composer and writer. Played violin in the Los Angeles Philharmonic. Was on the editorial staff of the *Musical Courier*. Wrote several operas, including *The Echo, Caprice*, and *Through the Narrow Gate*. Short operas include *Beggar's Love* (*A Little Girl at Play*), *Mountain Blood*, and *The Forest Dwellers*.

Pearson, Eugene. American bass vocalist and teacher. Sang the role of Wotan in Richard Wagner's *Die Walküre*.

Phillips, Ted, Jr. (1945–   ). Negro American artist.

Phillips, Theodore (Sowande, Fela) (1905–   ). Nigerian composer. Became a leading jazz musician in London. Served as director of the Nigerian Broadcasting Service in Lagos, and established the Sowande School of Music at Nsukka. Works include *African Suite* for strings, *A Folk Symphony*, and organ settings of African folk songs and Negro spirituals.

Piatigorsky, Gregor (1903–1976). Russian cellist. Was principal cellist with the Berlin Philharmonic (1924–28). Made numerous recordings and appeared with most major orchestras all over the world. Besides his solo playing, he is known for his performances of chamber music, often in ensembles with Jascha Heifetz, Artur Rubinstein, etc.

Pomar, Jose (1880–   ). Mexican composer. After emulation of European composers, began composing music to represent class struggles in Mexico. Works include *Sonata in F sharp*, and *Prelude and Fugue* for percussion, harp and xylophone.

Ponce, Manuel Maria (1882–1948). Mexican composer. Works include orchestral pieces, concerti for violin and guitar, sonatas, piano pieces and many arrangements of Mexican folk songs.

Portanova, Joseph Domenico (1909–1979). American portrait sculptor and designer.

Portanova, Mary Spalding. Principal harpist with the Indianapolis, Atlanta, and Miami Symphony orchestras. Wife of Joseph Portanova, sculptor.

Powers, Marie (–1973). American actress and opera singer. Renowned for her performances of Gian Carlo Menotti's *The Medium.*

Price, William. American violinist who lived briefly in Little Rock, Arkansas about 1908. His residence was at 1418 Chester Street. He played violin at the Crystal Theater. William Grant Still's violin teacher.

Princi, Carl, (1920–). American broadcaster. Joined Los Angeles station KFAC in 1953, becoming Director of Programming and Community Involvement in 1972, and Vice-President in 1983.

Putterman, David J. (1900–79). Cantor at Park Avenue Synagogue (New York City) from 1933 through 1976.

Reis, Claire R. American writer and music educator. Studied at the Institute of Musical Art (N.Y.) and in Europe. Served as executive director of the International Composers Guild, executive chairman of the League of Composers (1923–48). Author of *Composers, Conductors, and Critics* (New York, 1955). See League of Composers.

Respighi, Ottorino (1879–1936). Italian composer. Composed operas, ballets, choral works, chamber music (including several string quartets), songs, and works for orchestra of which the most famous are *Le Fontane di Roma, I Pini di Roma,* and *Feste Romane.*

Revueltas, Silvestre (1899–1940). Mexican composer. Works include ballets, several orchestral works, film scores, chamber works, piano pieces, and songs. From his film music *Redes* (an orchestral suite) is often performed. His *Sensemaya* is frequently heard in Mexico and the U.S.

Rhines, Howard (1912–   ). Staff member of Los Angeles station KFAC (1945–70).

Rivera, Diego. Mexican artist. Championed nationalistic movement for Mexican art in the 1930's.

Robeson, Paul (1898–1976). American Negro singer. Studied law (B.A., Rutgers University, 1919; LL.B., Columbia University, 1923). Appeared in plays throughout the U.S. and England. Was featured in the title role of Shakespeare's *Othello* in London (1930). His success as a recitalist was tempered by his leftist political views. In 1952 he was awarded the International Stalin Peace Prize ($25,000).

Robinson, Bill "Bojangles" (1878–1949). American Negro dancer and vaudeville entertainer. Went from a young boy who danced for pennies on the streets of Washington, D.C., to become one of the highest paid dancers in Hollywood films. Began in vaudeville in 1896. Starred in the musical show *Blackbirds*, in 1927. Appeared in such films as *Harlem is Heaven* (1932), *The Little Colonel* with Shirley Temple, and *Stormy Weather* with Lena Horne.

Robinson, Dollye M. E. (1927–   ). Negro American music educator.

Robinson, Richard. American tenor; involved with the Los Angeles Bureau of Music. Conducted performances of William Grant Still's ballet, *Sahdji*.

Robison, Willard (1894–   ). American Negro composer, author, and singer. Organized The Deep River Orchestra. Appeared frequently on radio programs and recordings. Works include *Six Studies in Modern Syncopation*, *Rural Revelations*, *Heads Low*, *A Cottage for Sale*, *The Devil is Afraid of Music*, *Peaceful Valley*, and *Lonely Acres*.

Rodzinski, Artur (1894–1958). Dalmation-Austrian conductor. Studied law at the University of Vienna and music at the Vienna Academy of Music. Held posts as conductor of the Los Angeles Philharmonic, the Cleveland Orchestra, the NBC Symphony (with Toscanini), the New York Philharmonic, and the Chicago Symphony orchestra. Conducted the American premiere of Dmitri Shostakovich's opera, *Lady Macbeth of Mtzensk*.

Rosenfeld, Paul (1890–1946). American author and music critic. Wrote music criticisms for *The Dial*. Promoted new American music. His books include *Musical Portraits* (on 20 modern composers), *Musical Chronical, An Hour with American Music*, and *Discoveries of a Music Critic*.

Rostropovich, Mstislav (1927–). Russian cellist and conductor. Taught at the Moscow and Leningrad Conservatories. Won the International Competition of Cellists in Prague, after which he played concerts throughout the world. He received the Lenin Prize for conductors in 1963, but left Russia after difficulties with Soviet authorities. He was appointed in 1977 as conductor of the National Symphony Orchestra (Washington, D.C.). In 1978, he and his wife were stripped of their Soviet citizenship and labeled "ideological renegades."

Rubinstein, Artur, (1886–). Polish pianist. From his tours of Spain and South America he became an exponent of the music of Spanish composers and the Brazilian Heitor Villa-Lobos. In 1946 he became an American citizen.

Ruby, Harry (1895–1974). American composer and lyricist. Wrote for several Broadway musicals and Hollywood films. Began as a pianist in vaudeville. Among his shows were *The Ramblers, The Five O'Clock Girl, Good Boy*, and *Animal Crackers*.

Ruggles, Carl (1876–1971). American composer. His compositions are sharply dissonant and mostly atonal; most notable among his works are *Angles; Men and Mountains; Men, Lilacs*, and *Marching Mountains; Evocations;* and *Organum*. In his last years, he devoted himself mainly to painting.

Ryder, Georgia (1924–   ). American Negro educator. In 1979, he became dean of the School of Arts and Letters at Norfolk State University (Virginia).

Salzedo, Carlos (1885–1961). French harpist and composer. Settled in New York City in 1909, where he served as first harpist with the Metropolitan Opera Company. In 1913, he founded the Trio de Lutècé with George Barrere (flutist) and Paul Kéfer (cellist). Co-founded the International Composers Guild with Edgar Varese. Established the Salzedo Harp Colony at Camden, Maine. Composed numerous works for solo harp, as well as many chamber works for harp and other instruments. Made transcriptions of pieces by Bach, Corelli, Rameau, Haydn and Brahms.

Saminsky, Lazare (1882–1959). Russian composer, conductor and writer. Studied mathematics and philosophy at the University of St. Petersburg. Emigrated to the U.S. in 1920. Co-founder of the League of Composers in 1923. Works include operas, symphonies, and choral and chamber works.

Sandi, Luis (1905–   ). Mexican composer. Specialized in choral music. Founded the *Coro de Madrigalistas*. Compiled collections of choral pieces for schools. Wrote *Norte* (a symphonic suite), *Carlota* (a one-act opera), *Bonampak* (ballet), and film music.

Sargeant, Winthrop (1903–   ). American music critic. Served on the editorial staff of *Musical America*, as music critic of the *Brooklyn Daily Eagle* and the *New York American*, and as music editor of *Time* magazine. He is also the author of several books.

Saunders, Gertrude. American Negro singer and Broadway entertainer. Began her career on stage at the age of 17 with the Billy King Company. Noticed by Eubie Blake and Noble Sissle, she was chosen to be the feminine star of the original show, *Shuffle Along*, a role later filled by Florence Mills. Performed in burlesque before joining a vaudeville company on the Keith, Lowe and Toher circuits. In 1924, she appeared in Irvin C. Miller's production of *Liza*. Other shows included *The Board of Education*; *Bon Bon Buddy, Jr*; *Dinah*; *Exploits in Africa*; *The Heart Breakers*; *Over the Top*; *Strutt your Stuff*; and *They're Off*. Her last major appearance was in *Run Little Chillun'*.

Sawhill, Clarence (1906–83). American music educator. Director of Bands at UCLA (1952–72).

Schoenberg, Arnold (1874–1951). Viennese composer. Pupil of Alexander von Zemlinsky, whose sister he married. Early works, of which *Verklärte Nacht* is most famous, followed the spirit of Romantic poetry and the influences of Richard Wagner, Gustav Mahler, and Richard Strauss. After composing and teaching in Berlin, Vienna, and Paris, he came to the U.S. in 1933. Became an American citizen in 1941. Leader in the movement to establish the 12-tone technique as a widely accepted method for composing music. Followers included Alban Berg, Anton von Webern, Egon Wellesz, Ernst Krenek, and Luigi Dallapiccola. Composed prolifically for orchestra, chorus, chamber ensembles, piano, organ, and wrote many songs. Among the works most performed are *Pelleas und Melisande, Kammer-symphonie, 5 Orchester-Stücke*, for orchestra; and *Gurre-Lieder*, for soli, mixed chorus, and orchestra.

Schuyler, George S. (1895–1977). Negro American satirist, journalist, and essayist. Wrote *Black No More*, the first full-length satire by a black American. Distinguished newspaperman for more than 50 years. His novel, *Slaves Today*, exposed slave traffic in Liberia in the 1920's, and was the first African novel by a major black writer. Among his best known essays is "The Negro Art Hokum." His autobiography is entitled *Black and Conservative*.

Schuyller, Philippa Duke (1932–1967). American Negro pianist. Began playing publicly at the age of four. Made her debut in 1946 with the New York Philharmonic, and appeared the same year with the Boston Symphony Orchestra. Works include *Manhattan Nocturne*, for orchestra; *Rhapsody for Youth*; *Nile Phantasy*, for piano and orchestra; and *Fairy Tale Symphony*.

Scott, Cyril Meir (1879–1970). English composer. His works, most often performed in England and Germany, reflect descriptions and poetic legends under exotic titles. His harmonic style and orchestration were clearly impressionistic, and he often utilized unresolved dissonant chords. He was also a student of occult philosophy, and wrote on the relationship between music and colors. His works include chamber music, choral works, a piano concerto, a concerto for oboe and strings, many piano pieces and over 100 songs.

Senghor, Léopold Sédar (1906–). First President of Senegal (1960–). Political leader and poet. Studied at the Sorbonne. Taught at Tours and in Paris. Served in the French Army in World War II. Deputy to the French legislature. Exponent of the philosophy of *negritude*. With Alioune Diop, founded *Présence Africaine*, a Paris magazine.

Sevitsky, Fabien (1893–1967). Russian conductor. Born Koussevitsky (nephew of Sergei Koussevitsky). Conducted in Russia until 1922 before performing for a year with the Warsaw Philharmonic. After a year in Mexico, he joined the Philadelphia Orchestra, and in 1925 organized the Philadelphia Chamber String Sinfanietta. Served for nearly 20 years as conductor of the Indianapolis Symphony Orchestra.

Shaw, Artie (1910–). American jazz band leader, clarinetist, and composer. Formed his own band in 1935. Songs and instrumental works include "Comin' On," "Back Bay Shuffle," "Any Old Time," "Traffic Jam," "Non-Stop Flight," "Summit Ridge Drive," "Nightmare," "Chant," "Monsoon," "Moonray," "Easy to Love," and "Concert for Clarinet." His recording of "Gloomy Sunday" (arr. by William Grant Still) created an uproar when it was thought to contribute to an increase in suicides.

Shaw, George Bernard (1856–1950). British dramatist.

Sheer, Leo. American conductor. Conductor of the Lexington, Kentucky, and Abilene, Texas, Symphony Orchestras.

Shepperson, Charles B. Second husband of Carrie Fambro and step-father of William Grant Still. He was a clerk for many years. His Little Rock address was 1415 Chester. He moved to 912 W. 14th, the Fambro home, when he married Carrie Fambro in 1904.

Shostakovitch, Dmitri Dmitrievitch (1906–1975). Russian composer. During the Stalin Purges, he became the primary target for persecution and was used as an example of failure to write acceptably under "socialist realism." His opera, *Lady Macbeth of the District of Mtzensk*, became a *cause célèbre* bringing forth the wrath of the Kremlin, Pravda, and various communist leaders. Of his many symphonies, No. 5 remains widely performed all over the world. In addition to the symphonies, his works include ballets, operas, concerti, choral and chamber works, songs, solo works for piano and music for numerous films.

Sibelius, Jean (1865–1957). A romantic, best known for *Finlandia*, he is Finland's most honored composer.

Simon, Henry W. American journalist and music critic. Brother of Richard Simon, one of the founders of Simon and Schuster. Author of numerous articles and books. Music critic for *PM*, a New York newspaper in the 1940's.

Sissle, Noble (1889–1975). American Negro lyricist, singer, and dance band leader. Teamed with Eubie Blake to write several highly successful musicals including *Shuffle Along*, *Follies Bergere*, and *Brown-Skin Models*. In 1965 a special Town Hall concert, "Sissie and Blake," was sponsored by ASCAP to honor their 50 years of contributions to musical shows. Along with other leading Negro musicians, Sissle contributed to the three great world's fairs of the 1930's (Chicago, San Francisco, and New York).

Sokol, Vilem (1915–). Czechoslovakian-American conductor and violinist. Conductor and Musical Director of the Seattle Youth Symphony (1960–).

Smith, Hale (1925–   ). American Negro composer. Studied at the Cleveland Institute of Music (B.M. and M.M.). Was one of several poets and composers whose works were performed regularly at the Karamu House in Cleveland. His works include orchestral and band pieces, concerti, and solo compositions. His *Contours for Orchestra*, a twelve-tone work, was recorded by the Louisville Orchestra.

Smith, Hezekiah Leroy Gordon "Stuff" (1909–1967). American Negro violinist. Began study with his father and joined his father's band at the age of 12. Played with such groups as the Aunt Jemima Touring Show, Alphonso Treut, "Jelly Roll" Morton, and Joe Bushkin. Among the musicians who played with him were Jonah Jones, Clyde Hart, William "Cozy" Cole, Lloyd Trotman, Erroll Garner, and "Billy" Taylor. Toured in Europe as soloist with Norman Granz's "Jazz at the Philharmonic." Helped pioneer the electrically-amplified jazz violin.

Solomon, Izler (1910–   ). American conductor. Conducted the Columbus, Ohio; Hollywood Bowl; Israel Philharmonic; Buffalo Philharmonic; and Indianapolis Symphonic Orchestras.

Stowkoski, Leopold (1882–1977). Conductor. Born in London. Came to the U.S. in 1905. Served as conductor of the Cincinnati, Philadelphia, Houston Symphonies, the New York Philharmonic, and Hollywood Bowl Symphony Orchestra. Known for transcriptions of works by Bach, and for work in motion pictures, particularly Walt Disney's *Fantasia*.

Stone, Carol. American actress. Daughter of Fred Stone (the original Scarecrow in the Broadway production of *Wizard of Oz*).

Stone, Lloyd. American tenor. Soloist for the National Champion Elk's Chorus. Sang on radio programs. Director of the Los Angeles Bureau of Music.

Stravinsky, Igor (1882–1971). Russian composer. Studied law. Did not begin serious study of music until after meeting with Rimsky-Korsakov at the age of 19. Settled in the U.S. and became an American citizen in 1945. From a long association with Sergei Diaghilev came the ballets *The Firebird*, *The Rite of Spring*, *Petrouchka*, *Le Rossignol* (after Hans Christian Anderson), and *Pulcinella*. Stravinsky often used Russian subjects, including folk tales, yet his works have been banned in Russia. He wrote in nearly every genre and employed a remarkable range of musical techniques, including twelve-tone scales, revolutionary orchestral effects and colors, and economical scoring. Works include ballets, operas, symphonies, concerti, soli, chamber, and choral music.

Strong, George Templeton (1856–1948). American composer. Included among his works are three symphonies and two symphonic poems.

Swift, Day (1905–). American composer. Wrote several Broadway shows, revues, and songs. Best known for her score for *Fine and Dandy*.

Szell, George (1897–1970). Hungarian conductor and pianist. Appeared as pianist with the Vienna Symphony Orchestra at the age of 11. Conducted his own symphony and played Beethoven's "Emperor" Concerto with the Berlin Philharmonic at the age of 17. After high recommendations from Richard Strauss, he held operatic conducting posts in Strasbourg, Prague, Darmstedt, Dusseldorf, and Berlin. Became conductor of the Scottish Orchestra (Glasgow). After arriving in the U.S., he appeared as guest conductor of the NBC Symphony, after which he conducted at the Metropolitan Opera Company. In 1956, he became the conductor of the Cleveland Orchestra, leading it to a position among the world's greatest orchestras.

Talbert, Florence Cole (1890–1961). American Negro soprano. Toured with Hahn's Jubilee Singers. Made her debut at Aeolian Hall (New York) in 1918.

Taylor, Deems (1885–1966). American composer and writer. His operas *The King's Henchmen* and *Peter Ibbetson* set records for an American opera at the Metropolitan Opera Company (1926–28 and 1931–34). Other important works include a suite *Through the Looking Glass*, and two cantatas: *The Chambered Nautilus* and *The Highwayman*. Was president of the American Society of Composers, Authors, and Publishers (ASCAP) from 1942–48.

Teske, Charles. American adagio dancer. Premier dancer in *Tropical Lion*, produced at the Hollywood Bowl by Kurt Baer.

Thigpen, Helen. Negro American soprano. Performed at Town Hall (New York) and with the Los Angeles Philharmonic under Eugene Ormandy at the Hollywood Bowl in 1949.

Thomas, John Charles (1891–1960). American baritone. Studied at the Peabody Conservatory in Baltimore. After first singing in musical comedy in New York City, he became a member of the Theatre de La Monnaie in Brussels, the Chicago Opera Company, Covent Garden (London), and the Metropolitan Opera Company.

Thompson, Randall (1899–). American composer. He is best known for his choral works which include *Allelulia*, *The Testament of Freedom*, *Rosemary*, and *The Peaceable Kingdom*.

Thompson, Ulysses "Slow Kid" (1888–). American Negro comedian and dancer. Innovator of the slow motion dance. Ran away from home at the age of 14 to tour with a medicine show. Played vaudeville as a tap dancer and acrobat on the Keith-Orpheum circuit. Developed an act with Florence Mills, who became his wife. Appeared with Florence Mills in *Shuffle Along* and *Dixie to Broadway*. Also appeared in a revue with Will Vodery's Band and Shelton Brooks as master of ceremonies.

Tiomkin, Dimitri (1899–). Russian composer and pianist. Made his U.S. debut with a recital in Carnegie Hall in 1926. Settled in Hollywood, where he has written scores for more than 120 films. Recipient of four Academy Awards.

Toch, Ernst (1887–1964). Austrian composer. First studied medicine and philosophy. Self-taught in music. Won numerous prizes in Austria for youthful compositions. His music is Romantic in spirit, but embraces a wide range of techniques. He experimented with 12-tone rows, spoken voices, etc. Wrote symphonies; concerti; chamber music, including several string quartets. His Third Symphony won the Pulitzer Prize (1955). Other writings included concert études for beginners, incidental music for various plays, and several song cycles.

Torkanowsky, Werner (1926–   ). German born conductor. Appointed conductor of the New Orleans Symphony Orchestra in 1963. Has appeared as guest conductor with major orchestras throughout the world.

Toscanini, Arturo (1867–1957). Italian conductor preeminent on the world stage.

Tucker, Adrian. American artist. Maintains a studio in Los Angeles.

Tucker, Sophie (1884–1966). Russian-American singer and actress. Self-proclaimed the "Last of the Red Hot Mamas," she became a night club star until her death. She appeared in such shows as *Shubert Gaieties, Earl Carroll Vanities, Leave It to Me,* and *High Kickers.* The 1962 Broadway musical, *Sophie,* was based on her life. Author of an autobiography entitled *Some of these Days.*

Van Vechten, Carl (1880–1964). American novelist. Encouraged the careers of such artists as Isadore Duncan, Anna Pavlova, Sergei Rachmaninoff, Erik Satie, Igor Stravinsky, Gertrude Stein, George Gershwin, Ethel Waters, and Paul Robeson. One of the first to rediscover Herman Melville. Largely responsible for the popular recognition of the Negro as a creative artist during the Harlem Renaissance. Author of more than 20 fictional works of which the most renowned is *Nigger Heaven*.

Várèse, Edgar (1885–1965). French composer. Came to New York in 1915. Founded the New Symphony Orchestra for performances of modern music. Organized the Pan American Society for promoting music of the Americas. Earlier works are impressionistic and romantic. Became one of the boldest innovators in 20th century music. His compositions are governed by functional efficiency and aural impact. Works employ varying combinations of instruments, voices, and sources of sounds without definite pitch. Performances of his works in Europe and America evoked violent demonstrations.

Villa-Lobos, Heitor (1887–1959). Brazilian composer. Played cello in cafes and restaurants before formal study at the National Institute of Music. Traveled extensively throughout Brazil collecting priceless folk music. Devoted ardently to Brazil and its music education, he produced numerous works for children. Founded the National Conservatory of Orpheanic Song, and the Brazilian Academy of Music. He is best known for his series *Bachianas Brasileiras*, in which Brazilian melodies and rhythms are treated with Bachian counterpoint. A prolific composer, his more than 2,000 works include operas, ballets, symphonies, chamber music, concerti, choral pieces, works for piano (many performed by Artur Rubinstein), and songs.

Vodery, Will (1885–1951). American Negro band leader and arranger. From 1911 to 1932, he was music supervisor for the Florenz Ziegfeld productions. During World War I, he directed the 807th Infantry Band, for which he received an award for excellence from Robert Casadesus. Served as a consultant to Duke Ellington. Joined other distinguished Negro musicians in contributing to the three great World's Fairs in the 1930's (Chicago, San Francisco, and New York).

Voorhees, Donald. American arranger and conductor. Led his own dance band in the 1920's. Conducted the band in the Broadway musical *Earl Carroll's Vanities of 1925*. Formed a band with Red Nichols for Newark radio station WOR, and soon afterwards the CBS radio network. Conducted such shows as "Albert Spaulding," "Ed Wynn Colgate House Party," "Gibson Family," "Lawrence Tibbett," "Calvacade of America," 1939 Ford summer show, and for many years, "The Bell Telephone Hour" on both radio and television. Made more than 20 recordings, many for Columbia.

Waldeen. (Waldeen Falkenstein). American dancer. Appeared at the Norma Gould Studio (Theatre) in Los Angeles. Toured Mexico as a dancer and settled there.

Waldo, Elizabeth (1923–). American violinist and composer. Author of *Latin American Music, Spanish American Folk Songs,* and other books. Among her compositions are several works for orchestra, chamber ensembles, and mixed chorus. Nominated for an Emmy Award.

Waller, William Lowe (1926–). Governor of Mississippi (1972– 76).

Waters, Ethel (1900–1977). American Negro singer. Began singing publicly at the age of five. Joined a vaudeville company at the age of 17. One of the first two singers to sing W. C. Handy's "The St. Louis Blues". Renowned for her recordings of "Stormy Weather," "Am I Blue," "Heat Wave," "Down Home Blues," and "Oh, Daddy." Appeared in such Broadway musicals as *Africana, Blackbirds of 1930, Rhapsody in Black, As Thousands Cheer,* and *Cabin in the Sky.* Toured for nearly 20 years with Billy Graham Crusades, where she regularly sang "His Eye Is On the Sparrow."

Wardell, Bertha. American dancer and stage manager.

Watkins, William A. T. Negro American educator. Principal of Union School in Little Rock, Arkansas. Lived at 1702 Ringo.

Weber, Morris "Joe" (1867–1942). American actor, producer and director. Won greatest fame with his partner as Dutch comics in a series of musical burlesques which they presented for eight years at the Weber Fields Broadway Music Hall. Of the many musicals produced by Weber, four had scores by Victor Herbert. Weber productions included *The Geezer, Fiddle-Dee-Dee, Twirly Whirly, The Only Girl, The Merry Widow Burlesque, Eileen, Hip! Hip! Hooray*, and *Honeydew*.

Weede, Robert (1903–). American baritone. Was a member of the Metropolitan Opera Company for several seasons. In 1956, he sang the leading role in Frank Loesser's *Most Happy Fella'*.

Whalen, Grover A. President of the 1939 New York World's Fair Organization. William Grant Still, who wrote the Fair's theme music, was forced to stay at the Y.M.C.A. in Harlem while other dignitaries stayed in luxury hotels. Whalen issued a special invitation for Still to join him for dinner at the Terrace Club.

Whalen, Michael (1902–1974). Leading actor in many Hollywood B features of the 1930's and 40's.

Whisonant, Lawrence (Winters, Lawrence) (1915–1965). American Negro baritone. Made his debut in 1947, at Town Hall, New York. Made his operatic debut with the New York City Opera in 1948. Made his European debut with the Hamburg (Germany) State Opera in 1952. Appeared in the Broadway musical *Call Me Mister* (1946).

White, Clarence Cameron (1880–1960). American Negro violinist and composer. Born in Clarksville, Tennessee. Held various positions as a violinist in Boston and elsewhere. Taught at the Washington Conservatory of Music. Later headed the Department of Music at West Virginia State College. His compositions for violin were performed by Fritz Kreisler and Albert Spalding.

White, Paul (1895–1973). American composer, violinist, and conductor. Served as associate conductor of the Rochester Civic Orchestra.

Works include several compositions for orchestra, chamber and solo pieces.

Whitelow, Pearl. American singer. Appeared in many concerts and on radio and television on the west coast.

Whiteman, Paul (1890–1967). American conductor and band leader. In World War I, he conducted a 40-member band in the U.S. Navy and organized hotel bands. Developed symphonic jazz. In 1924, at a concert in Aeolian Hall in New York City he introduced George Gershwin's *Rhapsody in Blue*. Author of several books, including *Jazz, How to Be a Bandleader*, etc.

Williams, Paul R. (1894–). American Negro architect.

Willson, Meridith (1902–). American composer, librettist, and lyricist. Best known for his Broadway show, *The Music Man*. Other shows included *The Unsinkable Molly Brown* and *Hero's Love*.

Winant, John G. The U.S. ambassador to Great Britain from 1941–1946. He was a former governor of New Hampshire.

Wincenc, Joseph (1915–). American conductor and educator. Violinist in and conductor of numerous symphony orchestras.

Winstead, Kenneth. American double bassist. Played in the Kansas City Philharmonic. Member of the Los Angeles Philharmonic (1941–46).

Winter, William Forrest (1923–). Governor of Mississippi (1979–83).

Yorty, Samuel William (1909–). American political leader. Member of California State Assembly, member of U.S. Congress. Mayor of Los Angeles.

Young, Charles (1864–1922). American Negro military officer. One of the first among his race to enter West Point. Rode with Teddy Roosevelt's Rough Riders. Wrote the song "There's a Service Flag in the Window," which boosted morale in World War I. Taught military science at Wilberforce College. Was a student of languages, a collector of books and African folk songs, and an accomplished musician.

Zemach, Benjamin (1900–   ). Russian-American concert dancer and choreographer. Member of the Moscow Habeina. Emigrated to the U.S. in the late 1920's. Served as a dialogue coach at RKO Studios. Staged numerous plays. Served as Director of Dance and Drama at the University of Judaism in Los Angeles.

Appendix 3

THE WORKS OF WILLIAM GRANT STILL

Title	Length in minutes	Publisher

WORKS FOR THE STAGE

Title	Length in minutes	Publisher
La Guiablesse (ballet)	30	WGS Music
Sahdji (choral ballet)	45	CFI-ESM
Blue Steel (opera)	120	ms.
Lenox Avenue (ballet)	23	WGS Music
Miss Sally's Party (ballet)	30	WGS Music
Troubled Island (opera in 3 acts)	120	SMC
A Bayou Legend (opera in 3 acts)	120	WGS Music
A Southern Interlude (opera)	60	ms.
Costaso (opera in 3 acts)	120	WGS Music
Mota (opera in 3 acts)	120	WGS Music
The Pillar (opera in 3 acts)	120	WGS Music
Minette Fontaine (opera in 3 acts)	120	WGS Music
Highway 1, U.S.A. (opera in 2 acts)	60	WGS Music
Incidental music for *The Prince and the Mermaid* (a children's play)	20	WGS Music

WORKS FOR ORCHESTRA

Title	Length in minutes	Publisher
Three Negro Songs	10	ms.
Black Bottom	10	ms.
Darker America	17	CFI-ESM
From the Land of Dreams	8	ms.
From the Journal of a Wanderer	20	ms.
From the Black Belt (a."Lil' Scamp" b."Honeysuckle" c."Mah Bones is Creakin'" d."Blue" e."Brown Girl")	20	CFI
From the Heart of a Believer	10	ms.
Log Cabin Ballads	10	ms.
Africa (a."Land of Peace" b."Land of Romance" c."Land of Superstition")	30	ms.

Florida Blues (an arrangement)		Handy Bros.
Afro-American Symphony	28	Novello
A Deserted Plantation (a."Spiritual" b."Young Missy" c."Dance")	15	Robbins
Ebon Chronicle	9	ms.
The Black Man Dances	10	ms.
Dismal Swamp	15	Theodore Presser
Beyond Tomorrow	9	WGS Music
Symphony in G Minor	25	WGS Music
Can'tcha Line 'Em	10	WGS Music
Old California	10	WGS Music
In Memoriam: The Colored Soldiers Who Died for Democracy	6	MCA Music
Fanfare for American War Heroes	1	WGS Music
Pages from Negro History (a."Africa" b."Slavery" c."Emancipation")	10	CFI
Poem for Orchestra	15	MCA Music
Bells	7	MCA Music
Festive Overture	10	WGS Music
Symphony No. 5 (*Western Hemisphere*)	25	WGS Music
Fanfare for the 99th Fighter Squadron	1	WGS Music
Archaic Ritual	20	WGS Music
Symphony No. 4 (*Autochthonous*)	27	WGS Music
Wood Notes	20	SMC
Danzas de Panamá (string orchestra, quartet)	15	SMC
The American Scene (Suite 1: *The East* a."On the Village Green" b."Berkshire Night" c."Manhattan Skyline" Suite 2: *The South* a."Florida Night" b."Levee Land" c."A New Orleans Street" Suite 3: *The Old West* a."Song of the Plainsmen" b."Sioux Love Song" c."Tribal Dance" Suite 4: *The Far West* a."The Plaza"	50	WGS Music

b."Sundown Land" c."Navaho
Country"
Suite 5: *A Mountain, A Memorial
and a Song* a."Grand Teton"
b."Tomb of the Unknown Soldier"
c."Song of the Rivermen")

Little Red Schoolhouse	15	SMC
(a. "Little Conqueror" b. "Egyptian Princess" c. "Captain Kidd, Jr." d. "Colleen Brown" e. "Petey")		
Serenade	8	WGS Music
Symphony No. 3	25	WGS Music
Patterns	15	WGS Music
The Peaceful Land	9	American Music Edition, Publs.
Los Alnados de España	12	WGS Music
Preludes	12	WGS Music
Threnody: In Memory of Jan Sibelius	4	WGS Music
Miniature Overture	2	WGS Music
Choreographic Prelude	5	WGS Music

WORKS FOR ORCHESTRA WITH SOLOISTS OR CHORUS

Levee Land	10	WGS Music
Kaintuck' (with piano solo)	13	WGS Music
Song of a City (Rising Tide, Victory Tide)		WGS Music
And They Lynched Him on a Tree (with two choruses, narrator, contralto, soloist)	19	WGS Music
Plain-Chant for America	10	WGS Music
Those Who Wait	10	WGS Music
Wailing Woman	10	WGS Music
From a Lost Continent (with chorus)	15	WGS Music
The Little Song That Wanted To Be a Symphony (with narrator and women's vocal trio)	19	CFI
A Psalm for the Living (with chorus)	10	Bourne Co.

Rhapsody (a. "Pastorale" b. "Romance" c. "Lullaby" d. "Paean")	15	WGS Music
Ennanga (with harp solo)	15	WGS Music
The Path of Glory (a. "Prologue" b. "Invocation" c. "Call to Battle" d. "Judgment" e. "Elegy")	15	WGS Music
Christmas in the Western World (Las Pascuas) (strings and chorus) (a. "A Maiden Was Adoring God, The Lord" b. "Ven, Niño Divino" c. "Aguinaldo" d. "Jesous Ahatonhia" e. "Tell Me, Shepherdess" f. "De Virgin Mary Had a Baby Boy." g. "Los Reyes Magos" h. "La Piñata" i. "Glad Christmas Bells" j. "Sing, Shout, Tell the Story!")	20	SMC

WORKS FOR BAND

From the Delta	8	MCA Music
To You, America!	11	SMC
Folk Suite for Band	8	Bourne Co.
Little Red Schoolhouse	15	SMC

CHAMBER MUSIC

Suite for Violin and Piano (orchestral version available) (a. "African Dancer" b. "Mother and Child" c. "Gamin")	15	MCA Music
Incantation and Dance (oboe and piano)	5	CFI
Pastorela	11	Warner Bros.
Danzas de Panamá (string orchestra, quartet)	15	SMC
Miniatures (flute, oboe and piano)	12	Oxford U.P.

(a. "I Ride an Old Paint"
b. "Adolorido" c. "Jesus Is a Rock in a
Weary Land" d. "Yaravi" e. "Frog
Went a'Courtin'")

Romance (saxophone and piano)	3	Bourne Co.
Four Indigenous Portraits (string	10	WGS Music

quartet and flute)
(a. "North American Negro"
b. "South American Negro" c. "South
American Indian" d. "North
American Indian")

Lyric String Quartet	9	WGS Music
Vignettes (oboe, bassoon, and piano)	11:30	SMC

(a. "Winnebago Moccasin Game"
b. "Carmela" c. "Peruvian Melody"
d. "Clinch Mountain" e. "Garde Piti
Mulet La" or "M'sieu Banjo")

Folk Suite #1 (flute, piano and string)	8:52	SMC

(a. "Bambalele" b. "Sometimes I Feel
Like a Motherless Child" c. "Two
Hebraic Songs")

Folk Suite #2 (flute, clarinet, cello and	9	SMC

piano)
(a. "El Zapatero" b. "Mo'le" c. "Mom'
zelle Zizi" d. "Peruvian Melody")

Folk Suite #2 (flute, clarinet, cello and	9	SMC

piano)
(a. "An Inca Dance" b. "An Inca Song"
c. "Bow and Arrow Dance Song")

Folk Suite #4 (flute, clarinet, 'cello and	5:30	WGS Music

piano)
(a. "El Monigote" b. "Anda Buscando
de Rosa en Rosa" c. "Tayeras")

Little Folk Suite from the *Western*	2:30	SMC

Hemisphere (brass quintet)
(a. "Where Shall I Be When the Great
Trumpet Sounds?" b. "En Roulant Ma
Boule")

Little Folk Suite from the *Western Hemisphere #1* (string quartet) (a. "Salangadou" b. "El Capotin")	3:45	SMC
Little Folk Suite from the *Western Hemisphere #2* (string quartet) (a. "El Nido" b. "Sweet Betsy from Pike")	4	SMC
Little Folk Suite from the *Western Hemisphere #3* (string quartet) (a. "Aurore Pradere and Tant Sirop Est Doux" b. "Wade in the Water")	3	SMC
Little Folk Suite from the *Western Hemisphere #4* (string quartet) (a. "Los Indios and Yaravi" b. "The Crawdad Song")	3:30	SMC
Little Folk Suite from the *Western Hemisphere #5* (string quartet) (a. "Tutu Maramba" b. "La Varsoviana")	4	SMC

WORKS FOR PIANO

Three Visions (a. "Dark Horsemen" b. "Summerland" c. "Radiant Pinnacle") ("Summerland" also available for small and full orchestra)	11	WGS Music
Quit Dat Fool'nish	2	Belwin
Seven Traceries (a. "Cloud Cradles" b. "Mystic Pool" c. "Muted Laughter" d. "Out of the Silence" e. "Woven Silver" f. "Wailing Dawn" g. "A Bit of Wit") ("Out of the Silence" also available for flute, piano and string orchestra.) ("Muted Laughter" is in *Piano Repertoire* by Bernice Frost, J. Fischer, publishers.)	17	WGS Music

Swanee River	2	Robbins
Bells	6	MCA Music
(a. "Phantom Chapel" b. "Fairy Knoll" (orchestral version also available)		
Marionette	1	MCA Music
Prelude		Scribner's
(in *The New Scribner Music Library*, Vol. 4)		
Five Animal Sketches		Silver Burdett Co.
(In *Music for Early Childhood*, New Music Horizons Series)		
Ring Play	1	Belwin
(In *Twentieth Century Piano Music* by Bernice Frost)		

WORKS FOR ORGAN

Reverie	3	F. Rayner Brown
Elegy	3	F. Rayner Brown
"Summerland" (from *Three Visions*)	6	WGS Music

WORKS FOR ACCORDION

Aria	5	Sam Fox Pub. Co.
Lilt	4	Pietro Deiro Pub.

WORKS FOR VOICE, OR VOICE AND PIANO

Winter's Approach (solo voice and piano)	3	G. Schirmer
The Breath of a Rose (solo voice and piano)	5	G. Schirmer
(In *A New Anthology of American Song*)		
Twelve Negro Spirituals	25	Handy Bros., Francis, Day, etc.

(a. "I Got a Home in-a Dat Rock"
b. "All God's Chillun Got Shoes"
c. "Camp Meetin'" d. "Didn't My
Lord Deliver Daniel?" e. "Good
News" f. "Great Day" g. "Gwinter
Sing All Along de Way" h. "Keep Me
From Sinkin' Down" i. "Listen to the
Lambs" j. "Lord, I Wants To Be a
Christian" k. "My Lord Says He Is
Goin' to Rain Down Fiah" l. "Peter,
Go Ring Dem Bells")
(published for solo voice and piano,
with g, h, and j published for S.A.T.B.
also)

Victory Tide or *Rising Tide* (for S.A.T.B. and T.T.B.B.)	3	Belwin
Here's One (for solo voice and piano, also for S.A.T.B.)	4	John Church Co.
Caribbean Melodies (solo voice, chorus, piano and percussion) (the concluding song, "Carry Him Along," is published separately for S.A.T.B.)	60	Oliver Ditson Co.
Bayou Home (solo voice and piano)	3	Robbins
The Voice of the Lord (tenor solo and S.A.T.B.; also included in the anthology *Synagogue Music by Contemporary Composers*)	5	Witmark
Ev'ry Time I Feel the Spirit (solo voice and piano)	2	Galaxy
Mississippi (voices and piano)	3	WGS Music
Songs of Separation (solo voice and piano) (a. "Idolatry" b. "Poeme" c. "Parted" d. "If You Should Go" e. "A Black Pierrot")	12	MCA Music

Lament (women's trio and piano) (In *American Music Horizons*, part of the New Music Horizons Series)	3	Silver Burdett Co.
Up There (In *World Music Horizons*, part of the New Music Horizons Series)	1:30	Silver Burdett Co.
Sinner, Please Don't Let This Harvest Pass (a spiritual in *Let Music Ring*, California State Series) (for S.A.T.B. and piano)	3	California State Department of Ed.
Song for the Valiant (solo voice and piano)	3	WGS Music
Song for the Valiant (solo voice and piano)	3	WGS Music
Song for the Lonely (solo voice and piano)	4	WGS Music
Grief (solo voice and piano) (In *Anthology of Art Songs by Black American Composers*)	3	Marks
Citadel (solo voice and piano)	2	WGS Music
I Feel Like My Time Ain't Long (a spiritual for S.A.T.B. and piano)	3	Presser
Is There Anybody Here? (a spiritual for S.A.T.B. and piano)	3	Presser
Three Rhythmic Spirituals (S.A.T.B. or solo voice and orchestra) (a. "Lord, I Looked Down the Road" b. "Hard Trials" c. "Holy Spirit, Don't You Leave Me")	9	Bourne Co.
From the Hearts of Women (a. "Little Mother" b. "Midtide" c. "Coquette" d. "Bereft") (for solo voice and piano, or solo voice, flute, oboe, string quartet and piano)	9	WGS Music
All That I Am (hymn for S.A.T.B. and piano)	2	WGS Music

Song of the Hunter (solo voice and piano)	1	Holt, Rinehart
(In the textbook, *Exploring Music*)		
God's Goin' To Set This World on Fire	1	Holt, Rinehart
(In the textbook, *Exploring Music*)		
Your World	3	Ginn and Co.
(voices and piano, in the textbook *The Magic of Music*)		
My Brother American	2	Amer. Book Co.
(In the textbook *Sound, Beat and Feeling* of the New Dimensions in Music Series)		
We Sang Our Songs	3	WGS Music
A Psalm for the Living (S.A.T.B. and piano)	10	Bourne Co.
Christmas in the Western World (Las Pascuas)	20	SMC
Arkansas (solo voice)	3	WGS Music
Four Octavo Songs (S.A.T.B. and mixed voices)	10	Gemini Press
(a. "Ev'ry Time I Feel the Spirit" b. "The Blind Man" c. "Toward Distant Shores" d. "Where Shall I Be?")		

KEY TO PUBLISHERS

AMERICAN BOOK COMPANY, Litton Educational Publishing, Inc., Litton Industries, 450 West 33rd Street, New York, NY 10001.

AMERICAN MUSIC EDITION, PUBLISHERS, 263 East 7th Street, New York, NY 10009.

BELWIN, INC., Rockville Center, L.I., New York 11571.

BELWIN-MILLS PUBLISHING CORPORATION, Melville, New York 11746.

BOURNE COMPANY, INC., 1212 Avenue of the Americas, New York, NY 10036.

CFI or CARL FISCHER, INC., 56-62 Cooper Square, New York, NY 10003. (They also distribute for the EASTMAN SCHOOL OF MUSIC: ESM).

CALIFORNIA STATE DEPARTMENT OF EDUCATION, Publishing Division, 721 Capitol Mall, Sacramento, CA 95814.

F. RAYNER BROWN, 2423 Panorama Terrace, Los Angeles, CA 90039.

FRANCIS, DAY & HUNTER, 138-140 Charing Cross Road, London, W.C.2, England.

G. SCHIRMER, INC., 609 Fifth Avenue, New York, NY 10017.

GALAXY MUSIC CORPORATION, 2121 Broadway, New York, NY 10023.

GEMINI PRESS, INC., PILGRIM PRESS, 132 West 31st Street, New York, NY 10001.

GINN & COMPANY, Boston, MA 02117.

HANDY BROTHERS MUSIC COMPANY, 1650 Broadway, New York, NY 10019.

HOLT, RINEHART & WINSTON, 383 Madison Avenue, New York, NY 10017.

J. FISCHER & BROTHERS, Glen Rock, New Jersey 07452.

JOHN CHURCH, THEODORE PRESSER, OLIVER DITSON, Presser Place, Bryn Mawr, Pennsylvania 19010.

MARKS, EDWARD B. MARKS MUSIC CORPORATION, 1790 Broadway, New York, NY 10019.

MCA MUSIC, 543 West 43rd Street, New York, NY 10036.

NOVELLO & COMPANY, LTD., 27 Soho Square, London, W.I. England, or Borough Green, Sevenoaks, Kent, TN158DT. (The American representative is BELWIN, INC.).

OLIVER DITSON, see JOHN CHURCH.

OXFORD UNIVERSITY PRESS, INC., 44 Conduit Street, London, W.I. England, or 200 Madison Avenue, New York, NY 10016.

PIETRO DEIRO, 133 Seventh Avenue South, New York, NY 10014.

PRESSER, THEODORE PRESSER, see JOHN CHURCH.

ROBBINS MUSIC CORPORATION, 799 Seventh Avenue, New York, NY 10019.

SAM FOX PUBLISHING COMPANY, 11 West 60th Street, New York, NY 10023.

SCRIBNER'S, CHARLES SCRIBNER'S SONS, 597 Fifth Avenue, New York, NY 10017.

SILVER BURDETT, 250 James Street, Morristown, NJ 07960.

SMC, SOUTHERN MUSIC PUBLISHING CO., INC., 1740 Broadway, New York, NY 10019.

THEODORE PRESSER, see JOHN CHURCH.

WARNER BROTHERS MUSIC, WITMARK, RCA Building, Rockefeller Center, New York, NY 10020, or 9200 Sunset Blvd, Los Angeles, Ca 90069.

WGS MUSIC, WILLIAM GRANT STILL MUSIC, 26892 Preciados Drive, Mission Viejo, CA 92691.

DISCOGRAPHY

Scherzo from the *Afro-American Symphony*, recorded by Howard Hanson and the Eastman-Rochester Symphony Orchestra for Victor Records, no. 2059-B.

Excerpts from the *Seven Traceries*, recorded by Verna Arvey, pianist, for Co-Art Records, no. 5037 A and B.

"The Flirtation" from *Lenox Avenue*, played by the Hancock Ensemble under the direction of Loren Powell and issued by the Hancock Foundation at USC, no. 395.

The "Blues" from *Lenox Avenue*, recorded by Artie Shaw and his orchestra for Victor Records, no. 27411 A and B.

Scherzo from the *Afro-American Symphony*, recorded by Leopold Stokowski and the All-American Orchestra for Columbia Records, no. 11992-D.

Here's One and the "Blues" from *Lenox Avenue*, recorded by Louis Kaufman, violinist, and Annette Kaufman, pianist, in an American album for Vox, no. 667-A. This album was reissued by Concert Hall Records as "Contemporary American Violin Music," no. H-1640, CHS 1140.

"Work Song" from *From the Delta*, recorded by Morton Gould and his symphonic band for Columbia Records, no. 4519-M, CO 39622.

The *Afro-American Symphony*, recorded by Karl Krueger and the Vienna Opera Orchestra for New Records, Inc. NRLP 105.

Excerpts from the *Seven Traceries*, *Lenox Avenue* and *Three Visions*, played by Gordon Manley, pianist, and available from Belwin-Mills Publishing Corporation.

To You, America! recorded by Lt. Col. Francis E. Resta and West Point Symphonic Band and included in the recordings of the Pittsburgh

International Contemporary Music Festival, issued by ASCAP for non-commercial use by educational institutions.

Here's One, recorded by Robert McFerrin, baritone, for Riverside Records, no. 812.

A tape of the Fourth Symphony (*Autochthonous*) available from the National Association of Educational Broadcasters to educators only. Taken from a 1959 UNESCO concert in Denver, the composer conducting.

Suite from the ballet *Sahdji*, recorded by Howard Hanson with the Eastman-Rochester Orchestra and the Eastman School Chorus for Mercury Records, no. MG 50257 B.

Here's One, recorded by Bill Mann (tenor) and Paul Mickelson (organist) for Work Records, Inc., W-3061 LP.

The *Afro-American Symphony*, recorded by Karl Krueger and the Royal Philharmonic Orchestra of London in an album called "Music in America," MIA 118, obtainable from Soc. for Preservation of American Musical Heritage, Box 4244, GCS, New York, NY 10017.

Festive Overture, recorded by Arthur Bennett Lipkin and the Royal Philharmonic Orchestra of London, album, no. CRI SD 259, obtainable from Composer's Recordings, Inc., 170 W. 74th Street, New York, NY 10023.

Songs of Separation, recorded by Cynthia Bedford and the Oakland Youth Symphony Orchestra in an album called "The Black Composer in America," DC 7107, obtainable from Desto Records, CMS Records, Inc., 14 Warren Street, New York, NY 10007.

Three Visions, played by Natalie Hinderas, pianist, on an album called "Music by Black Composers," DC 7102-3, available from Desto Records, CMS Records, Inc., 14 Warren Street, New York, NY 10007.

Suite for Violin, Pastorela, "Summerland," "Blues" (from *Lenox Avenue*), "Carmela" and *Here's One*, played by Louis and Annette Kaufman, ORS 7152, obtainable from Orion Records, Box 24332, Los Angeles, CA 90024.

From the Black Belt and *Darker America*, recorded by Siegfried Landau and the Westchester Symphony Orchestra on an album called "The Contemporary Composer in the U.S.A." TV-S 34546, Turnabout Records.

"Lawd I Wants To Be a Christian," recorded by John Patton in "Black Spirituals and Art Songs," a Narthex Recording, 2909 Wayzata Blvd., Minneapolis, MN 55405.

Excerpts from Suite #3 from *The American Scene* (*The Old West*), recorded by the All State group of the National Music Camp at Interlochen.

Ennanga, recorded by Lois Adele Craft (harpist), pianist Annette Kaufman, and string quartet; *Songs of Separation* and *Song for the Lonely* recorded by Claudine Kaufman, George Berres, Alex Neiman and Terry King, all on album no. ORS 7278, obtainable from Orion Records, Box 24332, Los Angeles, CA 90024.

Excerpts from *Lenox Avenue* (the "Blues") and *Here's One*, recorded by Louis Kaufman, on an album called "The Kaufman Legacy," (Masters of the Bow), Volume 2, MB 1032, available from James Lesley Creighton, Discopaedia, c/o Recordings Archive, Edward Johnson Music Library, University of Toronto, 80 Queen's Park Crescent, Toronto, Ontario M5S1A1.

Three Visions, recorded by Felipe Hall on an album called "Black American Piano Music," no. SM 93144, available from Da Camera Schallplatten records, 10 bis 12 Lameystrasse, Mannheim, Germany.

The "Blues" from *Lenox Avenue*, recorded by Artie Shaw and his orchestra, reissued by RCA records, Bluebird Label no. AXM2/ AXK2-5572, from Volume IV, "The Complete Artie Shaw," obtainable from RCA, 1133 Avenue of the Americas, New York, NY 10036.

Grief, recorded by Susan Matthews, available from the University of Michigan School of Music, Records, Ann Arbor, Michigan 48109.

The Major Piano Works, recorded by Albert Dominguez.

Appendix 4

ORCHESTRAS AND CONDUCTORS PERFORMING THE WORKS OF WILLIAM GRANT STILL

———————— Orchestras ————————

Eastman-Rochester
Berlin Philharmonic
New York Philharmonic
Pittsburgh Symphony
BBC
Hollywood Bowl
Chicago Symphony
Boston Symphony
Kansas City Philharmonic
Bell Telephone Hour
London Symphony Orchestra
Los Angeles Philharmonic
San Francisco Symphony
Detroit Symphony
Helsinki Municipal Orchestra
Utah Symphony
San Antonio
Dallas
St. Louis
Cleveland
Philadelphia
Minneapolis
Royal Philharmonic
NHK

Tokyo Philharmonic
New Orleans Philharmonic
Buffalo Philharmonic
Indianapolis Symphony
Oklahoma Symphony
NBC Symphony
Sinfonía de Mexico City
Cincinnati Symphony
National Gallery Orchestra
Valencia (Spain) Symphony
   Orchestra
National Symphony Orchestra
Liverpool Philharmonic
Honolulu
Rochester Civic Orchestra
Denver Symphony
Baltimore Symphony
San Diego Symphony
Boston Pops
Monte Carlo Orchestra
Nashville Symphony Orchestra
Birmingham (Alabama)
   Symphony
Seattle Symphony

———————— Conductors ————————

Eugene Goossens
Paul Whiteman
Howard Hanson

Hans Lange
Leopold Stokowski
Sir Hamilton Harty

Arthur Fiedler

Karl Krueger

Alfred Wallenstein

Donald Voorhees

Rudolph Dunbar

William Steinberg

Rudolph Ganz

Maurice Abravanel

Walter Hendl

John Barnett

Joseph Wincenc

Paul Freeman

Leonard Slatkin

Sidney Harth

Georges Barrere

Frederick Stock

Otto Klemperer

Fabien Sevitsky

Rudolph Ringwall

Andre Kostelanetz

Victor Alessandro

Vladimir Bakaleinikoff

Edwin Franko Goldman

Dean Dixon

Pierre Monteux

Artur Rodzinski

Vladimir Golschmann

Antal Dorati

Merideth Wilson

Carlos Chavez

Thor Johnson

Raphael Kubelik

José Iturbi

Sir John Barbirolli

Fritz Reiner

Frances Antori

Eugene Ormandy

Donald Johanos

William Smith

Gunther Schuller

Werner Torkanowsky

Guy Fraser Harrison

Eric Leinsdorf

George Szell

Izler Solomon

Dimitri Mitropoulos

Leon Thompson

Edgar Várèse

Saul Caston

Leon Barzin

Zubin Mehta

Arthur Bennett Lipkin

Albert Stoessel

Werner Janssen

Robert Russell Bennett

Richard Bales

Joseph Levine

William F. Santelmann

Richard Lert